ADVENTURES *in* SOLITUDE

ADVENTURES

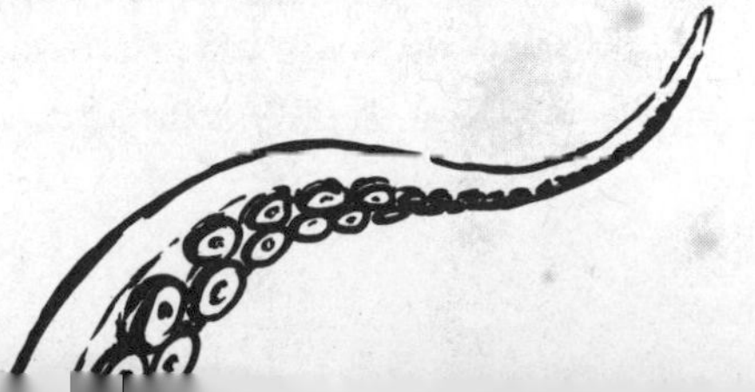

What Not To Wear

to a Nude Potluck

and other stories from

DESOLATION SOUND

in SOLITUDE

by **Grant Lawrence**

HARBOUR PUBLISHING CO. LTD.

6 7 8 9 — 15 14 13 12

Harbour Publishing Co. Ltd.
P.O. Box 219, Madeira Park, BC, VON 2HO
www.harbourpublishing.com

Edited by Silas White.
Cover design by Naomi MacDougall. Cover photograph by Julie Mendgen. Back cover photo by Megan Barnes. Inside cover: Detail from "A Chart shewing part of the Coast of N.W America with the tracks of His Majesty's Sloop *Discovery* and Armed Tender *Chatham*; Commanded by George Vancouver Efq. and prepared under his immediate inspection by Lieu. Joseph Baker," courtesy David Rumsey Map Collection, www.davidrumsey.com. All interior photographs from the author's collection, with the following exceptions: table of contents, Ken Kelly; page 25 by Nadine Sander-Green; page 93 courtesy Brian-Desmond Couche; page 102 from the collection of Andrew Scott; page 196 courtesy Richard Blanchet.
Illustrations by Christy Nyiri. Interior design by Five Seventeen.

Printed on 100% post consumer waste recycled stock using soy-based inks.
Printed and bound in Canada.

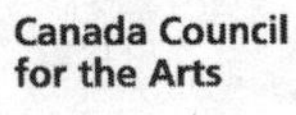

Conseil des Arts
du Canada

Harbour Publishing acknowledges financial support from the Government of Canada through the Canada Book Fund and the Canada Council for the Arts, and from the Province of British Columbia through the BC Arts Council and the Book Publishing Tax Credit.

LIBRARY AND ARCHIVES CANADA CATALOGUING IN PUBLICATION

Lawrence, Grant, 1971–
Adventures in solitude : what not to wear to a nude potluck and other stories from Desolation Sound / Grant Lawrence.
Includes bibliographical references.
ISBN 978-1-55017-514-1
1. Lawrence, Grant, 1971–.
2. Radio broadcasters—Canada—Biography.
3. Desolation Sound (B.C.)—Biography—Anecdotes.
I. Title.

FC3845.D47L39 2010 971.1'31 C2010-904401-0

for Dad

TABLE *of* CONTENTS

Prologue . . . 9

PART ONE

1 A Little Place in the Wilderness . . . 15

2 Fjord Rowboat . . . 23

3 C'mon Sea Legs . . . 33

4 Shine a Light . . . 43

5 The Beautiful Failure . . . 63

6 Smoke on the Water . . . 73

7 Harvest Moon . . . 79

8 Hermit of Desolation Sound . . . 83

9 Lund . . . 95

10 Blood's Too Rich . . . 101

11 Wishing Well . . . 107

12 Captains Courageous . . . 117

13 Take Me to the Riot . . . 129

PART TWO

14 Somewhere Else . . . 135

15 Going Bush . . . 147

16 Cloudy with a Chance of Drunk . . . 161

17 Hangover Days . . . 175

18 Welcome to the Night Sky . . . 183

19 When Animals (Don't) Attack . . . 195

20 My Sword Hand's Anger . . . 205

21 Purple Haze . . . 221

22 Stormy High . . . 229

23 *Big Buck$*, Terror of the Inlet . . . 239

24 Lorenzo's Inferno . . . 251

25 Left and Leaving . . . 257

26 Proof of Love . . . 263

Recommended Reading . . . 279

Recommended Listening . . . 281

Thank You . . . 285

Prologue

It was nearing the end of another gorgeous day in Desolation Sound. Nick and Soraya were busy cooking our annual long-weekend seafood feast: grilled lingcod, steamed clams, boiled red rock crab, barbecued oysters and skewered prawns, all caught within the last two days in the surrounding waters. I volunteered to make a last-minute check of the prawn trap, to top up our menu of the freshest food in the world. Climbing into the boat, I looked into the clear, bottle-green salt water and saw the reflection of my face: relaxed, unwashed and grizzled from weeks in the wilderness.

There was no place I would rather be. The eighteen-year-old Mercury outboard managed to start up one more time, on the third pull. I plunked myself down on the salt-encrusted bench seat, cracked an almost-cold Black Label beer and opened up the throttle. Speeding through the inlet's main current while squinting with my hand over my brow at the reflective ocean surface, I eventually spotted the Styrofoam buoy with "Lawrence" scrawled on the side of it. I slowed down, pulled alongside and, in one tipsy motion, killed the engine, reached over the side and grabbed the buoy rubbing against the skiff's beat-up aluminum hull. I hopped to my feet and started hauling the trap up from the bottom of the ocean.

Prawning in coastal BC waters generally calls for a depth of about three hundred feet. That's the height of a thirty-storey skyscraper, pointing straight down. I kept pulling, hand over hand, the workout and the warmth of the setting sun causing a trickle of sweat down the back of my neck. After a few minutes of heavy hauling, the two-pound weight marking two hundred feet clanked against the side of the boat like a mallet to a gong. In another minute or so the trap was at last visible, now just twenty feet below in translucent jade water.

The ocean let go of the trap with a righteous splash. Much lighter without water holding it down, I hauled the trap over the side and onto the floor of the boat. On a good haul, the trap is alive with chaos, prawns snapping their Sea-Monkey-like forms in every direction, their scales a bright pink, their tiny eyes black and bulging . . . But on that midsummer's eve, the contents of the trap moved slowly, thickly as one mass: a living lava lamp. A mound of red, pimply slime rolled over against the mesh, revealing a large, menacing yellow eye glaring back at me. I stumbled backwards, sloshing beer onto my dirty shorts.

I was staring into the eye of the great Pacific octopus, the first I had ever seen in the wild, filling my prawn trap with its red, lumpy skin and intertwined gelatin arms. Without taking my eyes off it, I nervously cracked a fresh beer with one hand; with the other, I reached around for my fishing knife but found only the empty sheath.

Never that comfortable with large wild animals, I wanted the octopus out of the boat as fast as possible. I reached forward and flipped the release catch, causing the trap to spring open. The octopus slid out onto the floor of the boat like spilled Jell-O, sending me scrambling in panic up to the very edge of the bow. The eight-armed beast made for the opposite end, still glaring, gills flaring, tentacles outstretched, feeling up its foreign surroundings in every direction.

While I stared on in morbid trepidation, one of the octopus's tentacles crept out to the right to wrap itself around a wrench I occasionally used to bang-start the outboard. Its eyes were locked onto mine as another tentacle slithered out to the left, feeling around the floor of the boat like someone looking for their glasses on a bedside table. To my horror, the octopus found my fishing knife before I could, loose amid fishing tackle and empty beer cans. The octopus appeared to be arming itself and it had six arms to go.

My eyes darted around the bow for something I could protect myself with. The octopus began to advance, slithering like Jabba the Hut in my direction. Then I saw the oar, seven feet long, lying lengthwise along the side of the boat. I snapped myself out of my frozen fear and grabbed it, pointed it at the octopus, and went over my options. I didn't want to kill it; I wanted it to return to its octopus's garden beneath the waves. Instead of positioning the oar as a club, I fashioned it more as a giant spatula. I edged forward and, with one thrust, slid the blade of the oar under the octopus's body. The octopus paused, its eyes widened, then it dropped its weaponry and wrapped all eight arms around the oar like a little girl hugging her daddy's leg.

Bending down, I took a deep breath and hoisted the oar high into the air. The octopus stared down at me, still clinging tightly. For that split airborne moment, the wet, red body contrasted brilliantly against the summer evening's still-light, blue sky like the flag of Swaziland. With a downward thrust, I plunged oar and beast into the ocean. The octopus held on for another second, and then with ballet-like grace released itself. With all eight arms in perfect synchronicity, the octopus propelled itself back to the depths, leaving behind a black cloud of ink.

I held the dripping oar, gazing down into the dark water in awe. I straightened up, looked around me and exhaled. A smile crossed my face as I pulled the cord to start up the cranky outboard, thinking of the feast that Nick and Soraya were preparing back at the cabin. I wasn't coming home empty-handed; I had a story to tell.

PART ONE

"Language has created the word loneliness to express the pain of being alone, and the word solitude to express the glory of being alone."

– Paul Tillich, theologian

1
A Little Place in the Wilderness

For all of the adventures, fishing tales, mishaps, characters and serenity that I have encountered in Desolation Sound over the past thirty years, I have my father to thank. Many decades ago, it was Dad who noticed a tiny two-line ad in the real estate section of the *Vancouver Sun* daily evening newspaper:

> Five kilometres oceanfront, 180 acres land, coastal wilderness, British Columbia. $155,000.

Dad was a "recreational real estate developer." That meant he would comb our home province of British Columbia essentially looking for unwanted, undeveloped hinterland. If the setting was nice and price was right (extremely cheap), he'd buy it, divide the property up into lots, sell the lots to individual owners and hopefully turn that unwanted rugged landscape into a rural haven where average people could seek out their own slices of paradise. His vision was pure of heart: never did he want to ravage tranquility, displace wildlife or pave paradise. Dad's ideal was to build rustic, livable cottages, constructed far enough apart from one another so as to provide natural privacy by the lay of the land, and to disrupt the surrounding wilderness as little as possible. Dad told me years later that to him that two-line ad, whether on purpose or not, sounded like much more than a place: it sounded like an experience.

When I was a kid, I loved and adored my dad. He was a larger-than-life hero throughout my childhood. To me he looked like Robert Redford, Harrison Ford or Steve McQueen. He was rugged, athletic, handsome and suave, and seemed to possess great physical strength. He held a degree in mechanical engineering, had an adventuresome spirit and seemed to know just about everything about anything. Dad grew up a prairie kid in Winnipeg in a crowded household of six children, himself a twin. His mother passed away when he was only sixteen, which deeply affected him, bottling up many emotions for the rest of his life. He had never gotten along with his own father, which eventually caused him to leave home, change his name and strike out into the world at an early age. This departure from the family home foreshadowed a deep need in my father to always seek escape. He went to Toronto first, where he met Mom working as a secretary at an engineering firm in a downtown office tower. Dad's bolt-mechanism soon kicked in again and together they travelled to the edge of the world to live in Perth, on the western fringe of Australia, which proved a little too distant for both of them. After a stop in Japan, they eventually settled in Vancouver, Canada's equivalent to Perth, on the northwestern edge of North America. There they started our family and Dad's entrepreneurial real-estate business. Because so many of his properties were remote, he earned a recreational pilot's licence so he could scope out prospective pockets of land and fly clients to the properties in small floatplanes. He crashed twice while on solo flights, both times ending up upside down and hanging by his seatbelt, but on both occasions he was able to walk away and fly another day. Dad was always looking for the end of the road.

In many ways, even as a child, I was the opposite of my father. I was a scrawny, uncoordinated geek and extremely self-conscious. By the time I was in grade two I needed big, thick glasses to see the chalkboard. I had horribly wonky knees that would dislocate if I didn't look exactly where I was walking, which forced me to wear bulky, *Forrest Gump*–like knee braces. I would often squint up at the bulk strength and *Cool Hand Luke*–like steadiness of my father and wonder what went wrong. He was outdoorsy and handsome; I was bookish, "artistic" and always pushing my geek-goggle glasses up from the end of my nose. He insisted on taking me out into the wilderness where it was all I could do to keep up with him; a whimpering mess, fearful of my own shadow. We'd travel by car, plane and boat, all three of which gave me projectile-vomit nausea and diarrhea. Thoroughly soiled failure though I felt, to his credit he never showed anything but pure love and support for me. I still couldn't help but feel inadequate around him.

Dad called the seven-digit number listed in the *Vancouver Sun*. Within a few months, he and I were sputtering over a remote and unforgiving landscape in a pontooned sheet-metal seaplane with Dad at the controls. Flights with Dad were a sickening, frightening and deafening experience. The little propeller plane would hit an air pocket and freefall twenty or thirty feet like an elevator with its cable cut, sending my stomach into convulsions as Dad would fight to regain altitude, noting my green complexion with a smile and shouting reassuring phrases that were incomprehensible over the earsplitting volume of the engine. We were buzzing over a lonely section of the BC coastline called Desolation Sound, a collection of deep inlets, islands and coastal mountains found at the northern end of the Strait of Georgia. It was beyond the end of the road: it was the backwoods, the boondocks, a far-flung place where there were no roads, no cars and very few people.

Desolation Sound was "boat access only." The people who lived there clung close to the coast like barnacles: a few hardy oyster farmers, First Nations fishermen, draft dodgers, wayward hippies, and one infamous "cougar lady." Each summer, the area received a two-month population boost from adventure-seeking tourists in yachts, sailboats and kayaks. The end of the pavement was thirty kilometres to the south of the Sound, where the final foot of the famed Pan-American Highway 101 came to a blunt, unceremonious full-stop in the tiny fishing village of Lund. Dad dipped the wings of our flying tin can from side to side so he could marvel at sights below out of the side windows. I missed it all, huddled in the passenger seat with my head between my knees, retching violently into an airsickness bag, my face streaked with tears of embarrassment. Dad was too awestruck to pay much attention to me. What he instantly fell in love with from the air, the British navigation legend Captain George Vancouver had originally surveyed with complete disdain from the bridge of his HMS *Discovery* in the summer of 1792.

It had barely changed in the two hundred years since: a rocky, jagged coastline dotted with islands and islets, coves, bays, lagoons and inlets, creeks and lakes, towering cliffs and granite outcrops, backdropped by a thick, coniferous forest that stretched straight up, unbroken, to the snowy coast mountain peaks and the BC interior beyond. Captain Vancouver sailed the *Discovery*, and his company's smaller ship, the *Chatham*, into the area on an unseasonably dark and rainy night. Both ships felt their way through the waters in a "very unpleasant navigation," as if "blindfolded" according to Vancouver, trying to find a place to anchor. They were shocked to find the water incredibly deep even close to shore. What Vancouver had no way of knowing is that Desolation Sound has the most dramatic drop in altitude from mountain peak to ocean floor in all of North America.

Finally, nearing midnight, they tucked in safely near what is now Kinghorn Island in the middle of the Sound. Vancouver and his crew of 170 men then spent a storm-soaked three weeks charting the region in rowboats. He was continually unimpressed by what he saw, noting in his captain's log, "This [area] afforded not a single prospect that was pleasing to the eye." Vancouver was under orders to chart the entire northwest coast of North America and find the secret, undiscovered waterway known as the Northwest Passage. The *Discovery* and the *Chatham* had already been at sea for over two years, painstakingly fulfilling other orders to survey parts of the New Zealand, Australian, Hawaiian and North American coastlines.

George Vancouver was desperate to live up to his predecessor Captain Cook's untouchable reputation as a tough, fair and brilliant captain with a long list of legendary maritime achievements. But Vancouver was battling a mysterious illness for much of his maiden voyage as captain, and by the time they hit North America in the stormy summer of 1792, he was also prone to sudden fits of rage followed by long bouts of depression. He drove his crew relentlessly, often accompanying his men as they rowed the lengths of the fjords and circumferences of the islands from dawn to well past dusk. Vancouver was possessed to do as thorough a job as possible, and did such excellent work that his charts were used for the next century. But in his frustration at hitting dead end after dead end of the deep, dark and winding fjords of coastal BC, Vancouver's anger and depression engulfed him.

Anchored near what is now Teakerne Arm on the Island of West Redonda and staring up at a wall of impassable mountains, Vancouver dismissively bestowed the negative and foreboding moniker of "Desolation Sound" upon the area. Since no road has ever been built, the name remains fitting to this day. For the most part, after the once-flourishing First Nations settlements were either wiped out by European-spread disease or entirely relocated, no relatively significant human population has ever taken up permanent and lasting residency on the shores of the Sound, though many have tried.

After four or five more low passes over Desolation Sound in the careening seaplane, Dad pulled back on the steering wheel, letting the little plane climb up high over the Coast Mountains as I white-knuckled the armrests, the back of my sweaty, little head pinned against the seat by inertia. He then levelled us out and pointed our winged rollercoaster cart homeward, finally bringing the pontoons down softly and safely on the Fraser River near Vancouver. I was desperately hoping Dad would take a pass on the empty and isolated Desolation Sound.

The Desolation Sound Marine Park as snapped from the cockpit of Dad's bucket-of-bolts seaplane. I missed this view completely because my head was between my knees while I was vomiting. The area had just recently been deemed a park and there is nary a human structure in sight. That would change.

2
Fjord Rowboat

Through various means of creative banking in the middle of a deep national recession, Dad managed to scrape together the funding to purchase the land in Desolation Sound. It was ours. My mind fogged with shuddering apprehension when Dad shared the news. His next initiative was to force Mom and me up to the property to "try it out" (we left my younger sister, Heather, at home with my grandparents). The plan was to strap our heavy, wooden rowboat to the roof of our cranky old Fiat, drive up the coast, park the car at the end of the road and row over to the property to camp out for a few days. Mom and I would experience what it took to actually get to this distant outpost by land and water.

When it came to the great outdoors, Mom was a lot like me. She just wasn't that comfortable with the whole "nature thing." Mom was always a lot more comfortable in a mall than a marsh, in a spa than a speedboat, at a country club rather than a campground. She liked her comfort, she loved her fashion and she was a self-professed "preppy" from Etobicoke, Ontario. She looked the part, refusing to "dress down" to the locals, as Dad always tried to convince her to do before our journeys beyond the end of the road. Mom likely would have preferred to remain in our tony West Vancouver neighbourhood than brave an ocean adventure, but she deeply loved and supported Dad. She proved time and again that she would follow him just about anywhere.

To find Desolation Sound, if not by air, one must embrace the provincial rite of passage known as BC Ferries, an ever-maligned but remarkably trustworthy fleet of car-barges covered evenly in barnacles, streaks of oil and rust, and infinite coats of thick white paint on every surface above the water line. Each boat is named after an area of BC, such as the *Queen of Surrey* or the *Queen of Chilliwack* — titles that unwittingly inspired endless gags for me and my sister once we were old enough to realize these floating hulks were named after areas that have been the butt end of jokes for decades: *Why wasn't Jesus born in Surrey? Because they couldn't find three wise men and a virgin.* The BC Ferries fleet is the largest of its kind in the world — once considered a governmental extension of our coastal highways before becoming a private company. The ferries are something every tourist adores but every coastal British Columbian loves to hate. Be the last car to make the sailing and it's a fist-pumping, spine-tingling, near-orgasmic, shout-out-loud victory. Miss that sailing by one car and the mixed feelings of depression and boredom set in as the gape-mouthed leviathan pulls away without you, not to return for hours, if at all.

The ferry terminals along the Sunshine Coast seem to have been constructed in an effort to create the most mind-numbingly dreary waiting atmosphere imaginable. Holding a spiritless, captive audience within a chain-link fence — sometimes for several hours on end — the average ferry terminal's entertainment usually consists of a large, sloped parking lot the size of a football field with little shade or shelter. It would usually contain a rank public washroom, one or two concrete picnic tables, an out-of-order vending machine, an empty newspaper box, and maybe, if the time of year was right, a concession stand selling questionable corn dogs and ice cream. Just beyond the chain-link fence, natural beauty abounded . . . beaches, ocean and forest. But we had already entered the ferry terminal, and we would never dare leave for fear of losing our place in line, or not being able to re-enter. We were trapped on the inside staring out, waiting to be freed from a chain-linked purgatory so our vacations could finally start.

The Earl's Cove ferry terminal, where my family spent countless hours of our young lives waiting in purgatory. Heaven if we made the ferry; hell if we didn't. Beauty abounds beyond the chain-link fence, but "Shore Access Prohibited." In the meantime, please enjoy this concrete ashtray!

It took two of these semi-mighty vessels to drop us onto a patch of the coastline within an hour's drive of our boat-launching point for Desolation Sound. The ferries ached and groaned their way across the mouths of those dark fjords like giant iron toads. The inlets they crossed were the same that caused Captain Vancouver so much grief, cutting so deeply inland that roads still haven't been built all the way around them. Between the ferry routes, on either side, is the Sunshine Coast Highway, an extension of the famed Highway 101. The two-hour drive between ferries winds through picturesque seaside towns such as Gibsons, Sechelt and Powell River with their curiously named side streets we could never explore, such as Redrooffs Road, Monkey Tree Lane and Sea Fiddler Road. For anyone taking part in the white-knuckle, lead-foot *Cannonball Run* from ferry to ferry, these street signs and towns were but a blur while we raced along some of the wildest, windiest, hairpin coastal roads that a stomach could manage. Or couldn't, as we discovered on that initial trek . . .

The Fiat lurched from side to side, twisting its way up the rain-soaked alder corridors of the Sunshine Coast Highway. The ropes holding down the rooftop rowboat strained with every turn, as did I. Curled on the vinyl back seat in the fetal position, hands on my gut, I wondered to what fresh hell Dad was leading us to this time. Mom was doing only marginally better in the front seat and was much more top-of-her-lungs vocal about it. In an attempt to ease our nausea, Dad slid in our favourite tape: *Endless Summer*, the end-all-be-all greatest hits compilation by the Beach Boys. It was no use. To the four-part harmonies of "Fun, Fun, Fun," I sat bolt-upright, hot saliva and stomach acid filling my mouth. I attempted to shove my face between Mom's headrest and the passenger window, managing only to get out the words, "Window, window, Mommy!" before I projectile-vomited a half-digested BC Ferries Sunshine Kids

Special directly into the side of my mother's face. Her ear, hair and shoulder all took direct hits, as did the inside of the passenger window. Collapsing into the back seat, my new summer jacket absorbed the second and third lurching mouthfuls. Mom flew into hysterics, demanding we pull over to clean up, but Dad kept cannonballing it, pedal to the metal, fearing we'd miss the next ferry.

When we finally screeched to a halt at the Earl's Cove ferry lineup, Mom and I staggered from the little green Fiat like vomit-encrusted lepers. We took what would be the first of many Earl's Cove ferry terminal walks of shame, past all the other waiting cars and their terminally bored, gawking occupants, to the clammy public washroom located at the front of the lineup, where we attempted to clean ourselves up with cold water and toilet paper. That first trip we had plenty of time; we missed the ferry by two cars, the journey far from over. Hours later, we rattled and bounced up and down a muddy ditch of a road through the rainforest, Dad holding off our weakening protests, telling us we were just minutes away from the Sound. The Fiat, the ropes and the rowboat groaned in unison one last time as we crested a final hill, and saw it. An opening in the forest wall allowed us to look down upon an ocean wilderness, perfectly still and silent in the falling rain. Dense cedar rose sharply from the rocky shoreline. A wispy white mist clung to the treetops like cotton on a Christmas tree. No living thing could be seen or heard. The sight filled Dad with a sense of achievement and excitement, but left Mom and I seriously questioning why we had come to this wet, lonely place.

In 1927 a little girl named Nancy Crowther made the very same trip with her parents, on foot. The Crowthers trekked twenty kilometres north over land from the coastal mill town of Powell River. From the tiny Okeover settlement just to the south of

Foreboding and frightening when I was a kid, this narrow opening through the dark wall of trees at the end of the road would eventually become my "view of serenity." The government wharf is at the bottom of the hill, and the ridges and mountains of Desolation Sound can be seen beyond.

Desolation Sound, the Crowthers bushwhacked their own trail two kilometres north along the shoreline to an isthmus of level, low-lying land between two deep and narrow bays. Nancy's father bought the 135-acre parcel for $10 and built a sturdy log cabin that remains there to this day. Fifty years later, this was the exact spot we looked down upon.

Sputtering and skidding down the hill on what felt like the Fiat's last gasp, we pulled alongside a wooden fence overtaken by moss and ivy, its pickets rotten and overlapping like English teeth. The sagging gate was adorned with a weathered sign. The message upon it could still clearly be read: WARNING. PRIVATE PROPERTY. NO TRESPASSING. BEWARE OF DOGS. Beyond the sign was a yard, a garden, an orchard and a cabin. Beyond that was a pebble beach covered in driftwood and oyster shells, inconsequential waves rearranging the round stones with each earthly push and pull. The only way to get to the beach was through the yard. "That's ridiculous," Dad reasoned, essentially to himself. "This person can't legally block us from the beach. No one owns what's below the tide line and it's low tide, so let's just unpack the car here, scoot across the yard and put the boat in."

Still not knowing who lived there, or how serious the warnings were, we soon found ourselves tiptoeing across the yard to the water, making trip after trip from the car to the shoreline as quickly and quietly as we could. Finally it was time to move the heavy, wooden rowboat, which Dad hoisted from the roof and onto his shoulders. The sheer weight of it caused him to tip from side to side, front to back, while trying to maintain balance and keep an eye on his footing. He reminded me of one of those tipsy waltzing toadstools from *Fantasia*. Manoeuvring through the gate, he whacked the rowboat against a wet fencepost. Dad had just squeezed through when we heard the dogs. The teeter-tottering wooden blue rowboat waltz turned into a desperate sprint.

A pack of hellhounds burst out of the orchard. They were at full speed and volume, heading straight for us, saliva dripping off gleaming teeth, shoulder muscles rippling with every thrust of their front legs. I was terrified; Mom was screaming for Dad to hurry. Dad skidded along the pebbles, flipped the boat off his shoulders and slammed the hull into the water. "Load it up, let's go, let's go!" Dad yelled with clear and unfamiliar panic in his voice. We threw the sleeping bags, tent, food and clothes into the bottom of the already leaking dingy as the dogs hurdled the edge of the yard and hit the pebble beach behind us with a crash. Dad chucked the last of our goods into the boat, including me, then grabbed an oar and spun around to meet the pack. I began to cry, my teeth chattering in fear, my glasses fogging in the rain. The dogs formed a semicircle around us at the water's edge — heads down, teeth bared, snarling, snapping, barking, closing in.

"QUIET!"

The dogs' violent cacophony instantly dropped to a whimper, as they turned their heads subserviently in the direction of their master's voice. We did, too, turning from a ferocious bush-dog standoff to staring down the barrel of a .303-calibre rifle. She was a heavy-set, stout, older woman with grey, unkempt hair that she had attempted to tame into a bun. Her face was broad, pierced with small, dark eyes. Her skin had deep wrinkles crossing it in every direction like a European road map. She wore a red and black checkered mackinaw jacket over a knee-length colourless dress and a faded, yellow apron. Thick wool socks protruded over the edge of her muddy rubber boots. She handled the rifle with the comfort and familiarity that most elderly ladies show a pair of knitting needles. We didn't know it at the time, but we were face to gun barrel with the Cougar Lady of Okeover Inlet.

In a surprisingly refined British accent, she asked in a low tone, "Who are you and what are you doing here?"

One of the lessons Nancy Crowther's father taught her at an early age was how to shoot a rifle, a life-saving skill when living in the remote bush. Predators were prevalent: bears, wolves, coyotes and cougars. Nancy shot her first cougar when she was thirteen years old and protecting the family goats. When she was fourteen, she survived a cougar attack, saved only by her dog leaping to her defence. The dog wasn't so lucky. Over the course of her long life in Okeover Inlet, Nancy Crowther was said to have shot and killed an astounding twenty-two cougars. She became a local legend but the Cougar Lady did not welcome celebrity. After both her parents passed away, she was rarely seen off her little farm. As luck would have it, Ms. Crowther also lived on the closest and most convenient launching point to the Desolation Sound property Dad had just purchased.

Slowly lowering the oar, Dad apologized for the trespass and explained our intentions in his most calm and charming demeanour possible. He introduced himself as a "new neighbour," introduced Mom, and then me, peeking over the gunwale of the boat in my puke-stained, rain-soaked jacket, still recovering from the trauma of the dogs. Without lowering her .303, Nancy Crowther listened to Dad's story with unimpressed suspicion. Her dogs were now gathered calmly at her feet or sniffing around the beach. One even nuzzled my forearm with his nose, giving his tail a friendly wag.

After sizing us up for a few more strained moments, the muzzle of the rifle soon threatened only the muddy earth. Either she figured we were genuinely naïve, or possibly it was an act of pity, but Ms. Crowther graciously allowed us to park our car on her property and to use her beach to come and go as we needed. Later, she explained to Dad that after years of being left almost totally alone, "civilization" had been slowly creeping into the area over the last ten years in the form of drifting hippies, draft dodgers and end-of-the-road freedom seekers. Previously, her only threat was from wild creatures — but now it was the human kind that stole from her . . . Honey, grain, hay, tools and even groceries were disappearing, leaving her justifiably suspicious of any strangers. As Dad rowed us out into the still water of the bay, disturbed only by the falling rain and the rhythm of the oars dipping into the dark water, I looked back at the Cougar Lady as she walked across her land, rifle cradled in her arm, as she had done for almost her entire life.

It was in this log cabin that the legendary Nancy Crowther, the Cougar Lady of Okeover Inlet, lived almost her entire life, from the 1920s to the 1980s. While she lived here she was said to have shot and killed an amazing twenty-two cougars, "the ghost of the forest." The cabin is now owned by Powell River Sea Kayak.

3
C'mon Sea Legs

Desolation Sound will never seem quite as miserable as the time we rowed across the inlet on that first trip. As Dad silently paddled away from the Crowther homestead and around the tip of Dead Man's Island, we had our first view of the actual property through the mist. To my eyes it was an unfriendly, south-facing coastline made up of two broad bays, several little coves, a saltwater lagoon and two distinct points. We rowed straight to the nearest point of land, our boat's momentum slowed only by the floating garden of bull-kelp bulbs just offshore. We eventually came to a shuddering halt as the wooden hull hit the seaweed and barnacle–encrusted rock that jutted out to meet us. We had arrived.

Mom and I learned quickly that banana peel–slippery seaweed and ginzu-sharp barnacles are a cruel combination on Desolation's shores. Soaking wet, numbingly cold and still puke-encrusted, my first step on land slipped out from underneath me, slamming me headfirst onto the rocks, my glasses clattering off my face. I was now bruised, bleeding, blind and crying. We gingerly hauled our camping gear up above the tide line onto the moss-covered rocky point, about thirty feet before the forest wall. Our body language was obvious as we surveyed our surroundings: Dad had his chest pumped out and his hands on his hips; Mom had her arms crossed; while my arms hung limply, my head lolled to one side, defeated. Two-thirds miserable in the pouring rain, we were totally and utterly alone. There was not a sound nor a soul nor a living thing to be seen in any direction. We were way beyond the end of the road, in the middle of nowhere, and the only way in or out was via our leaky rowboat. Dad loved it, busying himself by pitching our mouldy canvas army surplus tent on the flattest spot of open rock he could find.

This photo captures my first memories of Desolation Sound: cold, wet, empty and grey. My childhood sentiments eerily echoed Captain Vancouver's 1792 log entry: "As gloomy and dismal as nature could well be supposed to exhibit . . . dull and uninteresting . . . dreary rocks and precipices compose these desolate shores . . . an awful silence pervaded the gloomy forests, whilst animated nature seemed to have deserted the neighbouring country altogether."

One hundred and eighty-five years earlier, a morose note in Captain Vancouver's log perfectly echoed our two-thirds majority: "As gloomy and dismal as nature could well be supposed to exhibit . . . dull and uninteresting . . . dreary rocks and precipices compose these desolate shores . . . an awful silence pervaded the gloomy forests, whilst animated nature seemed to have deserted the neighbouring country altogether." For the next two days it continued to pour relentlessly. Undaunted in the slightest, Dad rowed the length of the property, hopping out of the boat and over the rocks like a mountain goat, hammering in the white wooden property stakes of what would be the individual lots for cabins including one of our own. Meanwhile, Mom and I did not leave the dripping tent. Mom entertained herself with romance novels and knitting, while I buried my head in a soggy copy of *Tintin and the Black Island*. I also sketched whatever I could spot through the tent flap, which wasn't much beyond a line of dripping clothes and a smouldering campfire.

One of the primary reasons Dad was so giddy about the property was that he had quietly pulled off the recreational real-estate equivalent of a royal flush. He had just purchased 180 acres of private, free-title land in the middle of the largest marine park in BC — literally the only large-scale marine park on the entire Pacific coast of Canada. In 1973, after much analysis, the government of BC had set aside the 14,000 coastal acres now known as the Desolation Sound Marine Park. Of those 14,000 acres, only one-tenth remains privately owned; if the government of the time had had their way, there would be no private land whatsoever within the park. After the park's borders were established, the government's goal was to purchase all remaining private homesteads within park boundaries as they came up for sale. Many were abandoned by the original homesteaders and were either already owned by the bank, or on the market for a song. The government was able to scoop up prime Desolation Sound homesteads in places like Prideaux

Haven, Isabel Bay and Kakaykay Bay, the deep and narrow inlet directly beside where our tent stood. However in 1975 there was a change in government, and a strict new provincial budget was introduced. Thus, the very few privately owned lands would remain private, creating an unbelievably unique opportunity to own coastal property within a massive and pristine marine park, with no threat of further development on all sides for all time.

The original owners of our property were a Swedish immigrant family called Bloom. There was Gus Bloom, his wife, Alice, and their two young children, William and Alice. Some time after Dad bought the property, he tracked down the younger Alice Bloom, who was by then an elderly woman living in Sechelt. She was able to recall many fascinating and harrowing stories of her youth growing up in Desolation Sound. At the time of her family's arrival in 1911, the most common language in the Sound was Swedish, as many Swedes had come to the West Coast pursuing the logging trade. The Blooms purchased the 180-acre homestead from the Crown for $15 (Dad purchased it over sixty years later for $155,000). They built a log cabin in a sheltered little cove with a freshwater creek. For the next several years, the Bloom family made Desolation Sound their home, clearing land and planting an orchard. Gus found work with a nearby logging company as a hand-logger, an extremely dangerous profession that often involved single-handedly cutting down massive old-growth fir trees on steep mountain slopes, angling the cut so the logs would slide down into a lake or the ocean below.

At the time, Desolation Sound was filled with hand-loggers of all types vying for the valuable timber. Scandinavian families like the Blooms were looking to settle, while plenty of single men from the Maritimes, Quebec and the States were just looking for work. Accidents and deaths were a daily occurrence. In remote areas, loggers could be crushed by a falling tree or a rolling log, yanked over a cliff along with their fresh cut, drowned between logs on a floating boom, or wounded or killed by their own axe or saw. A logger working alone would die alone, often with no one realizing he was missing. Gus's life came to a predictably tragic end on the last night of January, 1920; unpredictably, his death had nothing to do with logging.

Alice Bloom told Dad she could remember the night clearly. The Blooms were just sitting down for dinner in their cabin when they heard angry shouting coming from just offshore. In the fading light of the short winter day, Alice's father went outside and saw a fishing boat owned by their popular fellow-Swede neighbour, Oskar Roos, one of the largest suppliers of illegal moonshine in Desolation Sound. Gus heard the sounds of men fighting on the boat, and shouts for help. Against his wife's protests, Gus told the family to hold dinner for him while he climbed into his little skiff and motored out into the blustery and rapidly darkening night.

When he was within a few feet of the fish boat, he saw Oskar Roos engaged in a violent, drunken struggle with a local Finn named Charlie Anderson. Gus cut the speed of his skiff and swung alongside the fishing boat. Oskar Roos was hanging on to the butt end of a rifle, while Charlie grappled with the barrel. Right away Gus realized it was Charlie who was yelling for help. Without turning off his engine, Gus shouted for the men to stop fighting, then threw himself between them, straddling both boats. All three men struggled back and forth until finally, Gus got both hands on the muzzle of the rifle and yanked it hard toward him.

From their cabin, the remaining Bloom family members heard an explosion from the water and rushed outside, but by now it was too dark to see anything. The rifle had fired. The force of the blast had sent Gus Bloom hurtling into the rear of his own boat where he collapsed. The bullet had shattered his left knee. Startled sober, Oskar Roos and Charlie Anderson quickly forgot about their conflict. Possibly unaware that Bloom was injured, they fired up the fishing boat and took off, leaving Bloom to writhe in agony. Gus's boat, which was still running, was now steering itself. By sheer luck, the skiff swung around and headed back to the Bloom homestead instead of toward the open waters of the dark inlet.

Alice and her mother and brother were now hurrying across the rocks to meet the boat where it came to a thudding halt. They found Gus clinging to what was left of his knee, blood soaking his wool pants, dark pools forming between the wooden ribs of the boat. The three of them managed to drag Gus to shore, and then, leaving the children to tend to him, Mrs. Bloom left in the boat to seek help. Hours later, in a larger launch run by a neighbour, young Alice and her brother were dropped off with friends while their parents made a desperate, late-night, stormy voyage several hours down the coast to the Powell River hospital, Gus slipping in and out of consciousness the entire way.

Alice's dad died the next morning, February 1, 1920, at approximately 8 a.m. on the operating table at the Powell River hospital with her mom at his side. Gus was thirty-five. The official cause of death was listed on his death certificate: "Hemorrhage and shock. Gunshot wound inflicted by another party. Compound, comminuted fracture of leg." Before he died, Gus was coherent enough to give a statement to Inspector Owen of the local police detachment. From the operating table, Gus gasped that Oskar Roos and Charlie Anderson had shot him, with Roos pulling the trigger then throwing the rifle overboard.

Owen immediately dispatched a tough young cop named Constable Hadley in a police launch piloted by another junior officer. When they reached the Scandinavian logging enclave of Lund, Hadley attempted to form a posse of locals to help capture Roos and Anderson but quickly got stonewalled, receiving no help from the Swedish community. Hadley sensed everyone knew of the situation, but no one would talk, many insisting they didn't speak English. Sure enough, word travelled quickly to Roos, who took off into the forest behind his cabin, armed with a double-barrelled shotgun. He told his neighbour to send a brazen message back to the cops: he would shoot anyone who came after him.

Hadley eventually figured out the residence of Charlie Anderson and found the hapless accomplice passed out on his bed in his decrepit shack, littered with empty moonshine jars, on the shore of Okeover Inlet. Hadley easily locked him up in the police launch. As he continued to search the area, he heard word of Roos's threat, which did not have its desired effect. Instead, Hadley determined where Roos lived and powered the police launch straight there to search the property with his guns drawn. In the woods just a few hundred feet behind the house, he stumbled upon one of "the largest moonshine stills ever discovered on the coast of British Columbia," according to the *Daily Province*. "There was little doubt in the constable's mind that the moonshine from the still was responsible for Roos's condition when the shooting occurred." With the butt end of his rifle, Hadley smashed the elaborate distillery to pieces.

After searching the woods further with no sign of Roos, Hadley laid a trap for Roos by instructing the junior officer on the police launch to drive it out of sight. Hadley then snuck up the hill and into Roos's cabin, a rifle in one hand and a handgun in the other. Sure enough, within half an hour of the boat leaving, Roos casually entered his cabin, with shotgun at his side. Hadley leaped out from behind the door, jammed both guns into Roos's back and put him under arrest. Outside the cabin, with Roos captured, Hadley signalled for the return of the police boat by firing two quick rounds into the air, then proceeded to lead Roos at gunpoint to the shore.

The path from Roos's cabin to the beach was extremely steep, and in the dimming evening light, Hadley slipped on some rocks and fell. In a split-second, Roos made a break for it, diving through the window of a shed and out the back door into the woods. Hadley bushwhacked twenty minutes in the dark in pursuit of Roos, eventually deciding to call off the search for the night. After an early-morning, no-nonsense interrogation of a neighbour, Constable Hadley learned that a Roos accomplice was to leave a rifle on the trail behind the cabin later that day. Hadley hatched another trap, planting an unloaded decoy rifle at the rendezvous point then waited in the bushes. Again Roos appeared on the trail, and again he was captured at Hadley's gunpoint without a shot fired. This time, Roos was tightly handcuffed when brought down to the shore.

After a night together in the Powell River jail, Roos and Anderson were delivered by police launch down the coast to Vancouver. The shooting and subsequent manhunt had been in all the papers and the brazen Constable Hadley arrived in the city to a hero's welcome. Roos and Anderson were locked up in the notorious Oakalla Prison to stand trial for murder, which was back then still a hanging offence. At the initial inquest, with Mrs. Bloom present, both pleaded not guilty. When interviewed separately, each man blamed the other for pulling the trigger, Anderson going so far as to say he saw the safety on when the two men were grappling over the gun, and that Roos must have moved it before he pulled the trigger. Back in Desolation Sound, a petition made the rounds citing Oskar Roos's good character and upstanding reputation. Not only was he the chief supplier of illegal whiskey, but he was also charmingly handsome, popular and funny. Everyone signed, including the influential Thulin Brothers, founders of the settlement of Lund, and the petition was hand-delivered to Vancouver in time for the trial.

The death of Gus Bloom was eventually ruled an accident, and both Roos and Anderson were set free to return to the Sound. It was a verdict the surviving Bloom family accepted, though they may not have had much choice in the tight-knit community as they had nowhere else to turn. It is unknown what charges, if any, Roos faced for the moonshine distillery. After Gus's death, the Blooms couldn't tend to their farm themselves so they moved to a nearby bay to live with a group of family friends. Mrs. Bloom held onto the original homestead and 180-acre parcel of coastline for another eighteen years before selling it in 1938 to a Danish family named Wallen who were looking to escape the impending war in Europe.

The Blooms stayed on in the area but Gus's death would not be the last tragedy they would suffer in Desolation Sound. Alice's brother, William Bloom, followed his father's footsteps into logging, and was killed in a floatplane crash in the mountains of the Sound in the winter of 1958, his body never found. Alice, however, lived a long life, dying a few years after sharing many pioneering stories with Dad. Bloom descendants reside on the Sunshine Coast to this day.

Although the Wallen family eventually settled in Seattle, they spent every summer in the Sound until 1965, but never built. They sold the property to a Mr. Noon of Los Angeles in 1970. When first approached by the BC government to sell the land for the newly formed Desolation Sound Marine Park, Mr. Noon wasn't interested. He changed his mind a few years later, but the government had also changed, leading Mr. Noon to place his two-line ad in the *Vancouver Sun*.

Dad, Mom and I eventually made it safely back to civilization from that first camping trip. I'll never forget how warm and cozy our damp old Fiat felt when I collapsed on its familiar vinyl back-seat bench and curled back into the fetal position, nibbling on a tea biscuit kindly provided by the Cougar Lady. Puttering back down the coast, we missed two more ferries, I threw up three more times and *Endless Summer* got mangled in the tape deck. Our first trip to Desolation Sound was complete. I had no perception how intertwined I would become with the ghosts, lore and legends of this lonely Canadian place dismissed by Captain Vancouver as "broken country."

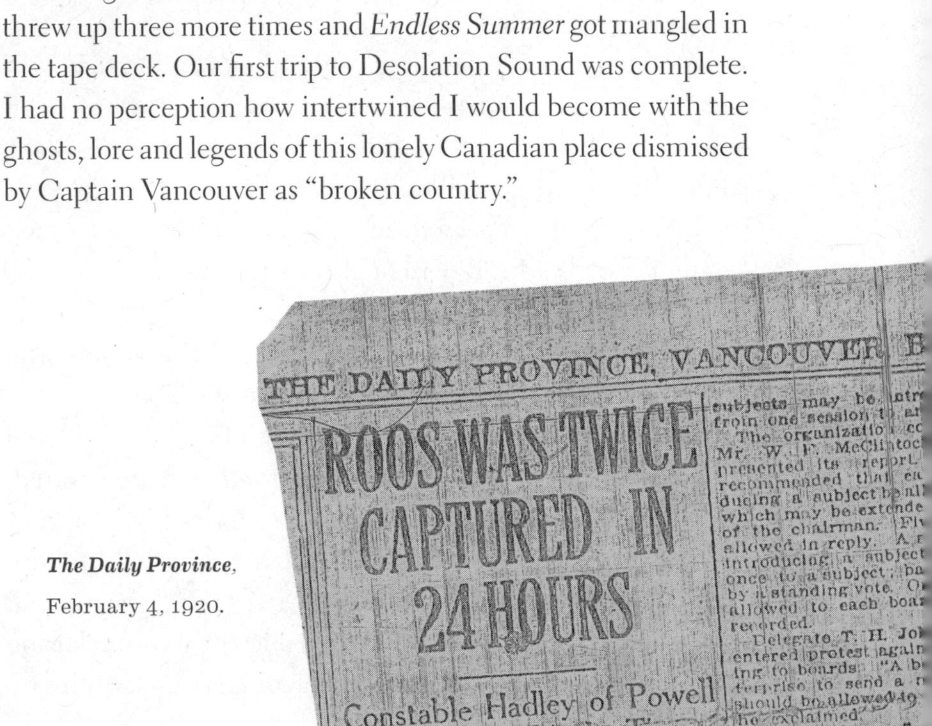

THE DAILY PROVINCE, VANCOUVER, B

ROOS WAS TWICE CAPTURED IN 24 HOURS

Constable Hadley of Powell River Has Lively Time With Prisoner.

Interesting Facts Are Related of Tragic Death of Coast Rancher.

Big Seizure of Moonshine at Home of Man Now Under Arrest.

Typical Story of Northern Woods Related in Official Police Documents.

Seldom have the records of the provincial police in Vancouver disclosed more interesting details of a hunt for a "wanted" man than those related today by Constable W. H. Hadley of Powell River, who arrived in town with two prisoners, Charles Anderson and Oscar Roos. Of this pair Anderson is regarded as comparatively inoffensive, but the capture of Roos and his safe arrival in handcuffs is regarded as a big achievement for the Powell River officer. Both men are being held in connection with the slaying of Gus Bloom, a well-known [illegible] rancher, [illegible] Constable Hadley [illegible]

subjects may be intr
from one session to a
The organization c
Mr. W. F. McClintoc
presented its report
recommended that ea
ducing a subject be all
which may be extende
of the chairman. Fi
allowed in reply. A
introducing a subject
once to a subject; ba
by a standing vote. O
allowed to each boa
recorded.
Delegate T. H. Jo
entered protest agai
ing to boards: "A b
terprise to send a
should be allowed to
he exclaimed.
"In which case,"
E. Waterman, Prin
ver Board of Tra
room with delegates
vention on any su
Mr. McClintock e
only after careful
the committee deci
of voting, believing
most equitable me
Upon a vote be
was accepted.
Mr. C. E. Dis
Terminal City Cl
pitality of the club
ing delegates, an
erously applauded
The Kiwanis G
H. Falconer of t
mittee, announced
vices in any capa
in the smoking
night.

AMENDED AG

The agenda
amended by the
and approved b
follows, the su
the order in wh
Completion a
E. Railway (P
immigration, w
its bearing on a
(Okanagan); Im
services (Sum
and Mission);
tion and servi
couver); Irriga
development
Interprovincial
Princeton, Su
Coast (Prince
ver); Universi
continuation
(South Vanco
Surrey); pre
ests (Victori
(Vancouver);

***The Daily Province*,**
February 4, 1920.

4
Shine a Light

Our family's next excursion to Desolation Sound didn't occur until several summers later, mostly due to my and Mom's complete lack of enthusiasm, which at times bordered on hysteria whenever Dad brought up the topic. "Not until there is a solid roof over our heads!" was Mom's oft-repeated response, while I usually just ran out of the room in screaming protest whenever Dad mentioned the Sound. Finally, Dad informed us that there was in fact a roof on our cabin site. A deal was a deal. With extreme reluctance, we stuffed the car with our entire small 'c' conservative West Vancouver family, including my younger sister, Heather, and our big, black beloved mutt, Aggie. My sister and I, in our early tweens, had blundered into the deepest trenches of nerdom: me with ever-thicker glasses, knobby knees and short-shorts; my sister with French braids, wobbly glasses of her own and nose planted permanently in her *Little House on the Prairie* books.

We hit the Sunshine Coast Highway on a stovetop-hot July day—the sheer opposite weather to our first rain-soaked voyage. All the windows were rolled down and various bare limbs hung out of the car to catch the breeze, as the cassette player blasted out the sounds of Billy Joel's *Glass Houses* and ABBA's *Greatest Hits*. Between singing along at the top of our lungs to "It's Still Rock 'n' Roll to Me" and "Waterloo," my sister and I still managed to puke repeatedly, the stench of which triggered Mom and Aggie to also start vomiting, causing a sickening scene of rollin', rockin' chaos. Dad blocked out the retching by turning up the stereo and pressing down on the gas pedal. No matter how recklessly Dad took the hairpin curves, slamming brother, sister and large, black dog from side to side in the back seat, we still missed the second ferry, which forced us to kill hours in the blazing sunshine at the Earl's Cove concrete ferry dock. We would wonder over the years if the person who had designed the ferry terminals had actually modelled them after prison camps.

Heather and I trudged the inside perimeter of the terminal's chain-link fence, caged nerds, seeking just a sliver of shade. I led the way with my new copy of *Tintin in Tibet* tucked under my arm, while my sister stumbled along behind, her view blocked by her open hardcover copy of *On the Banks of Plum Creek*, held up with both hands at face level. Back at the car, Mom painted her nails and kept a small dish of water in the rare shade beneath the car for Aggie, whose long, pink tongue was panting. Dad had wandered to the front of the line and was fearlessly mingling with a motorcycle gang, a common sight on the Sunshine Coast in the summer. They had rumbled into the terminal in a rolling thunderstorm of leather, steel and exhaust fumes, straight to the front of the line, as was BC Ferries' custom with motorcycles. Everybody else tried to be coy, but we couldn't help but stare at the bikers in their patch-covered, dirty denim vests, their oil-encrusted Levi's, their heavy, square-toed leather boots, red bandanas, beards, tattoos, long hair, big bellies and bigger voices.

Whenever police cracked down on the motorcycle gangs in the city, or there was a tip that the cops were about to raid the clubhouse, the bikers would make themselves scarce, often splitting up to the Sunshine Coast to wait it out until the heat had cooled off. The winding, picturesque highway was dotted with pubs every ten or twenty kilometres and made for a great run on a motorcycle. It was a wonder they were so amicable when shooting the shit with Dad, rather than suspecting him to be a narc . . . what with his close-cropped hair, mirrored aviator sunglasses and athletic build. Sitting cross-legged with my back against the fence while fiddling with the hinges on my knee braces, I pushed my glasses up my nose and squinted in awe at Dad interacting with the motorcycle gang.

Hours later, the ferries, motorcycles and chain-link fences behind us, we rolled down steep and winding Malaspina Road in the afternoon sun. As we rounded our last turn, we saw a view that would, many years later, become my visual definition of serenity. Outstretched before us was nothing like the foreboding black waters of our first foray but rather a sparkling ocean playground. The water was a calm and shocking blue. The summer sun heated up the sheltered inlets of the Sound to lizard-basking temperatures. We were bound for the Okeover government wharf, where our new motorboat waited patiently—lashed to the dock like a racehorse at a starting gate, eager to bolt. The Okeover government wharf (or "the dock," as everyone called it) was considered by locals as the "back door" to Desolation Sound, the town of Lund being the front. In coastal end-of-the-road country, it doesn't get any more end of the road than the government wharf, a sturdy wooden pier that stretched seventy-five feet from the shoreline, out over the water, wide and strong enough to hold cars on its thick, wooden planks. At the end of the wharf was a gangplank leading down to the wooden floats where the boats were tied. Out in the Sound, "next-door neighbours" could spend their summers in adjacent coves or bays yet never see each other in person. More likely they would cross paths at the wharf, which became the floating, transient community centre for the ocean-bound. Its towering wooden gateway was the starting and finishing line for seagoing adventures that could last an hour or a lifetime.

Dad drove the car up onto the wharf, the tires *thump-thump-thumping* as they rolled over each plank. We clambered out of the car and felt waves of warmth bounce off the granite rocks, melting the weatherproofing tar on the wharf. Defiant mussels and barnacles clung on to sides of the pilings, their shells shut tight, waiting for the high tide to return. Our nostrils filled with the scents of summer on the coast . . . salt air, seaweed, tar and gasoline. It was invigorating, and hard to believe that this was the place Mom and I had been so steadfastly avoiding for several years. Our dorky family stood together at the top of the gangplank, looking down at the hive of activity on the dock. Boats of all shapes and sizes were lashed onto the floating "T": dirty wooden tugs, aluminum oyster barges that looked like giant bathtubs, customized sailboats and half-sunken dinghies. The foot traffic was a mixture of loggers, oyster farmers, fishermen and end-of-the-road hippies that generally looked like a cross between the cast of *The Beachcombers* and the Manson Family, with a light sprinkle of summer tourists — everyone awkwardly united by an early summer's worth of weathered relaxation.

On any waterway, much more than on a highway, there is a distinct hierarchy of vehicles. When Captain Vancouver sailed the *Discovery* and the *Chatham* into Desolation Sound, those ships were the largest vessels that had ever sailed into the waters, dwarfing even the Spanish ships that were already there. When the Sliammon people first saw European ships they were flabbergasted, frightened and curious, thinking they were moving islands covered in dead trees. The *Discovery* was about one hundred feet long and thirty feet wide, while the *Chatham* was considerably smaller, both stuffed with 170 men between them. The European boats were still much larger than even the biggest Native dugout canoes, some of which could hold up to thirty people. All of these crafts were Lilliputian compared to the modern-day BC Ferries.

One of the BC Ferries, part of the largest ferry fleet in the world, and one of the boats that every BC coast dweller loves to hate (even if they are extremely dependable and wind us through some of the most breathtaking scenery in the world). It took two of these lumbering giants to get us to within an hour of our launching point for Desolation Sound.

In the present waters of BC, the ferry is at the very top of the food chain—lumbering white whales of steel, frothing forward, giant mouths agape, ready to swallow anything in their paths. They are the rulers and queens. Get out of their way or die. The *Queen of Surrey*, which powers between Horseshoe Bay and the Sunshine Coast, is just under four hundred feet long and one hundred feet wide. After the ferries come the yachts, floating mansions of the rich and famous, some with helicopter landing pads, uniformed crews and secondary "skiffs" larger and faster than most of our primary Desolation Sound boats. Over the years various Hollywood celebrities have cruised the Sound in their floating white palaces. Johnny Carson, Merv Griffin and John Wayne (whom Mom and I met at the government wharf, getting the Duke's autograph, which I still have to this day) have all enjoyed vacationing in the Sound. More recently, Brad Pitt and Jennifer Aniston were through, and Oprah Winfrey thrilled many when she spent a couple of weeks in the area a few years back. A few rungs below the yachts are sailboats. The thin, graceful little sister to the yacht, sailboats are far less intrusive than their wide, hard-charging, gas-guzzling big brothers. They are captained by the romantics and the adventurers—lovers of the sea and lovers of boats.

Well below the yachts and sailboats in the unnatural order of the ocean are the local flotsam and jetsam of the residential boats: our often-barely-floating ragtag fleet of *Beachcombers*-style workboats, tugs, oyster skiffs, aluminum and fibreglass speedboats, all in various states of disrepair. Dinged propellers, oil-burning carburetors, leaky hulls, seats with the Styrofoam poking through, interiors littered with soggy garbage and empty beer cans—these boats are both the very scourge and pure character of the Sound. And while the yachts and sailboats have romantic or punny names like *Knot a Care*, *Even Keel* or

Wind Weaver, the local boats of the Sound have another style of moniker, such as *Aquaholic, Booz'r Cruis'r, Beer O'Clock,* or *Tuna Colada.* When Heather and I finally figured out some of the meanings behind the names, Heather asked Dad, "Why doesn't someone just name their boat *I'm Really Drunk Right Now?*" Ranking below even the aluminum skiffs are the tippy canoes, their squatting occupants often shaking an angry paddle at the charging speedboats. At the very bottom of the floating food chain is the lowly kayaker, rare in those early days. Kayaks are so close to the water and so hard to see when everyone is roaring around, that the local powerboaters have commonly referred to them as speed bumps.

We'd often take our little aluminum skiff out for picnics in nearby coves and beaches, and here is my little sister, Heather, pictured at Lover's Beach. She's either adjusting the boat on a dropping tide or making a run for it.

Standing at the top of the dock surveying the ragged nautical scene, we West Vancouver imports stood out like a three-piece suit at Woodstock. Glaring brighter than the sunshine was Mom's outfit: spotless pink shorts, a pink sweater slung over a pink polo shirt, knee-high pink-and-white-striped tube socks, all topped with matching, freshly applied pink nail polish and perfume that overpowered the dripping dock tar. Even our dog Aggie was trim and refined compared to the ragamuffin local mutts that came sniffing at the butt of the canine from the city. Luckily, Dad had been coming and going for the last couple of years and fit right in with the locals in his dirty jeans, well-worn white V-neck T-shirt and crumpled Winnipeg Blue Bombers baseball cap.

While Dad chatted with various characters on the dock, the rest of us delicately climbed into our new boat: a twelve-foot aluminum skiff with three bench seats and an eighteen-horsepower pull-start outboard motor, which was steered with a tiller from the back of the boat. Dad hopped in and we took an exhilarating twenty-minute ride through glassy seas and warm salt air, up through the inlets, past large rocks covered by dozens of curious harbour seals and their pups craning their necks to see us, their big eyes questioning our possible threat. Dad pointed out eagles sitting atop towering fir trees, their white heads easy to spot against the steep dark green hillsides. We rounded a point and came into our bay, where we caught our first view of Dad's development. Along the shore, six or seven cabins were in various stages of construction, giving the area somewhat of a shantytown look. As we approached our very own half-built cabin — roof intact as promised — Dad eased up on the throttle, slid it into neutral and brought us in to shore. We didn't have a dock, nor would we ever get one. We just climbed out of the boat onto the rocks and schlepped our backpacks and groceries up to the cabin.

I couldn't believe the difference sunshine made to the Sound. It had come alive. Looking up, the blue sky juxtaposed brilliantly with the evergreen tips of the trees; I had never seen colour like that. Everywhere there were birds, and Dad knelt down and pointed out each one to Heather and me. The eagles now tittered and soared high overhead. *Whoosh-whoosh-whoosh* went the powerful wings of a low-flying, coal-black raven, staring straight at us, checking us out. A blue kingfisher dive-bombed into the water, coming up with wriggling, silver flash in its sharp, black beak. A family of merganser ducks swam in a "V" formation along the shoreline, Mama upfront looking stern with her woodpecker-shaped head and fancy feather-plume cowlick, teaching her half-dozen playful babies how to dive for needlefish. If a threat came near, Mama would let out a low squawk and five ducklings would jump on her back, one wild child racing to catch up after wandering too far. Tiny hummingbirds buzzed by our heads, pausing in mid-air like giant mosquitoes, then gone. A great blue heron stood like a statue at the water's edge, neck like a snake, beak like a pair of barber's scissors, head cocked slightly to one side, fishing. Ugly turkey vultures with shrivelled, bald heads sat high in the treetops, bulging eyes scanning the rocks and ocean for dead things. I could feel myself starting to come around on Desolation Sound. My sister, however, was not.

Innocently, Heather only associated the word "cottage" with "lake," "comfort," and "fun." She had experienced a few in her young life, when our family visited friends in Muskoka (classic Ontario cottage country), the Okanagan Valley (BC's interior summer land), and for our family reunions in Clear Lake, Manitoba (a 1950s-style resort village). A few days before we left for the cabin we had seen *Dirty Dancing*, which is exactly what Heather thought Desolation Sound would be like . . . a romantic summer lifestyle at a lakeside resort, cabins on a hill sloping down to the lakeshore, a path lined with neatly trimmed laurel hedges leading to the beach, the tennis courts and the dining hall. If the lake wasn't to her fancy, she'd have the option of a pool. Nearby would be a quaint little town with an old movie theatre and an ice-cream parlour that stayed open late on a hot summer night, where a Patrick Swayze-like dude would be waiting to serve her two scoops of strawberry ice cream and sweep her off her feet.

While Dad is loving this boat ride in our twelve-foot aluminum skiff with antique outboard motor, please note my little sister's scowl, gritted teeth and the immediate proximity of her security blanket. Also of note: no life jackets anywhere in sight.

Instead what she got was a wild ride in a twelve-foot aluminum boat across a saltwater expanse to a half-built cabin on stilts, poised like a giant spider on a moss-covered rock with a few knurly arbutus trees sticking out around it, in front of a forest that no doubt contained wild things, be they beast or human. We could see a few neighbouring cabins, but the granite shoreline was so vertical there was no way we could walk over to visit. Even our neighbours were "boat-access only." Like the rest of us, Heather noticed our cabin deck had no railings, even though the deck stretched out above jagged cliffs and deep ocean below like a diving board. Her heart sank with confused disappointment.

Our almost-completed cabin's beauty was clearly in the eye of the beholder, and Dad couldn't wait to show us around. At first squint it looked like a superintendent's lodge, scooped up from Banff National Park and dropped onto a rocky outcrop in the middle of nowhere. Since Dad grew up in Manitoba, he had always admired the prairie railway stations with their gently sloped, overhanging roofs and French windows, a design he painstakingly recreated for our cabin, lining the entire front three sides in those French windows. Mom's love of the sun was taken into account with three different levels of sprawling decks, all drenched in windswept sunshine — safety railings and small children be damned. Inside, the cabin offered the soothing aroma of fresh cedar. Towering log poles and heavy crossbeams held up the high, peaked ceiling and cedar-shake roof. The living room had a few pieces of familiar, random furniture from our house in the city — the rest were purchases from the recently opened IKEA outlet in Vancouver — all of it surrounding a wood-burning, cast-iron fireplace. There was a small kitchen, separated from the living room by a half-wall, with a Coleman stove, fridge and lamps — all powered by propane gas — and cupboards filled with enough mismatched cups, plates, pots, pans and utensils to make a Value Village manager blush. Up three stairs was our bathroom, with a sink, shower stall and toilet — none of which worked yet. There was a master bedroom for Mom and Dad, and a smaller bedroom for Heather and me with bunk beds.

Here are my parents enjoying a sunny evening on the deck, before we had any actual chairs to sit in. Dad's looking like Ryan O'Neal in *Love Story*, Mom is as unabashedly preppy as ever, with her knee-high argyle socks and pink sweater tied around her shoulders. Dad would often try to convince her to "dress down" to the locals, which she would vehemently refuse to do.

From wherever we stood in the cabin, we could look out the surrounding French windows that were mostly glass from top to bottom, and see the ocean from every angle. It felt like the cabin was floating on the sea and caused me to feel slightly nauseated, as if the cabin was undulating with every wave. Dad's beloved overhanging eaves covered off the upper level of decking on the front three sides of the cabin, which allowed us to sit outside and still stay cool in the shade and dry in the rain. Various critters came to depend on the eaves as much as we did. Pretty little barn swallows darted in and out of the upper corners, feeding chirping babies in nests that looked like they were constructed from a combination of bird shit and papier mâché.

We also found out quickly that a burgeoning colony of little brown bats had discovered the eaves. They apparently loved sleeping deep between the slats of the warm, cedar-shake shingles that made up our roof; heated by the sun, the wood had the effect of a miniature Swedish sauna. At dusk that first night, Mom, Heather and I watched in horror as dozens of bats dropped from the eaves above our picnic table like fighter jets, scattering pell-mell into the night sky. They flew out over the ocean, and then circled back, swooping down en masse upon us to assumingly seize upon our necks with their tiny fangs. Our instinct was to wave our arms madly, scream at the top of our lungs and run across the deck to dive inside the cabin doors. Even Aggie scrambled for cover with her tail between her legs, yelping in fear. We watched in wide-eyed amazement, our noses pressed against the glass, as the bats fluttered around Dad's head like the disciples of Dracula, never touching him. As he calmly but loudly explained to us through the glass, the bats have a natural sonar that allows them to track their prey—like mosquitoes and no-see-ums, creatures that actually *were* out to suck our blood. Since the mosquitoes were buzzing around us, that's where the bats followed. They ate their weight in mosquitoes every night, and their plentiful guano we found on the deck below the eaves each morning was great for the flower garden we would eventually plant, too. It wasn't until much later that we found out that little brown bats are the number-one carrier of rabies in British Columbia.

One of the first routines I established at the cabin was to hop out of bed and run to the east-side cabin windows. From there, I could look directly downward into a perfect little tidal cove. Each morning the tide was always at a different and dramatic level, and there was always some new aquatic marvel to behold. Stepping out onto the deck and looking straight down, I could peer into the cove's clear, shallow, emerald-green water and spy on an entire other world. Hundreds of translucent jellyfish the size of softballs floated just below the surface, engaged in a collective, slow-motion waltz. Thousands of tiny minnows clung together like a dark cloud, darting suddenly in a different direction en masse from an unseen threat. Heavily armoured red rock crab the size of a boxer's fist moved sideways amid underwater seagrass that swayed to and fro like hula skirts. Bright and glistening purple and red starfish clung to the rocks just above the waterline, perfectly still but constantly moving.

Every morning I'd hop out of the bunk beds I shared with my sister and run to the east-side windows to look straight down into the clear waters of the neighbouring cove. The tide was always at a different level and there was a new sight to behold. On this day, it was a massive school of swirling needlefish, like a living, underwater tornado.

Just beyond the tide line was a little driftwood beach and the forest behind it. A few feet into the woods was the site of the original Bloom family homestead. Gus Bloom made the decision to build their cabin out of sight from the ocean in an attempt to go unnoticed by the local First Nations bands, which held winter ceremonies in nearby Kahkaykay Bay. Kahkaykay is a gorgeous, deep, natural safehaven from stormy weather, and although it has been now completely reclaimed by nature, it was once a winter village for thousands.

Kahkaykay Bay is one of those important but overlooked and misunderstood First Nations historical sites that Captain Vancouver "discovered," but imperialistically ignored because acknowledging the significant population there did not meet his interests. For many centuries, thousands of Natives from the peaceful Sliammon, Klahoose and Homalco tribes would gather in Kahkaykay each winter, living in grand longhouses that were up to two hundred feet long. They would come together amicably to escape both the raging winter weather and the warring peoples from the north: the Kwakiutl and the Haida. These northern tribes would swoop down and raid Coast Salish nations, slaughtering the men and carrying off the women and children as slaves. Kahkaykay's deep, narrow entrance with high cliffs on either side offered strategic maximum protection from both weather and war, and offered plenty of hiding places. The Salish continued to populate Kahkaykay through to the mid-1800s, until finally their populations were decimated by European diseases such as measles, smallpox and tuberculosis.

The government assigned the local Sliammon band to one of their traditional summer camps on the open waters of the Strait of Georgia. It is now the Sliammon First Nation reserve just north of Powell River, speed limit 30 km/h. A small portion of Kahkaykay Bay was eventually declared a reserve, as were areas near Lund and Okeover, but only for very occasional ceremonial purposes and not for permanent living. To add further insult to injury, in the late 1800s and early 1900s, many of the other village sites throughout Desolation Sound were surveyed, sold off, or given away free to pioneers and European settlers through land grant programs as a government enticement to move to Canada, including the current townsite of Lund.

In Kahkaykay Bay and throughout Desolation Sound, the Salish created elaborate, effective low-tide clam gardens and tidal fish traps, entire villages pitching in to move mounds of rocks and boulders to create growing plateaus. The evidence of the clam gardens, fish traps and canoe skids are still clearly visible to this day. The gardens were created to feed a village of hundreds, sometimes thousands, and though the villages are long gone, many of the gardens are still extremely fertile. One surface scrape of the gravel and sand off in any of these anthropological wonders exposes an immediate reward of bountiful and delicious clams. The looming danger remains "red tide," a saltwater algae bloom that creates a temporary toxin in all bivalve ocean creatures, such as clams, mussels and oysters. The toxin is very poisonous and can cause extreme food poisoning, paralysis and even death to humans. Today, there is constant testing to warn of an outbreak. Notices are posted on wharfs and shellfish farms are shut down immediately.

Red tide and an array of other hazards and sicknesses claimed many First Nations lives, their life expectancy was not much beyond fifty. When a tribe member died while they were in Kahkaykay Bay for the winter, the Salish would put the body in a cedar box and hoist it with cedar rope into a tree on a special island reserved for the dead. Upon the tribe's return the following winter, they would take some of the boxes down and cremate the remains in a ceremony, believing the souls of the dead would be reincarnated in nature, be it animal, vegetable or mineral. The small island that was used for the cedar boxes for the Kahkaykay village is located directly across the inlet from our cabin. When the Europeans arrived, loggers would heave an axe into a tree on that island and get the shock of their lives when human bones rattled down upon them. Years later, vacationing yachters would find human skulls and bones while exploring in the underbrush, earning it the nickname "Dead

Man's Island." Some yachts in the early days of vacation cruising were even said to have human skulls from Dead Man's Island perched on their dashboards, and given names like "Charlie" or "Smiley." Beside Dead Man's Island was the only island in the entire inlet upon which not a single mature coniferous tree grew, just low bushes and shrubbery.

No one could explain why trees wouldn't grow on this little island, until Dad told me a Sliammon legend. Each winter in Kahkaykay, some children would be among those that wouldn't survive the season. Legend has it that the bodies of the deceased children were put on this smaller island, a dead child's island. No one else has ever given me a better explanation as to why no tall, mature trees ever grew upon it. Kahkaykay Bay remains a sacred First Nations reserve, though it is rarely ever used or visited by the Salish. When Dad eventually tracked down Alice Bloom, she had clear memories of seeing the Natives passing by the mouth of their little cove in their dugout canoes. She also recalled with great fondness that on certain nights each winter, she and her family would secretly watch the Natives dance around a raging bonfire on the shores of Kahkaykay during their then-illegal potlatch celebrations, their singing filling the night.

Against my stuttering complaints, Dad would often drag me along with him into the forest for hikes—way too far from the safety of our cabin walls and open shoreline for my comfort. I had to watch the placement of every one of my North Star sneakers' steps for fear I would dislocate a knee, but I still made sure to stay right on Dad's heels, petrified that something would grab me from behind and drag me into the dense woods. I carefully plodded along, often glancing nervously over my shoulder, while Dad showed me where the Bloom cabin would have likely stood in the cove, and the clearing where their garden and farm would have been. Over the course of the half-century since the Blooms made the cove their home, the West Coast rainforest had swallowed all remnants of their time in the area, with the exception of a few remaining apple trees. At the end of each summer those trees still managed to poke their branches out of the wild wood to show off their yearly crop of fruit, long after those who planted them had departed.

Farther into the bush, Dad pointed out massive, rotting stumps that were the remains of the last hand-logging in the area, dating back to the mid-1950s. Two dark gouges carved six feet up the stump were still clearly visible, which Dad explained to me were "springboard holes." The loggers would insert boards into the holes to stand on, getting clearance above the base of the tree to enable them to cut it down. To me the holes looked like the glaring eyes of an eroded statue at the gates of the Temple of Doom. I made sure not to touch or even brush up against the stumps as we passed them by. Each time we came to a place where others had been, Dad paused to talk and reflect. He looked down at me as I panted beside him, catching my breath, pushing my steamed glasses up my nose. I was torn — I wanted to rest but I also wanted to turn around and head for home. Dad ignored my anxiety, calmly asking me to try to imagine the people that were there before us: the Salish, the Blooms and the loggers. Imagining all those ghosts just spooked me even more.

On those many hikes, against the odds, I not only survived, but also absorbed Dad's passionate lessons of the forest. He showed me animal tracks in the soft mud near the creek: raccoon, deer, bear, squirrel and other critters. The evidence of live animals large and small was nerve-rattling, but I quickly learned to identify several different footprints. Sometimes Dad would stop silently, mid-step, putting one hand on my shoulder. With the other, he'd point up to a great horned owl perched on a branch, staring furiously back down at us. We'd turn a corner and scare up a grouse, ruffling up its charcoal-coloured feathers in fear, noisily taking temporary flight. Dad taught me to identify every tree — fir, cedar, maple, hemlock, pine, spruce, alder and arbutus — by its bark, leaf or needle; and every plant — salal, manzanita, huckleberry, blackberry, fern, skunk cabbage — by its berry, leaf or flower. The arbutus, manzanita and pine grew in the sunniest spots, down by the ocean on the hard granite outcrop, whereas the cedar, maple and alder grew where it was wet, in a creekbed or a swamp. The towering and awesome Douglas fir tree, with its thick, fire-retardant bark, could grow anywhere and did. Dad explained that the best lots were the ones where the arbutus trees grew; they'd be sunny from dawn till dusk.

Down in Kahkaykay Bay, Dad and I carefully walked through long grass growing over the site of the abandoned First Nations village. Before setting foot on that land, my knowledge of First Nations culture extended about as far as Jesse from *The Beachcombers*; this was a whole other world. At low tide, Dad showed me how to identify the man-made stone walls of the clam gardens, and the cleared canoe launches near the village site. Once pointed out, these artifacts were suddenly very clearly and obviously man-made, yet so easily overlooked. He showed me ancient pictographs painted on the flat granite cliff face. Once I focused upon them, I could see obvious human figures and house-like dwellings depicted in red ink. I was stunned at the realization of the civilization that once existed in this mystical place. Dad walked me over to an island that could be reached by foot at low tide. Sliammon legend has it that during potlatch ceremonies, this island served as a stage, where each family was expected to climb up onto it and tell of their exploits from the summer, either in song or story. The resulting singing and laughter is likely what Alice Bloom so fondly remembered when she and her family would curiously spy on the potlatch celebrations from the opposite shore of the bay.

All the mighty longhouses and original Native dwellings were long gone. Besides the clam gardens and canoe skids, which disappeared underwater at high tide, the only physical structure that remained on the village site was a rotting, one-room cabin that had been desecrated by graffiti from visiting yachters and campers. The cabin was at one time the final home of an old Sliammon chief. The chief was born at the Kahkaykay winter camp many decades earlier, when the tribe still used Kahkaykay as a winter shelter before totally relocating to the reserve in Powell River. When the chief retired, his wish was to live out his days in Kahkaykay Bay. And so his little cabin was barged up the coast and into Kahkaykay, where they placed it on pilings right on the shoreline, directly beside a huge clam-garden lagoon. The chief is also now long gone, but his cabin still stands, barely. On the outside wall someone has painted the words "Kahkaykay Bay Hotel: Vacancy."

When I asked about who had written the graffiti, Dad told me dark stories of Desolation Sound hippie communes that made my glasses fog up.

5
The Beautiful Failure

"Where there is sunshine there is a shadow."
– Anvil, Canadian heavy metal band

The thirty-eight individual lots of the Desolation Sound property sold slowly. It wasn't the boon Dad predicted it would be, and it caused him great disappointment. He had to come up with all sorts of creative sale pitches to attract buyers, even offering to throw in a built cabin and a boat with a motor with the purchase of land. Eventually the lots, each including a small, one-room cabin, were sold for as low as $40,000 apiece to a first round of buyers that included a few teachers and professors, a bus driver, a newspaperman, and Aldo, an easygoing, bearded, rotund freedom-seeker who was a cracked-mirror image of Jerry Garcia. Aldo had spent time at a notorious and genuine hippie commune a short boat ride away. The experience had affected him enough to somehow scrape together the money to buy his own property in the area, and when Dad listed the property for sale, Aldo eventually figured out a way to make it happen. Desperate for sales though he was, Dad was reluctant to sell to Aldo because he couldn't stand hippies.

Dad had to come up with all sorts of sale pitches to attract buyers to a remote area with few amenities.

Neither of my parents had ever embraced any part of the hippie movement, Dad essentially condemning the lifestyle as dirty and lazy. Counterbalancing Aldo was the Reverend Jim Davies, Dad's kind of guy: a straight-laced, no-nonsense United Church minister, old-school outdoorsman and obsessed salmon fisherman. Reverend Jim taught me one of my inaugural life lessons of Desolation Sound: "If you fall out of the boat, pray to God, but swim for shore."

The new collection of neighbours soon urged Dad to form a strata council, which Dad was against, mostly because he didn't want rules in the first place. Dad believed the new owners in Desolation Sound should be able to get along with reason, civility, a large degree of privacy and natural space. He painstakingly surveyed each and every lot so they would all have natural boundaries and conform to the terrain: a ravine, a high bluff, a cove, or a stand of trees separated each cabin's building site. It pained him to set out even the most basic rules, and it pained him even more to hear of the formation of committees and councils in this wild place, worrying that politics would soon follow. Mom reasoned that Dad should just let the soon-to-be elected strata council of owners (who would be sworn in by raising their right beer) worry about rules, and to step aside. No one said Dad had to be on the council.

Mom and Dad in our finally finished cabin, a.k.a our IKEA showroom in the wilderness. Note the brand new pot-bellied fireplace, Dad's Winnipeg Blue Bombers cap and Mom's pearl earrings.

The unsteady sales of the individual lots and formations of committees were nothing compared to the problems Dad faced with the construction of the cabins. It proved to be a major challenge to build cabins on uneven granite cliffs, with no road access or electricity. When it came to the completion of our cottage, Dad had to halt construction constantly to return to Vancouver to handle the sales of other lots. A local scallywag and part-time carpenter named Mack saw a niche, formed a motley crew of locals and was offering his relatively cheap services to individual owners to help complete their cabins. Mack was a wiry Irish redhead, aggressive and industrious. Aldo the happy hippie was the first to hire Mack, and subsequently, Aldo was the first to have what resembled a cabin.

Dad was jealous but still resisted, as he had heard stories about Mack that made him cautious. Word around the Sound was that Mack had a wild temper and carried a razor-sharp chisel with him everywhere he went, sometimes using it as a weapon. Mack had apparently once feuded with a local fisherman. One time, when their boats passed within a few feet of one another in the inlet, Mack reportedly stood up and threw the chisel like an Ed Ames tomahawk, landing it with a loud *thunk* into the wooden bench right between the fisherman's legs, thus earning him the nickname "Mack the Knife." Mom thought it was the most ridiculous story she had ever heard. Alas, there were no other construction options that were going to be as cheap. Dad eventually enlisted Mack the Knife and his gang to help finish our cabin.

When our family arrived that summer amid the construction, the much less intimidating Aldo spotted us tooling around on the rocks in front of our half-built—but roofed—dwelling, so he stopped by in his ramshackle sailboat to greet us. Aldo had a friendly chat with my folks, which ended, much to Dad's chagrin, with Aldo inviting us over to his place for a potluck dinner party that night.

Dad in the midst of building our cabin. It remained like this for a long time due to persistent problems with financing, local builders, high tides and a hippie kid named Harvest Moon.

Ever since the Europeans arrived, Desolation Sound has always attracted a certain type of individual. Whether it was Captain Vancouver, the settlers of the late 1800s, the yachting elite, the wayward hippies or my very own father, the Sound's vast myriad of ocean, rock and forest has many times served as the final destination, the land beyond the map — a place of hope, refuge, hiding and escape. When the Vietnam War caused a generation of socially conscious Americans to turn on, tune in and drop out, rumours rippled down the west coast as far as California, and as far east as New York state, of fabled Canadian communes clear from any law, authority or city skyline. The Desolation Sound and Lund area was suddenly a sought-after destination for draft dodgers and commune idealists hoping to live by the rhythm of nature. In the late 1960s and during the 1970s, just down the inlet from the future site of our cabin, a real-life, certifiable hippie commune sprung up on an old homestead.

Hippies from across North America would hitchhike west to California. If they made it out of San Francisco, they would thumb their way up to Canada. If they made it across the border, they'd keep on hitchhiking up the Sunshine Coast, searching for their lost horizon. When they eventually made it to the town of Lund, they either crashed at one of the many nearby "mainland" communes, or caught a ride on a boat travelling north into Desolation Sound.

At the Desolation Sound commune's height, thirty to forty disillusioned, ambitious misfits lived among their dogs, cats, chickens and goats — attempting the Age of Aquarius, unplugged. They took over the deteriorating buildings of the original European homesteaders, which included a barn, a small, one-room schoolhouse and a main lodge. They planted gardens, fished for their dinner, collected oysters and harvested the long-gone homesteaders' still-producing orchard. Their goal was to eventually create a completely communal, self-sustaining lifestyle. They grew a lot of pot and mushrooms, too. In the first year, a baby was born in the commune without the aid of "outsiders," which the members took as a sure sign that their self-sustaining dream was becoming a reality.

As can be counted upon, summers in the Sound are hedonistic bliss, an unmatched Canadian ocean paradise. It was in the summer that most of the hippies would arrive, from 1968 all the way through the 1970s. The kids happily existed on a diet of pot, hash, acid, mushrooms and free love. At first, the commune threatened to become a tourist attraction among the yachting elite who anchored their boats in the bay just offshore. Naked hippies having sex along the shoreline were easily focused upon with a set of binoculars. But food and money were often scarce or nonexistent in the commune, so its members developed a routine of rowing their leaky skiff out to the yachts, often in the nude, offering the vacationers fruit and oysters in exchange for money and other provisions. This practice annoyed the tourists fairly quickly, and word spread through the yachting community that anchoring near the commune should be avoided.

The commune's goal was to create a permanent enclave, which meant living in Desolation Sound year-round. But as much as the summers of the Sound are blissful, the winters can be brutal. They are dark and dangerous to both mental and physical health. Hence, the nastiest stories from Desolation Sound always occur in the winter. Whether it was the Sliammon, Gus Bloom, William Bloom, the Cougar Lady or the hippies, tales of depression, insanity, fatal accidents, fire, suicide and murder almost always coincide with the cold, dark, wet months of winter between October and March.

Unabated and likely ignorant of the area's history and the harshness of the season, the hippies hunkered down for the long haul. But as the skies turned black, so did the mood of the commune. An accidental drowning in a raging winter storm cast a shadow of sadness many members couldn't shake. Free love turned to rampant jealousy, paranoia and violence. Spring orgies became winter pregnancies, with no clear indications as to who the fathers were. Almost everyone who lived in the commune contracted STDs, including communal crabs that kept going around and around. One winter the entire community came down with boils that they couldn't get rid of.

Brutal, physical fights among the men were common, as was bizarre behaviour likely brought on by drugs, darkness, rain, isolation and cabin fever, locally known as "going bush." One member barricaded himself in a cabin and fired a rifle at anyone who came near. Another tore apart the commune kitchen one night, throwing everything out the door and into the rain. Running out of firewood was routine, but everything that surrounded them was soaked through from the constant winter downpours and wouldn't burn. First, they raided other nearby homesteads, stripping the buildings of wood. When they exhausted that supply, they tore apart their own buildings one by one, burning the wood and leaving garbage everywhere.

Sadly, like so many dropout communes of the era, the hopeful Shangri-La of the Desolation Sound commune failed to materialize in the long term. Its members wanted to drop out of society, but couldn't (or wouldn't) form their own as hard as they honestly and idealistically tried to self-sustain themselves. After five devolving years, the property owners (a commune leader's absentee parents) eventually kicked everyone out. The commune's remaining members scattered, some to Lund and to other parts of the Sound (like Aldo), and some across North America from whence they came.

A bizarre and intriguing book entitled *Apple Bay*, written by commune member Paul Williams, was published in 1976. It's a firsthand drug-addled, diary-like account of what

Williams considered a necessary but failed life experiment. Williams summed up the many reasons for the commune's shortcomings: "Sex, territory, restlessness, stubborn egotism, the need for privacy, the need for togetherness, the need for moral leadership, it all adds up to ceaseless pain, an end to dreams, and someday, somedays, the beginning of real work, order out of chaos, the hardest job any of us ever imagined facing." Williams, a renowned music journalist who now lives in San Diego, has published several books and is credited for publishing *Crawdaddy*, the first critical American rock 'n' roll magazine and predecessor to *Rolling Stone*. While attending the Woodstock concert in 1969, Williams met a young girl who was hitchhiking west to San Francisco after the festival. Williams dropped everything, including his post as editor of *Crawdaddy*. When they arrived in San Francisco they were disillusioned with the scene, and that's when they heard about the Desolation Sound commune in Canada.

It seems that no matter how hard they try to abstain, human beings just can't help but form societies complete with law and order, rules and reason. Dad was already finding that out reluctantly, far as he was from a hippie. He was quickly realizing that he had purchased land that had a magnetic and insatiable appeal to hippies long after their 1960s Age of Aquarius had passed (Mom called them "leftover hippies"). The irony that Dad would be forced to work with, employ, trust and deal with neighbouring "leftover hippies" and outlaw bikers for many decades is still unfolding for him to this day.

Hesitantly, my parents accepted the invitation to Aldo's potluck.

6
Smoke on the Water

Pot would in fact be the keyword to Aldo's potluck invitation. Much to their consternation, my parents were figuring out that besides apples and oysters, there were a few other crops that could be successfully harvested in Desolation Sound. With its rare coastal microclimate of warm, wet air and long, hot summers, Desolation Sound is perfect for growing bountiful bushels of marijuana. Aldo's potluck was a five-minute boat ride away in the next bay. As our motorboat rounded the rocky finger that separated our bays, we heard the potluck before we saw it. The combined caterwaul of a party in full swing danced across the open water like radio waves. As we drew closer, my innocent young eyes widened upon seeing a scene of total hedonism.

Intertwined brown bodies lay outstretched all over the sun-drenched shoreline, smoking, drinking, laughing, singing, making out and making love. Seemingly wild, long-haired children ran among the cavorting adults, leaping off the rocks into the green ocean water. The aesthetic that united the party was a revealing one: every single man, woman and child was totally and utterly nude. It was like the moment Charlton Heston discovers the humans at the oasis in *Planet of the Apes*. Just add a cranked-up Deep Purple cassette and matching purple bong smoke that hung low across the bay: "Smoke on the Water," just like the stereo blasted. This outrageous scene was more than enough for Dad to start vigorously turning the boat around, but mom wouldn't let him, reasoning that:

a) she was bringing banana bread;
b) we were going to have to meet the rest of our neighbours eventually;
c) how would it look if the big, bad developer and his family suddenly swung their boat around in full view of the entire party and left without even saying hello?

We tied our skiff to a makeshift barge of boats, a barely floating, pell-mell parking lot of rafts, canoes, kayaks and rowboats in various states of sunken disrepair. We had to climb through several of them before we could make our way up the gang-plank to shore.

Throughout my childhood, whenever I was extremely uncomfortable or frightened, I developed a strange nervous reaction: my teeth would chatter like I was locked in a freezer. Walking up that gangplank on that hot summer night into a foreign, naked scene of hippie strangers, my teeth sounded like a death rattle. My little sister cowered behind me, pulling on the back of my *E.T.* turtleneck. We were greeted by a beaming Aldo and his festive, long, white beard, flowing down over his bulging brown belly, both of which almost covered his dangling penis. Almost. He gripped a half-full bottle of label-less red wine in one hand and waved a giant doobie in the other, which he transferred to his lips when he extended his leathery, brown hand in welcome. My sister and I stared on in shock, eyes like Keane Kids in pale, expressionless faces. My teeth continued to chatter uncontrollably.

Everyone at the party warmly welcomed us with extremely uncomfortable hugs, introducing us all around. Pungent pot clouds filled the air like a skunky London fog. Elaborate bongs gurgled and hissed, threatening to stain Mom's pink pedal pushers. Mom later said she had never maintained such steadfast eye contact in her life and took extra caution when reaching out to shake hands with the guys. When Aldo sat down on a stump and spread his legs like Santa in a sauna, she strategically placed the pan of banana bread directly on his lap. Painfully, my sister and I were torn away from our parents' side when two gregarious, naked kids bounded up to us and insisted that we try their rope swing. They pranced barefoot down the rocks with the effortless agility of nimble forest creatures while we gingerly followed as if blindfolded. At the edge of a cliff overlooking the water was a lineup of more naked brown children of various ages, all shrieking happily while taking turns on a thick, bristly rope swing that was looped around a branch of a giant fir tree that grew out over the water. They'd place a foot in a loop at the bottom, grab the rope with their hands, swing out over the ocean, and let go just at the right moment to plunge into the warm, green water below.

My sister and I were expected to follow suit. My teeth had stopped chattering long enough to politely refuse but these friendly naked children with names like Sunpatch and Birdsong urged us on, insisting that we remove our clothes and join in the fun. (Similar pressure in far more adult situations was being put on our parents back in the heat of the bash.) For whatever bizarre societal reason, being the only clothed individuals at a nudist party at the edge of the wilderness felt as uncomfortable as if one were to be suddenly dropped naked onto a downtown sidewalk. And there would be no "Grin and bear it"—literally—for the Lawrence family on this night. The closest thing we got to public nudity was in our bathing suits once or twice a summer on a Vancouver beach, and even then I would never dare take my shirt off.

I struck a deal with the Lost Boys. Neither my sister nor I would remove our clothes, but I would try the rope swing. A pair of naked, deeply tanned identical twin boys with matching shocks of shaggy black hair held the rope for me. I pushed my glasses up from the end of my nose and nervously placed my shaking Keds sneaker inside the loop. I took hold of the rope. Its fraying fibres bit into my silky city palms. With a simultaneous shove from the twins I was suddenly airborne, hanging on for my young life, all my tiny muscles contracted, my body wrapped around the rope in a kung fu grip.

As I arced out over the ocean, the setting rays of the sun spilled across the surface, turning it to gold, illuminating the shoreline rocks with an illustrious shimmer. I felt something deep within let go and give in. Panic turned to acceptance, then calmness, then serenity as I hung over the glimmering ocean, frozen in space. Time stood still and all sound ceased. As if in a dream I gazed back toward the cliff edge at my sister and the naked children. They were calling to me . . . waving, yelling something and making hand gestures. The moment of serenity evaporated as quickly as it began. Real life, sound and motion roared like a train from a tunnel. I heard the words "Jump! Now! Jump! Let go of the rope!"

I didn't jump, and I didn't let go. I held on. Momentum swung me back toward the ledge filled with children like a nerd pendulum. I heard the words "No!! No!!" as they began to scatter. I slammed into the crowd, knocking kids off the ledge, sending them plunging into the water like lemmings. My runners' toe grips scraped the rock ledge but couldn't hang on.

The rope took me swinging out over the water again. I shut my eyes and hung on so tight the fibres cut into my palms. This time, when momentum swung me back toward the cliff, since I had cleared it of children, I slammed face first into a wall of granite. My glasses clattered to the ledge. Blind and stunned, I dropped to my hands and knees and searched until my fingers found them, bent but not broken.

My sister was pushed out of harm's way thanks to a very kind older, fully developed naked girl, who also helped me with my bleeding nose, her perky brown breasts at my direct eye level. While the rest of the kids pulled themselves out of the water below, the kind girl suggested we head back to the main party and find our parents. Both my sister and I readily agreed and followed her round brown bum back to the party.

We spent another ninety excruciating minutes at the party. Since the only pot my parents touched sat on our stove simmering Kraft Dinner on Friday nights, they weren't blending in any better than Heather and I were. After the umpteenth uncircumcised male member bounced past my sister's eye level, she eventually slipped into something akin to a catatonic shock, desperate to escape back into the 1880s world of heavily clothed bonnet-to-boot characters of *Little House on the Prairie*. I pushed my bent glasses up my nose to get a better look at the bronzed, pregnant hippie ladies, spread out on the rocks like melted candles.

Mom eventually signalled our exit . . . "Aldo! Thank you so much for having us!" in a volume shrill enough to frighten birds into flight. "We'd better get the kids home now, but this has been an absolutely fabulous party!" On our mostly silent boat ride home, Dad muttered that the party had been an unpleasant cross between *Helter Skelter*, *Apocalypse Now* and a *National Geographic* special on orangutans. I have had a deep, personal aversion to potlucks ever since.

7
Harvest Moon

One of the ne'er-do-wells of Mack the Knife's construction gang was a young, out-of-work oyster farmer named Harvest Moon, or "Moony," as the locals called him. Moony was a bearded, skinny, undernourished and somewhat hapless hippie who had leased a local oyster farm from the government in an effort to create a self-sustaining utopian lifestyle at the edge of the world. Like so many before him, Moony was finding out quickly that Desolation Sound was a far harsher toke than he had imagined. Oyster farming in particular is incredibly laborious, finger-shredding, back-breaking, tedious work at all hours of the day and night, a long-term work schedule controlled by tides. There is little return unless you stick with it for years; oyster farming is not a quick buck. When Moony started asking around the inlets for extra work, Mack brought him on to do grunt work, which usually meant endless schlepping of construction materials and lumber from the government wharf to the cabin sites. That's what Moony was supposed to do for us.

Moony followed Mack the Knife's growled instructions to the syllable, meeting the lumber truck at the wharf first thing in the morning. He painstakingly loaded the heavy planks, beams and shingles into his twenty-five-foot oyster barge. He then slowly and cautiously motored it up the inlet and into our bay. By noon, Moony had unloaded the lumber at the exact spot Mack requested so the crew could get to work the next morning. By 2 p.m., Moony was headed for home across the inlet for a nice early bong hit, confident of a job well done. His work was indeed spot on, with just one glaring exception. Moony had left the lumber at Mack's desired location, but at half-tide, so the lumber was sitting a good seven feet below the high-tide line. By the time high tide rolled in that evening at 7 p.m., the entire load of what should have been our hardwood floors, bedroom walls and decking, all $5,000 worth, simply floated away. Within hours, word had spread through the inlet that all sorts of amazing building materials were drifting with the currents, and soon every oyster farmer, hippie and hermit was puttering out into the Sound to salvage as much of the prime lumber as their leaky tubs could handle.

Later that night, a heavily stoned, satisfied and oblivious Moony made his regular trip to the Lund pub and overheard some of his inlet friends discussing the unbelievable floating bounty of fresh-cut lumber. Moony's face turned the colour of his namesake as his mistake slowly dawned upon him. Shortly thereafter, fully aware of his boss's reputation with a certain hand tool, Moony made the hasty decision that odd jobs and oyster farming in Desolation Sound weren't for him. No one ever saw or heard from the skinny kid again, though plenty of the shacks and cabins along the inlets enjoyed brand-new sections of cedar-shake roofing, reinforced walls, new railings and pilings that summer, all an inadvertent ocean cash crop courtesy of a kid called Harvest Moon.

When the news reached Dad in Vancouver, he didn't appreciate the charitable benefits of Moony's folly as much as the rest of the inlet's residents did. Dad was furious, blamed Mack for hiring an inept kid and stopped all payments. Mack the Knife became enraged, telling anyone who would listen that Dad was ripping him off, and that he was truly "the big, bad developer" several of the locals had feared would ruin their Desolation Sound tranquility. Mack ceased all further construction on our cabin. They traded angry phone calls and ignored each other's invoices.

A couple weeks later, Dad hired a seaplane and flew in an elderly couple from Vancouver to check out a few of the lots still for sale. Word eventually made it to Mack the Knife that Dad was back in the Sound. As Dad was walking the customers along the shoreline of one of the properties, Mack's beat-up old boat roared into the bay at full speed, heading straight for them. Reaching shore, Mack cut his engine, leaped out of the boat and ran straight at Dad and his perplexed, startled customers. Mack the Knife was shirtless, sweaty and wild-eyed. His long red hair was sticking out in all directions from the boat ride. When he was within a couple of feet, Mack the Knife made good on local legend. He whipped out a sharpened chisel from his belt and held it up. "Where's my money, Lawrence?!"

Dad leaned back, *Matrix*-like, and spread his arms to the side showing no resistance. "Easy, Mack. Let's talk about this."

"There's nothing to talk about! You owe me money and I want it now!" Mack spat back, still holding the chisel up.

"Mack, your man let my entire load of lumber float away with the tide. Your man . . . He's on your crew, maybe we could . . . share the responsibility?" A glimmer of culpability flashed across Mack's wild green eyes. He looked beyond

Dad at the ghostly, near-cardiac complexion of the potential customers.

"That was one stupid kid," said Mack with a chuckle, lowering the chisel. To Dad's hardly breathing, now-former customers he amicably said, "Hi, I'm Mack. You looking to build?"

Dad didn't make the sale. Miraculously, he did manage to hammer out a temporary truce with Mack the Knife, in that Dad would eat most of the cost of the lost lumber and construction would proceed. By the end of the fall of that year, our cabin was completed without further major interruption or incident. Dad knew he needed Mack and his gang to finish it, but as soon as the last nail was driven, he would do his best to avoid Mack the Knife for the rest of his days in the Sound.

Little did our family know that we would soon be dealing long term with a homeless, university-educated hippie-philosopher who would decide to pitch a tent directly beside our cabin. Or, that that same radical man would become one of the greatest mentors in my life.

8
Hermit of Desolation Sound

Within a few years, Dad's shantytown development slowly turned into a micro-colony of makeshift vacation cottages. They were being customized to each family's needs, individual boats were purchased, and an awkward new community was beginning to form where borrowing a cup of sugar involved starting an outboard engine. When my family next forayed up the coast that summer, we found ourselves neighbours with a resident who didn't hold a title deed. We didn't notice him right away. As always, we unloaded our supplies from the boat onto the small rocky outcrop in front of the cabin and started making the multiple schleps from shore to door. Dad spotted him first, stopping suddenly. Out of the corner of his eye he thought he saw something moving along the shore in the cove. He squinted in the sunlight, raised his hand to his brow and saw the movement again. We were all startled by Dad's frozen posture and followed his stare toward the woods.

I saw him, too. Blending in perfectly with the foliage a few hundred feet away from us was a bearded man with a long, thin face. He was casually sitting cross-legged on a fallen log at the very edge of the forest. His clothes were the same colour as the earth, woods and rocks. The only reason Dad had spotted him was his Zippo lighter had winked at us in the sunshine as he lit his pipe. The man was looking right at us. "Who is that?" Mom whispered nervously, brushing a piece of seaweed from my sister's shoulder after Heather had picked herself up from a face-first tumble.

"I have no idea," Dad replied slowly, not taking his eyes off the figure from the woods. Dad knew that the cove land adjacent to our cabin was owned by a man from Kamloops, BC, named Tim, but this person was not Tim. Slowly the man rose to his feet, and in a loping, easygoing gait, he crossed the short stretch of pebble beach of the cove and began to climb up the rock ledge to where we stood. "Hello there!" he cheerily called out, a pleasant creak in his voice like the floorboards of my grandparents' house.

"Hello . . . there . . . " Dad answered cautiously.

When he was face to face with us, we observed a tall, lean, weathered bushman. He was about forty or so, with a friendly smile and warm, alert eyes. He had a salt-and-pepper beard thick as a scrub brush, and his greying hair was pulled back in a ponytail. His skin was dark from the dirt and the sun. His nose was long and pressed into his face like a hockey player's. More Willie Nelson than Patrick Swayze, he extended his right hand to Dad and introduced himself with a wide smile: "I'm Russ Letawsky. You must be the Lawrences!" Russell helped us carry the rest of our supplies up to the cabin, and then accepted a Labatt Blue stubby as we all sat down on the deck. I hadn't said a word beyond a meek hello, but this mysterious, friendly fellow from the forest already fascinated me. Russell explained that he had pitched a tent on the old Bloom cabin site, just a few feet into the woods from the cove. He had arrived just about a month earlier, and was living on the lot full-time. Upon hearing this, Dad's face turned a pale shade of grey.

Even though Russell's polite demeanour didn't show it, he wasn't all that enthusiastic about having neighbours in such close proximity either. He was silently getting over his own shock, as he had been in Powell River ("town") that day, cashing his monthly welfare cheque, and had seen Mom at the grocery store in her pink sweater, pink shorts, pink nail polish and pink-and-white-striped tube socks. Like everyone else, he had assumed such a blindingly bright character could only be bound for Savary Island, a nearby anomaly ringed with sandy beaches that attracted some of Vancouver's most privileged families. An hour or so later, to his surprise, he saw this very same woman at the Okeover government wharf, a long way from Savary. He assumed she was lost. He fired up his skiff and left her and her family to stuff their own boat with enough supplies for a year. When that very same woman and her two kids, dog and husband showed up an hour later in, of all places, his very own cove, he thought for certain he had mixed the wrong mushrooms into his spaghetti sauce. The peace and tranquility Russell had sought so badly was about to be interrupted each morning by a woman who dried her nail polish in the sun and would scream at anyone who came near, waving her hands as if she was being attacked by hornets. Cracking another of Dad's beers using the flat edge of a long and dramatic buck knife he kept in a smooth leather sheath on his belt, Russell stretched out on the stairs of the deck and told us his life story. It lasted until after dark.

Long, tall and cool: Russell Letawsky, the Toronto-yuppie-turned-Desolation-Sound-philosopher-hippie. Little did I know that this Cowichan sweater–clad, bearded, tent-dwelling, leaky-skiff-owning freedom seeker would become one of the greatest mentors in my life.

Russell Letawsky was the son of Ukrainian-Canadian farmers. He was born in Skaro, Alberta, on the northern prairie just outside Edmonton. He and his five brothers and sisters spent their teen years in Edmonton in the late 1950s, Russell remembering it fondly just like *Happy Days* (Russell more like Richie Cunningham than Arthur Fonzarelli). The minute Russell graduated from high school he shook the Alberta dust for the bright lights and big city, in search of an education and to make his fortune in business. Russell arrived in Toronto when the city's bohemian hippie counterculture was just starting to get into full swing down in Yorkville, Canada's answer to Greenwich Village. To a self-described "hayseed" from Alberta, the scene was a freak show, a zoo, and proved too much for him. Instead, after a series of respectable part-time jobs, he landed a high-paying full-time gig as a salesman in the heart of the financial district. Russell fashioned his hair in a close-cropped brush cut like Paul Newman, wore a starched white-collar shirt, a crisp three-button suit and a thin black tie every day. He married and had a young daughter. He was a yuppie when everyone else was a hippie.

While he worked, Russell took night classes at York University, then often compared to progressive American schools such as Berkeley or NYU. While attending classes in subjects as diverse as engineering and philosophy, Russell's view on the world, and what was important to him, began to change. He delved deep into the writings of David Hume and Friedrich Nietzsche, appreciating Nietzsche's radical questioning of societal norms, values and truths. Russell specifically became fixated with one of Nietzsche's favourite phrases, *Amor fati*: Latin for "love of fate," or more specifically, "love *your* fate." In Nietzsche's 1882 book *The Gay Science*, he writes:

> I want to learn more and more to see as beautiful what is necessary in things; then I shall be one of those who make things beautiful. *Amor fati*: let that be my love henceforth! I do not want to wage war against what is ugly. I do not want to accuse; I do not even want to accuse those who accuse. Looking away shall be my only negation. And all in all and on the whole: some day I wish to be only a Yes-sayer.

Russell would read the passage over and over again and slowly but surely he felt the clouds in his mind lifting. He could see life's distant horizons with polar clarity, but that horizon was beyond Toronto's city skyline. Russell's sought-after white-collar prestige, which he had worked so hard for, was beginning to feel like a noose. The status, the yuppie lifestyle, suddenly felt as empty as Bay Street on a Sunday.

On a searing-hot and humid summer day, Russell found himself standing among the sweat-soaked masses at the chaotic corner of Yonge and Dundas in downtown Toronto. Right then, something snapped in Russell Letawsky. He told us it hit him like a sledgehammer. He looked around and said loudly, to no one and to everyone, "What the fuck is this? What the fuck am I doing?" He thought of *Amor fati* and no longer wanted to battle the ugly city. He did not want to blame others for his unhappiness. He wanted to look away. He no longer wanted to attempt to control his fate. Russell interpreted Nietzsche to believe that the weak and insecure built cities and waged wars, and that the strong cast themselves to the wind, like a leaf (others over time have interpreted Nietzsche somewhat . . . differently).

Russell dropped out of university, quit his job and left his family. In his own words, he "went radical." He stopped shaving and cutting his hair. He traded his cigarettes for a pipe. He had to get out of the city and back to the very country living he had scorned years earlier. The hayseed's wild oats had been sown as a yuppie in downtown Toronto and now he sought the opposite: he wanted to get as far away from the rat race as possible. Like Nietzsche's leaf in the wind, Russell drifted west, hitchhiking his way back across Canada. With each kilometre, he felt his mood improving, his happiness returning. Russell eventually found temporary work in a photo lab in the dusty cowboy town of Kamloops, BC. He was spending as much time in Kamloops' natural environment as possible — hiking, hunting and even doing a little gold prospecting in the local creeks. He also paid special attention to avoid the hippie-hating cowboys who harassed him and his ever-lengthening hair and beard. He made friends with the local hippies and draft dodgers.

That's how Russell met Annie, a gorgeous, green-eyed, dark-haired flower child. Annie's sister Laura was living down on the coast, preparing to split from a commune gone wrong, and Annie wanted to join her. Annie's description of Desolation Sound's saltwater oasis beyond rules, cops and cowboys sounded like the fate Russell had dreamt of. Annie and Russell fell for each other, and soon she agreed to hang around town for the summer while Russell packed up, quit another job and prepared to move to the coast with Annie.

Being the dreamer that Russell was, he pitched Annie a crazy idea: to *walk* to Desolation Sound, over the rugged, towering and treacherous Coast Mountains. So ridiculously steep and impenetrable are these mountains that very few roads crossed over them to the coast, but Russell wanted to avoid them anyway. Russell wanted to walk to the coast due west as the crow flies, the plan being to emerge right into Desolation Sound. Annie was a dreamer, too, and immediately agreed. In the middle of the summer, friends dropped off Russell and Annie at the very end of an old logging road near a washed-out bridge. And so Russell and Annie, armed with a map, a compass, some food and an M1 rifle with a thirty-bullet clip, walked straight into the bush. No road, no trail, no nothing—just kilometre after kilometre of thick, dense West Coast forest. The trip was supposed to take two weeks. It lasted a month.

Russell had planned out the food perfectly for two people . . . for two weeks. What Russell didn't calculate in his planning was how much Annie would slow him down. She was tough and up for anything, but they had to take their time. Most wildlife steered clear; they once spotted a grizzly wandering through the low brush on the other side of a valley, but never saw it again. The hairiest experience of the month occurred when Russell was fishing in a little mountain creek. The food had run out, so they were getting by on squirrels, grouse and river trout. As Russell made his way around a tree to drop his hook into a promising pool in the creek, he came face to face with a wolverine, one of the most elusive and dangerous animals in western Canada.

Almost never seen by humans, the wolverine is a snarling, muscle-bound cross between a badger and a bear, though only as big as a medium-sized dog. Wolverines have been known to attack animals as large as moose and to engage in combat with bears when defending a kill. Both Russell and the wolverine stopped in their tracks, staring at each other in shock. Russell's nostrils immediately burned with the strong, skunk-like scent the wolverine is known to have, and which has earned it the occasional nickname "skunk bear." After a momentary standoff, both stinky man and beast simultaneously turned on their heels and took off at full speed in opposite directions, each checking over his shoulder to make sure the other was doing the same.

Russell and Annie were eventually forced to leave the forests and climb straight into the craggy Coast Mountain range. They hiked up through the alpine and then to the ever-sliding dangerous shale found on steep mountainsides above the treeline. Hiking through shale is like trying to walk up a hill covered in broken dinner plates. They scaled rock faces, hiked around glaciers of snow and ice, and balanced across treacherous crevices with a fifty-foot rope tied to each other's waist. Twenty-eight days after they were dropped off on the logging road, Russell and Annie traversed their final ridge, frail and near starving. Standing tall on a peak high above the treeline, Russell put his hands on his hips and exhaled. "Baby," he called to Annie, who was scrambling up the shale twenty feet behind him, "come and look at this."

Annie grabbed onto his hand and squeezed tight while he hoisted her up the last few feet to join him. Annie and Russell looked down upon a glittering ocean, the sun dancing off the calm, dark-green waters of the winding inlets of Desolation Sound far below. It turned out that Russell's compass orienteering was extremely accurate. Lining up the inlets and islands with the map, he concluded correctly that they had come out above the very remote and deep Toba Inlet, just kilometres north of the land where Annie's sister was moving. Russell and Annie wasted no time traversing down the western slope of the range, into the alpine meadows and finally through the cool, towering, coastal forest. The two skin-and-bones hippies eventually burst through the dark wall of green — stepping into the oven-like, broiling summer heat of a logging operation's clear-cut.

A few hundred feet away a logging tractor fought with a freshly cut log like a *Rock'em Sock'em Robot*. Russell and Annie jumped up and down, waving their arms, making their way toward the tractor. When they were within one hundred feet, the tractor stopped like a dinosaur interrupted while devouring lunch. Slowly the machine turned to face the two figures eagerly approaching. The lone logger driving the tractor was understandably shocked to see two skinny humans in the middle of his remote clear-cut. When he climbed out of the cab of the tractor, Russell and Annie saw their first human being in a month. They whooped for joy, causing the logger even further concern.

After a brief and giddy explanation from Russell, the stunned logger loaded them into his tractor for a long, bumpy ride down the hill to the logging camp at the head of Toba Inlet. That night, Russ and Annie stuffed themselves full in the loggers' kitchen, swam in the warm ocean, excitedly told the loggers tales of their month in the bush, and slept like the dead in what they nicknamed the "Toba Hilton," a barely furnished bunkhouse trailer with plywood floors. The next morning, they hitched a ride on a barge that took them out into Desolation Sound, winding through the inlets to Laura's new place. In the meantime, Laura had become increasingly concerned about her sister, now two weeks late with no word. Every day, Laura and her boyfriend had been sailing to the nearby inlet where Russell told them they were likely to emerge. They were preparing their boat for the daily trip just as the logging barge pulled into their bay.

For the next couple of months, Russell and Annie bummed around the inlets. They drifted into the tiny nearby town of Lund, crashing for a few days here or a week or two there at various hippie farms hidden in the alder forests. Eventually, Annie tired of the scene and announced she was moving back to Kamloops, leaving Russell heartbroken and alone. Even though he had never sailed in his life, Russell used the savings from his Kamloops job and bought a little sailboat. He tied it up at the Okeover government wharf where he spent the next year or so. He learned to sail the inlets, frequently visiting various communes, and spent time living on old homesteads throughout the Sound. He'd often pass by our cabins, slowly being constructed.

Russell had fallen in love with Desolation Sound, and dreamt of owning one of my father's lots, but his bank account was like his belly, mostly empty all of the time. Undaunted, Russell would sail across the inlet day after day. He was most taken with the Blooms' original homestead—the little cove with the fresh running creek, apple trees and gravel beach directly adjacent to the rocky outcrop where the foundation of our family cabin stood. Like the majority of the hippies in the neighbourhood, Russell's only income was his monthly welfare cheque. There was no way he could raise the $35,000 asking price for a lot. Instead, he called someone who could: a draft-dodging pal from Kamloops named Tim who held down a steady job. If Russell Letawsky was anything, he was charming. Over a series of letters and phone calls, Russell provided Tim

Here's Russell Letawsky looking triumphant after his harrowing hike across the Coast Mountains to Desolation Sound. A hippie from head to knee . . . note the no-nonsense, tightly laced old-school hiking boots that got him across that range.

with vivid, passionate descriptions of the land, sea and aura of the Sound. Eventually, Russell received a letter back from Tim: "Are you sitting down?" the letter began. Tim had purchased the little cove lot and was inviting Russell to live on the land until Tim had the time to come west to build.

When we arrived that day to find Russell sitting at the edge of the forest, that's just what Russell was doing: living in the cove. By this point in his story, Russell had polished off most of my parents' beer supply for the weekend. He stood up, belched, thanked us for the hospitality and ambled back down the rocks toward his tent. I hopped up onto my feet and watched him until he disappeared into the forest. I was in awe. For a bespectacled, knee-braced little city nerd like me, it felt like I had just met Crocodile Dundee, John Lennon and Grizzly Adams all rolled into one.

9
Lund

If you wanted to truly experience the end of the road, you went to Lund. If you wanted to experience a bustling and remote fishing outpost or watch a genuine bar brawl, you went to Lund. If you wanted to mingle with those who straddle the margins of society—loggers, artists, bikers, First Nations, draft dodgers, oyster farmers, pot farmers, fishermen, prawners, hippies and kayak guides—you went to Lund. To see them all painfully co-exist with some of Vancouver's richest aristocrats (who seemed to be holding their breath until they set foot on their island jewel of Savary, just a few kilometres away) you went to Lund in the summertime. That's when Lund transformed itself from a forgotten fishing village at the end of the road to "The Gateway to Desolation Sound": the launching point for the draft-dodging communes, kayak adventures, fishing trips and the white sands of Savary Island—spotless beaches which would soon lure my sister and me as well.

Lund locals have been known to show an almost-open hostility toward the first few tourists who rolled unsuspectingly into Lund after a long, dark, wet winter. Even though that three-month summer tourist trade kept most of Lund with firewood in the stove and booze in the fridge for the rest of the year, time and time again the locals took a while to warm up to the onslaught of tourists during Lund's short, sunny season. Lund was a constant source of cultural fascination to our family. We could barely fathom that a community so small could be so amusingly dysfunctional. Dave's Parking was run by John. John's Boat Repair was run by Steve. Steve's Garbage Pick-Up was run by Dave. The gas station didn't pump gas but did fix boats, and the fish market was always closed with a sign on the door that said, "Gone fishing." The local real-estate agent was Jody Fastabend, the carpenter was Jim Nailer. Besides Jim, who was a great nailer, we soon learned that everyone was a jack-of-all-trades and master of none, and nobody bothered to replace the signs when businesses changed hands. There were constant accidents, fights and brouhahas spilling out of the pub and onto the wharf. Everyone seemed a little drunk, stoned or both.

Lund is ingloriously hidden away at the very last stretch of pavement of one of the world's longest roads: the Pan-American, also known as the Pacific Coast Highway 101. The stretch of blacktop snakes up and down the west coast of the Americas, from Quellon, Chile on the southern tip of Chiloe Island, north through South America where it is broken briefly by the infamous Darien Gap, a fifty-kilometre–wide national park that straddles the border of Colombia and Panama. Once the road resumes, it continues up through Central America, the United States, into Canada, along the Sunshine Coast, and finally . . . to Lund. North of Lund, islands, mountains and deep fjords fracture the Pacific coast, preventing any north-south mainland routes of note. One might hazard to assume that such a worldly claim would be seized upon, marketed, celebrated or at the very least slapped on a T-shirt, yet for many years the only notice of having reached the end of one of the world's longest highways was a faded, crooked, hand-painted sign overlooking a couple of parking stalls that said "Welcome to Lund: End of Road 101." Someone had eventually crossed out the word "end" and wrote "start" over top. *Zing.* Quellon at least has a bronze plaque. But that wooden sign was as ceremonious as it got in Lund, and we had the feeling that's exactly the way the locals wanted it to be.

Lund is a dead-end bottleneck for those escaping, hiding and starting over. Curious tourists would read the one-line description of Lund in the tourist guide book and drive up the windy highway to see it, planning to explore for a couple of hours. When they arrived they quickly realized it would take about five minutes, unless there was a bar fight to watch. Lund couldn't really be called a town, it could barely be called a village. But it was a port, and like most ports of the world, large or small, there was usually some kind of action almost everywhere you looked, mostly from the grizzled characters — male and female — who climbed in and out of boats every day of their existence.

After the very last inch of pavement is Lund's hulking government wharf jutting out over the harbour, always a hive of activity. Floating below the wharf was Lund's dock, chock-a-block with an array of boats from the grand to the sunken. Overlooking the wharf sat the historic Lund Hotel, originally built in 1895 by Lund's European "founders," Charles and Frederik Thulin, who arrived in 1885. Over a century earlier, the site of Lund was a thriving First Nations village when Captain Vancouver first spotted it through his spyglass off the starboard bow of the *Discovery*. He avoided any description of the happening village, but described the natural harbour and surrounding coastline as "Being on every side encompassed by islands and small rocky islets; some lying along the continental shore, others confusedly scattered, of different forms and dimensions." They kept on sailing. The village would eventually be forcibly abandoned.

Charlie and Fred Thulin were two enterprising young loggers passing by in a steamship heading into Desolation Sound. They claimed the aesthetically pleasing site as their own and named it Lund after an old university town in Sweden. Soon after they arrived, they logged the area, built a wharf, piped in fresh water, and began building a settlement complete with hotels, restaurants, and the first licensed bar and post office north of Vancouver. Fred Thulin became the unofficial mayor of Lund for many years, known throughout the community as "Papa Thulin." Both brothers were deeply respected in the growing Scandinavian immigrant logging community. In 1918, the original hotel burnt to the ground, swept up in a massive forest fire, but the brothers rebuilt a structure that stands as the village's main hub to this day.

Lund was also the closest outpost of civilization to our cabin, a forty-five minute boat ride away. Walking up the gangplank of the wharf and surveying the scene, Mom, Heather and I initially regarded Lund in the same snobby way we viewed most of the Desolation Sound area: Hicksville. When we visited Lund for supplies and groceries, to us, the locals who hung around outside the General Store looked like everyone our parents had ever warned us to avoid, many resembling the leering animatronic figures from the Disneyland ride *Pirates of the Caribbean*. We dealt with our intimidation by muttering nervous wisecracks to each other. Mom and Heather and I would walk past the hotel and pub bound for the historically overpriced Lund General Store. The staff wrote the prices of their choice in black Jiffy marker directly over the original price tag, or directly on the product—whether it was an axe or a tomato.

Little did we know how much we'd soon pine for the layabout hippies, logger fights and Jiffy-markered-up goods of Lund after two weeks of total isolation at the cabin. Within a summer or two, we started appreciating Lund more and more . . . We'd race up the wharf with screaming seagulls overhead, up the boardwalk and into the general store, praying for a freshly stocked *Archie Digest* rack, stacking the latest issues up on the counter with chocolate bars, freezies and mouth-watering Big League chewing gum in its deliciously squeezable package. And while we were blowing bubbles and catching up on the latest sexually latent love-triangle adventures of Archie, Veronica, Betty and the gang, Dad braved the pub, meeting with local builders and contractors.

Dad witnessed plenty of vicious bar fights in the Lund Pub, but managed to always avoid direct involvement. It was Russell, mild-mannered though he always was, who had several violent altercations within the pub walls. Mack the Knife was a nasty drunk. He would often hold court over the pub, loudly denouncing and bullying anyone within blurry, wasted sight. One night he didn't like the way Russell may or may not have been looking at him and Mack was right pissed enough to do something about it. After words were exchanged, Mack made a charge for Russell. Russell managed to get the best of Mack, putting him in a tight headlock and twisting Mack's arm behind his back. Russell wrenched Mack's arm so hard he could feel the bone bend. "Stop! You're breaking my arm!" Mack gasped. Russell told him he would only let him go if he promised no more fighting. Mack did, and Russell let him collapse onto the bar. Russell turned and went back to his pint of Guinness.

Mack jumped to his feet, grabbed Russell's ponytail with one hand and with the other punched him hard in the back.

When Russell doubled over in pain, Mack the Knife kicked Russell in the face, gouging open Russell's chin with the steel toe of his workboot. With Russell spouting blood and down for the count, a big Sliammon fisherman named Wolf got up from his table where he had been quietly watching the altercation while sipping beer with his puny wife, Stella. "Mack, don't you touch another hair on his head." Mack spun around and looked up at the barrel-chested fisherman, then made good on his nickname, pulling his chisel from his belt.

"Mind your own fuckin' business, Indian," Mack snarled. That remark caused Stella to hop to her feet and strike a wobbly martial-arts pose, yelling at Mack, "I know my kung fu, asshole!" Mack made a lunge at Wolf, but Wolf was able to smack the chisel out of his hand, draw Mack in close and head-butt him, hard. Wolf then dragged Mack the Knife out of the pub to the railing of the deck, picked him up and threw him off it, Mack landing on the boardwalk one storey below. This time his arm was definitely broken. Russell retreated back to the cove to recover from the vicious kick to the face, his chin bleeding into his beard for days.

Lund would eventually go through a sorely needed facelift in cuisine, conduct and culture, thanks in part to the Sliammon First Nation — who were run off the place originally — and to a few ambitious women who realized the untapped potential of Lund's summer melting pot beyond the margins. But that wouldn't occur for years. In our childhood, Lund remained our ridiculed and adored "Dysfunction Junction" at the end of the road.

10
Blood's Too Rich

Sitting like a crescent moon in the Strait of Georgia, just a kilometre west of Lund, is the wondrous microclimate of Savary Island. When you sink your toes into its white sand shores, you might miraculously feel transported to Martha's Vineyard, Key West or Barbados . . . anywhere but the often cold and clammy BC coast. On Savary Island — nicknamed the "Magnetic Isle" for its long-time allure — the sun feels hotter, the water feels warmer and the people just stink of money. Old money. That such a serene and sandy paradise could exist so close to the foreboding rocky crags of Desolation Sound was downright depressing to my sister and me. How could Dad have missed this island jewel? How did we end up in a cabin hanging off the edge of a cliff, where one misstep threatened paraplegia, while the chosen people of Savary enjoyed actual houses, lawns, roads, pristine beaches, water taxis and a general store with candy — just a forty-five–minute boat ride away from our desolate rock? As much as Captain Vancouver and his sailors found surveying the endless nooks and crannies of the Sound tedious, dangerous and frustrating, the one location they loved in the entire area was Savary Island, collectively marvelling at its broad sandy beaches, plentiful clams and resemblance to their beloved islands of the South Seas; they even had a big bonfire on Savary to celebrate.

Savary Island depicted in a vintage Western Canada Airways postcard: the sandy, crescent moon crown jewel of the upper Strait of Georgia, and the island beyond our reach — physically, culturally, and financially — save for one uncomfortably eye-popping, soul-crushing visit.

My sister and I were slightly appeased by the fact that (almost) everyone going to Savary was forced to slum it along the same long, double-ferry Dramamine drive we took to Desolation Sound. Much to my family's constant observation, we'd always be side by side with the sparkling Savary People on the ferries. It didn't take us long before we could spot the Savary thoroughbreds from a distance. They were gorgeous. Mom helped us hone the skill. "There they are," she would point out under her breath. "What a bunch of snobs!" The ladies wore the finest in designer clothing . . . bright pink, blue and yellow, which was confusing to Heather and me, since Mom pretty much dressed exactly the same way. The Savary People drove Mercedes, BMWs and Volvos with personalized licence plates (one of which sickeningly read SAVARY). The Savary Parents looked like they had just strolled off the eighteenth green at the country club, while the Savary Kids looked like Hitler Youth decked out in the hottest flip-collared Ralph Lauren and Fred Perry fashions. Mom tried to dress Heather and me up as best she could, but we just couldn't muster the panache. We were stuck behind our Coke-bottle glasses, weird haircuts and church-rummage-sale leftovers, peering at them over our *Archie* comics while the Savary Kids laughed and caroused like an Abercrombie and Fitch advert come to life, dominating *Asteroids*, the ferry's only arcade game.

One summer, Mom shocked us with the news that we had received an actual invitation to visit this oceanic Garden of Eden. After hearing Mom's description, Heather was ecstatic, as it finally fulfilled her vision of cottage life. I didn't really know how to take it. I wanted to openly refuse, but oh how desperate both Heather and I were to get a taste of that lifestyle, if only for a weekend. The Thornhills were one of several old-money Savary families. Mom had met Hope Thornhill through a women's group in Vancouver. Heather and I assumed Hope pitied her. The Thornhills were a family of four, and filthy rich. What Heather and I didn't know was that Mom had first invited the Thornhills to come and visit us inside the Sound. They refused but, possibly out of guilt, insisted that we visit them on Savary Island instead. Mom accepted their invitation on behalf of all of us. I feigned disgust that Mom had given in. Dad wasn't able to go, so we went without him.

Upon arrival, it was confirmed: the Savary People had an outrageously good thing going. Instead of schlepping groceries, luggage, leaky propane tanks and oily gas cans back and forth along cliffs like Sherpas, the bronzed and beautiful bodies of the Savary People had not a care in the world. They simply pedalled their bicycles along the beachside country lanes to the choicest sandy spot they pleased. There they spread out their checkered picnic blankets, pulled out the latest edition of Italian *Vogue*, and settled in for a day in the sun. It was exactly how Heather had imagined it would be. After spending the first day getting acclimatized to the shockingly serene and easy environment, Heather and I were taking an awkward evening walk with the Thornhill kids, Tiffany and Charles, along the seaside lane early Friday evening. We were suddenly engulfed by a large group of shrieking, gorgeous children. My sister and I panicked, thinking the gig was up, that we had been spotted as the foreigner nerds we were, and that we were about to get a high-society beat-down. We would be bound and gagged and dragged behind their bicycles down the dusty lanes, buried up to our necks in the sand, urinated upon, live crabs dumped on our heads . . . We were surprised to watch the gang speed past us toward the beach.

Tiffany and Charles looked at each other with delight and squealed in sickening unison, "The Daddy plane!" They raced after the rest of the kids, leaving Heather and me in a cloud of dust and confusion. We hobbled along in our knee braces and short-shorts and eventually caught up, finding the group of perfect youth all gathered in anticipation on the beach near the wharf. Minutes later came an overhead roar from a glistening, silver floatplane. It took a dive-bomb swoop above us, then U-turned over the ocean and came in for a dramatic and graceful landing just offshore. The children jumped up and down, arms in the air, shrieking, "Daddy! Daddy!"

The plane's aluminum pontoons lightly skidded to a halt on the sand. The black rotors of the huge propeller *click-click-clicked* to stop like the *Wheel of Fortune*, as the riveted metal door swung open, revealing men in suits. Stockbrokers, lawyers and doctors, finished with a week of work in the city, were arriving on Friday night to join their families for the weekend on the island. About a dozen disembarked, their slacks rolled up, black socks and dress shoes in one hand, and briefcases in the other. They waded to shore as their children raced to meet them, arms outstretched. Heather and I could only stand as observers on the outskirts of this scene of love and money. We didn't have a rich, well-dressed father emerging Don Draper-style from a pontooned plane to throw our arms around. Our Dad was back at our cabin in the Sound in cut-off jean-shorts fixing a leaky septic tank.

In two shakes of a lamb's tail, our weekend in paradise was over and we found ourselves reluctantly boarding the water taxi that would return us to Lund, where Dad would meet us to take us back to . . . our cabin. Heather and I couldn't help but stare out longingly over the churning wake of the water taxi, aching to be back on the island's idyllic shoreline. We wanted it easy, too. We wanted to be elite and to fit effortlessly into a navy blue Polo shirt with the collar flipped up. We wanted to play tennis and croquet and drink tea on the lawn and stroll along the laurel hedge. We wanted their jeans and their genes. We wanted to be Savary People. Alas, it was never to be; instead of tennis courts and sand castles, we had barnacles and kelp. Instead of doctors and lawyers, we had welfare hobos and oyster farmers. For years after that visit, both my sister and I harboured a small slice of resentment toward Dad for passing on Savary. Heather vowed to return to the "Magnetic Isle."

11
Wishing Well

Over the course of the next few summers, the hermit Russell Letawsky figured very largely in our family. Since that original meeting, he had become a close family friend to all of us. He was funny, charming, worldly and full of incredible stories. Even Dad warmed up to him. Russell was a dreamer, Dad was a realist; together they made an unlikely but effective team. Side by side they ingeniously came up with all sorts of ideas to make life harder on themselves in the short term and easier on us in the long term. One of their first major projects together was attempting to dig a freshwater drinking well. When they announced it one morning at the breakfast table, my mind immediately raced to the myriad *Little House on the Prairie* episodes in which blind children unwittingly stumbled and fell to horrible injury or death in wells. I didn't volunteer to help, but they dragged me along anyway.

Up until the plan for the well was hatched, our source for fresh water was the little creek that emptied out into the cove. We'd carry down two soft, cubic, plastic water jugs, just like the kind they used in *Land of the Lost* with the red plastic handle and white circular spout. They were light as air to carry down to the creek, but after we submerged the bags in the icy water to fill them, the translucent sacks became as heavy as a bag of rocks to carry back up the ledge to the cabin. Dad could do it in a few leaps and bounds, but it would take me forever to lug the jugs up. It was a chore I loathed. Dad promised that if they were successful in digging a well, there would be no more lugging jugs of water up from the creek. I was skeptical. Dad and Russell had a theory that since the water in the creek was so fresh and cold, it must be coming up from a spring farther back in the forest, possibly located in the swampy area that the Blooms had cleared of trees for their garden homestead many years early. Armed with shovels, Dad and Russell marched into the woods, me following closely behind. They chose a muddy spot in the middle of the clearing ten feet away from the creek bed. Dad struck shovel to dirt and hoisted.

After the first day, they were down four or five feet with no significant signs of water, just heavy mud. By the next day, they were down a further four feet or so, and had sent me back to the cabin to get pickaxes so they could slice through layers of clay and gravel. With each significant depth, they lowered down a cylinder of corrugated steel so the walls wouldn't collapse inwards. Eventually, on the third day, they had dug a round hole that was four feet across and twelve feet deep. I spent most of the time sitting against a tree engrossed in *Tintin and the Red Sea Sharks,* but occasionally, with extreme caution, I would peer over the edge, kneeling on the long, flat boards they had spread around the topsoil near the edge of the hole. I'd see Russell down below in the muck, his beard and face thick with black mud, as he hoisted the dirt out from below on trays that Dad pulled up by rope. Way down below, there were still no significant signs of water, just a mucky mess. Both Dad and Russell were exhausted and discouraged. Dad and I were dumping out one of the trays when Russell yelled, "Shit! I hit rock!"

Dad and I both peered over the edge. "What'd you say?" Dad yelled back.

"I said, I hit rock, a flat slab of rock!" called Russell. "Listen!" He took his shovel and slammed it downwards, a hard *clank* reverberating up the well shaft. "It's over, man," he shouted up. "No spring water. We picked the wrong fuckin' spot." I was secretly relieved. My sister would never have to go berry-picking in the forest and blindly plunge headfirst into the well, and not be found for days. These macabre thoughts were quickly replaced by the living nightmare that I would have to go back to lugging the dead-weight water jugs up to the cabin from the creek. So be it. Dad flopped himself down onto the ground, crossed his legs and furrowed his brow in thought. "Lower down the ladder!" yelled Russell from the bottom of the hole. Dad didn't answer.

"Dad? Russell . . . wants the ladder." It was on the ground a few feet away. Ignoring me, Dad hopped to his feet, grabbed one of the pickaxes and moved quickly toward the deep pit.

"What are you doing? Lower down the ladder and let's fill this shit in," shouted Russell, when Dad's head appeared at the top.

"Russell, can you get a full swing of the pickaxe down there?"

Russell paused and looked around the cramped, damp hole. "Yeah . . . I think so . . . but why? You want me to try and break solid rock?"

"I don't think it's rock!" Dad answered. "I think its *hard pan*."

Years earlier, on another wilderness property, Dad remembered talking to an old cattle rancher about a well the rancher had dug. He told Dad that the trick was to not be fooled by the hard pan, an extremely hard-packed layer of soil that forms a solid, flat slab that has deceived many into thinking it was rock. Hard pan could exist at any depth, and would be solid and thick enough to impede the flow of water. Dad lowered down the pickaxe to Russell. With filthy black hands, Russell swung the pickaxe into the base of the hole where it hit with another hard clank, vibrating the tool out of Russell's grip. "Fuck!"

"Do it again!" yelled Dad. Russell's eyes glared up in a mud mask as he picked up the wooden handle and swung: nothing. Dad urged him on. I rolled away from the edge and went back to my comic book. On the fifth or sixth swing, the clank was replaced with a thunk. I looked up from the comic book. "There!" shouted Dad. "Again!" Russell yanked the pickaxe from the ground and swung hard. The axe buried itself deeper. "That's it, again!" Dad was at the edge of the hole, crouched with his hands on his knees, me beside him.

On Russell's next swing, the hard pan cracked like a sidewalk in an earthquake. The blade of the pickaxe sliced cleanly through the hard pan, creating a crooked vein. There was a gasping, hissing sound and up through the crack gurgled cold, clean, Canadian spring water. Russell tossed the tool aside and both he and Dad let out several loud whoops and cheers, fists in the air. I got swept up in the celebration and whooped along with them, asking Dad plenty of questions, most of which he ignored. At the bottom of the hole, Russell knelt down and washed his face, looking up with a broad smile on his lean, clean(er) face. The water was quickly filling the hole, gathering around Russell's boots. Dad lowered down the ladder so Russell could scramble out.

The hole became our freshwater well. Together Dad and Russell constructed a heavy wooden lid to keep animals, vegetation and little kids from falling in. To check the water level without ever having to lift the lid, Russell created a giant dipstick of sorts, a long fifteen-foot pole, numbered at each foot length. He cut a slot in the lid of the well just large enough for the end of the stick and attached a small foam buoy to the bottom end, then slid the measuring stick through the slot, foam buoy first. The buoy always floated on the surface of the well water, so if the well was full, the measuring stick would be high in the air. If the water was low, the top end of the stick would barely be poking through the slot. It was unconventional, but we always knew the level of the well. It worked for many years.

So Dad and Russell had done it—they had dug a well. Now all they had to do was get all that fresh, clean spring water into our cabin, which they did by running a line of black plastic piping from the well, up the bluff to a huge water bag they had placed there, then back down the bluff to the back of our cabin with more black plastic piping. A month after the well was dug, high-pressure, sparkling water was pouring through our faucets and filling up our toilet. We were all thrilled. Dad and Russell barely ever sat still. Together they sliced out a network of trails in the dense brush, providing an alternative means to get to neighbouring cabins that didn't involve a boat. They devised an ingenious pulley system that stretched from shore to shore across our little cove, and then tied our boat to it, so it was always floating and off the rocks at any tide level. It looked just like a clothesline, but with a floating boat attached. When we needed the boat, we'd reel in the clothesline, and when we didn't we'd reel it back out.

After the sun set on their adventures and ingenuity, Russell and Dad would talk late into the night about all of their ideas . . . windmills, breakwaters, orchards, flagpoles and bee farms. Soon Dad officially hired Russell as the caretaker for the entire property and all the cabins, and he became well-known and liked by many of our family friends and cabin neighbours.

Russell turned out to be quite the charmer with women, and would frequently hit on Mom's oversized-sunglasses-wearing West Vancouver single-white-female divorcee friends who would visit us every so often. Russell initiated the courting with the friendly, drunken and totally un-West Vancouver greeting of "Hey lady!" Mom swears it was even successful once or twice.

Russell and Dad in scheming mode, dreaming up new ways to make cabin life easier for us. They could have started by building a railing around our treacherous deck, but that never happened.

Russell's primary caretaking duty was to make sure that no one vandalized or stole from any of the cabins while the owners were away, especially during the winter months. Dad paid him a small amount and helped him collect the scrap wood left over from the cabins being built, which allowed Russell to upgrade from his canvas tent to a sturdy little one-room shack, which was another source of allure to me. They constructed Russell's shack-cabin on a slab of flat rock just above the shoreline in the cove. Constructed in the shade of a cedar sapling, the tiny dwelling had a sloping, cedar-shake roof capped by a protruding chimney, a window that looked out onto the cove, and a wraparound deck just wide enough for Russell to be able to walk along it, holding onto the smooth, bark-stripped cedar bow railings.

Inside, he fended off near-constant dampness with a jet-black, pot-bellied fireplace that doubled as a stove, a coffee pot on top. Beside the stove were two mismatched chairs tucked into a little wooden table. On the table was a chessboard and a little transistor radio that hissed out the strains of Powell River's CBC Radio signal all day long. Leaned up against the inside of the door was Russell's greasy, intimidating .303 rifle. A thick plank was nailed in place to serve as a kitchen countertop, with various utensils and plates strewn about. Above the counter were open cupboards that he stuffed with canned goods, bags of rice, boxes of pasta and tins of pipe tobacco. Just under the big window was Russell's bed, a wide, wooden bunk covered in wool blankets and dirty pillows with no cases. Above the foot of the bed was a sagging bookshelf overflowing with just slightly mouldy philosophy textbooks, alongside equally damp and well-worn paperback copies of science fiction, literature, pulp, and Beat classics. Aristotle, Nietzsche and Hume; Ginsberg, von Däniken and Atwood; Kesey, Michener and Bukowski . . . But Russell Letawsky was not the only well-read, well-armed philosopher to have reached the shores of Desolation Sound.

The very first non-Native settler to live year-round in Desolation Sound was thought to be an American roughneck named Mike Shuttler. Born in Michigan in the mid-1800s, Shuttler had a violent life growing up as a logger in the American west, and was once left for dead after being severely wounded in a barroom knife fight. When he came to days later, he was lying on a blood-soaked mattress infested with flies, and he had a permanent scar that ran down the length of his face. He decided to get out of America and get away from people. He needed to disappear and sought a life of solitude, alone in the wilderness for the rest of his days. Somehow, like so many that followed after him seeking the same spiritual cleansing, Mike Shuttler found Desolation Sound, eventually settling in the sheltered area of Prideaux Haven, once a winter camp for First Nations. It is thought that he arrived in the Sound around 1890. He was a colourful character in the Sound for many years, and didn't remain totally alone for long. He was chronicled and caricatured in such classic West Coast adventure books as *The Curve of Time* by M. Wylie Blanchet, *Skookum Chuk* by Stewart E. White and the recent *Desolation Sound: A History* by Heather Harbord.

Shuttler was also Desolation Sound's first hermit philosopher, some ninety years before Russell Letawsky. According to Blanchet, he had shelves full of books, including many classics by "Marcus Aurelius, Epictetus, Plato and Emerson" and, just like Russell, he loved to sit and discuss philosophical thoughts at length with visitors. Blanchet was so taken by Shuttler's "credo," which he had scrawled in pencil and hung above his door, that she copied the entire verse down in her journal: "Look well of today, for it is the Life of Life . . . for yesterday is but a dream and tomorrow a vision. But today well lived makes every yesterday a dream of happiness, and every tomorrow a vision of hope . . . " Blanchet assumed Shuttler hadn't come up with it on his own, but rather copied it out of a book, and she was right. It's a portion of an ancient, undated poem by the famed Sanskrit poet-philosopher Kalidasa.

Each time our family rounded the point and puttered our boat into the cove, my sister and I would eagerly peer over the bow looking for any signs of life of our own hobo philosopher. "I see smoke coming out of Russell's chimney!" my sister would point out. "His boat is there!" I yelled back to my parents. "And there's Loop!" Loop was Russell's friendly, sloppy, giant mutt, who got along splendidly with our city dog, Aggie. Also keeping

Russell company were two cute little kittens that he allowed my sister and me to name: Mizz Mew and Maude. Once or twice we even came across Russell bathing, which amounted to the grizzled hermit sitting naked on the gravel beach in the cove, waiting for the tide to come up around him, scrubbing himself as it did.

That beach also served as Russell's garden, as it was chock-a-block with oysters the size of basketball player shoes, lying all over the surface of the beach. Oyster farmers knew about Russell's fertile beach, too, but because it was within the boundaries of the Desolation Sound Marine Park, an official oyster lease wasn't allowed. Every once in a while the park beaches were victim to midnight poaching. The poachers would wait for an extremely low late-night tide, and under the cover of darkness, sneak onto various beaches in the park and gather up as many oysters as they could. One night the poachers hit Russell's beach.

Russell was awakened by the sound of an outboard purring at low speed. He peered out his window and saw flashlight beams along the beachfront. He kept his hand on Loop's head, speaking softly to the big dog to keep him quiet, as he reached for his high-powered searchlight and .303 rifle. He slipped out onto the deck of the shack and flipped on the light, illuminating the beach. The four or five poachers instantly stood up and shielded their eyes. "What the fuck do you think you're doing on my oyster lease?" Russell bluffed, in an uncharacteristically aggressive bellow. Still shielding their eyes from the blinding light, one of the poachers yelled back with mock surprise in his voice, "Lease? What's your lease number, buddy?"

"My lease number?" Russell answered, as he balanced the searchlight on the railing of his deck while taking up his rifle with both hands. "This is my lease number, asshole! Three-oh-three!" He loudly cocked his rifle with authority and blasted a shot high into the air, the booming sound of the powerful gun bouncing off the cliff walls and back again. The shot caused Loop to instantly start up with a deep, menacing yowl, a bark that came from an obviously large dog. The poachers wasted no time scrambling back into their boat and speeding off into the night. It was their last visit.

Russell let me trace his movements all over the Sound, whether by boat or on foot. Here we're pictured at one of Russell's meditation spots, a lookout high above Kahkaykay Bay. That's me in the foreground during my Indiana Jones phase, the glasses being rather unfortunate.

12
Captains Courageous

Unfortunately, Dad became increasingly busy going back and forth from the city to the Sound, dealing with prospective customers. The Canadian economy was in the dumps and it became stressful for him just to make ends meet. The sales of the individual lots had slowed to a crawl; banks were foreclosing on various neighbours' properties. Dad insisted that Mom, Heather and I still use the cabin as often as we could in the summer months, and we would nervously make the journey on our own without our tower of strength and knowledge. With Dad away, Heather spent most of her time near the cabin with Mom, and I spent more and more time with Russell. Unlike my father, Russell seemed much more imperfect. He smoked, swore and drank a lot, none of which Dad did. Dad started the morning with three hundred push-ups and three hundred sit-ups. Russell started the morning with a doobie, a West Coast wake 'n' bake. He lived in a wooden shack with no electricity in the middle of nowhere all year round. It was a marvel to me that someone like him could even exist in the flesh.

At my persistent urging, Russell slowly taught me things Dad wasn't ready to trust me with, but that I needed to learn without Dad around. Dad had occasionally let me drive the boat, but it was Russell who first taught me how to fire up our outboard motor, drive the boat all by myself, and even achieve something called "planing" which allowed the boat to reach a certain speed and practically skim across the surface of the ocean, hydroplaning. As the warm salt air whipped through our hair, I felt the freedom of the Sound in the grip of my hand. I revved the engine faster and faster, and it felt like we were flying. I laughed out loud, and Russell laughed, too.

Russell showed me his and Dad's network of trails in the forest, and the signs he made so no one got lost. He allowed me to add my own silly signs, like "You have now entered bear country," something I saw at Disneyland. Russell didn't mind. He showed me his meditation spots high up on cliffs overlooking the ocean, which herbs and berries were edible, and which ones to avoid. One of the main staples of Russell's diet (when we weren't around to feed him breakfast, lunch, dinner, snacks, wine and beer) was the plethora of fish, clams, crabs and oysters he gathered with ease each day. Russell was an expert fisherman by necessity. My parents just weren't the fishing types, but I was desperate to go fishing with Russell. He left the cove to go fishing in deeper water every couple of mornings, always returning an hour or two later with at least a couple of large, bug-eyed fish on the end of a gaff hook.

The morning Russell finally invited me to go fishing was a moment of pure joy. I was ecstatic, begging Mom's permission, which she gave without much convincing. Russell primarily jigged for medium-sized bottom fish, which in Desolation

Sound included the relatively docile quillback and copper rockfish, the brightly striped orange-and-black tiger rockfish, the elusive and larger red snapper found at greater depths, and the muscular lingcod—which fought the hook like a pit bull chomping on a rat. It was almost unfathomable to me when Russell explained the incredible lifespan of these fish, anywhere from 50 to 120 years. Russell made my eyes widen when he said that, if we were lucky, we might catch the very same fish that Gus Bloom had caught seventy years ago. Back then it would have been too small to keep so he would have thrown it back, but now, it would be huge and juicy, and might even show the scar of Gus's hook. If we were unlucky, we'd hook a dogfish: actually a genuine shark, with disturbingly vacant cat-like eyes, that can be anywhere from two to four feet in length; its sandpaper-like skin makes it very difficult to clean and prepare for eating. The bottom line was, as I discovered on that first day of fishing, we never failed to reel in some type of mysterious, beautiful and frightening creature from the depths below.

I didn't have a fishing rod, so I made my own. I found a young arbutus tree near the cabin, and sawed off a solid branch about the thickness of a hockey stick, but only about two feet in length. To this day, a stub still sticks out of that tree where I sawed it off at age twelve. My chosen piece of wood had a strong smaller limb at one end that was perfectly sized to hold my reel of fishing line. Two smaller branches stuck out in the middle and at the very end, which I could thread my line over. The arbutus's smooth, hard wood allowed the fishing line to glide over it easily. For our first fishing trip we hopped in Russell's leaky, derelict skiff, *putt-putting* out into the inlet by his tiny two-horsepower Seagull outboard. He killed the engine only two hundred feet away from the front door of our cabin. Russell's filthy fingers gracefully showed me how to tie the lure to the end of my line. We used "Codbusters": a gruesome-looking barbed hook slid through a pink lure with a squiggly rubber tail to fool the fish into thinking they had spotted a seriously out-of-it shrimp, ripe for the gobbling.

"Drop your hook!" Russell ordered with a smile. I let it go with a plop into the water, spooling out the line on my makeshift arbutus-branch fishing rod. With wonder I watched the weighted hook disappear into the green-black depths, the reflection of a pencil-neck geek with a messy bowl cut squinting back at me through oversized, thick glasses. Eventually I felt the clunk of the lure hit the ocean floor. Russell instructed me to wind the line up a few full turns of the reel, and to then "jig" . . . And together, like a scene from *Captains Courageous*, the little nerd from the city sat with the hermit from the woods, methodically and silently watching our lines, moving our fishing rods up and down, up and down. In nervous anticipation I mimicked the same graceful motion of Russell's rod, creating what I imagined was an underwater ballet that would prove irresistible for our gape-mouthed prey. Within ten minutes of dropping our hooks, I felt a strong, sudden downward tug on my tree branch. "Pull up!" shouted Russell. "That's a bite!"

"What do I do?" I yelled, jumping to my feet in the boat, gripping the smooth branch tightly with both hands. "Pull up and keep pressure on the line, and reel it up quick!" I strained to hurriedly reel it in and keep the line taut. Sweat dripped and my glasses fogged, sliding to the end of my nose. Whatever creature had bit the hook was fighting and struggling below, thrashing the fishing line from side to side, the reverberations of which I could feel in my fingertips. A few minutes later, appearing before my wide eyes under the hot sun, was a big, fat, juicy, bug-eyed fish, spiralling up from the depths, led by my line. It broke the surface without much fight left, lying on its side exhausted, the hook wedged firmly in its lower lip. Russell reached into the brine with a gaff hook, slipped it through the gills, and within seconds, the two-foot-long fish the colour of a penny was flipping and gasping on the bottom of the boat. I had to look away while Russell took the wooden handle of the gaff and whacked it three times between the eyes. We caught several more fish that day, Russell knowing exactly where to drop the hook each time.

Captains Courageous: the first fish I ever caught, a quillback rockfish. Russell's holding up a small tiger rockfish that we probably should have thrown back.

Captain Vancouver did not know where to drop the hook. Compounding the rotten weather, painstaking surveys and the constant threat of illness was the frustration that they could not seem to reap any fresh food from the waters or shores of Desolation Sound. When the *Discovery* and *Chatham* sailed into Desolation Sound on that dark and rainy June night, they originally anchored near the small and centrally located Kinghorn Island. Over the next few days, they were battered by an exhausting and stressful southeasterly gale: "Heavy squalls and much rain drove us, by its increased violence, from our anchorage." They relocated in the sheltered waters of Teakerne Arm on West Redonda Island for the rest of their survey of Desolation Sound, but according to Vancouver, their new location was no better, writing that they "found a more eligible anchorage, though in a situation equally dreary and unpleasant . . . Our residence here was truly forlorn . . . whose soil afforded only a few small onions, some samphire, and here and there bushes bearing a scanty crop of indifferent berries. Nor was the sea more favourable to our wants, the steep rocky shores prevented the use of the seine, and not a fish at the bottom could be tempted to take the hook." He also noted with disdain that the "stupendous rock mountains [rose] almost perpendicularly from the sea."

The long, flat fishing seine net, that hangs in the water like a curtain, would have been ineffective in Desolation Sound unless near a salmon spawning creek at the right time of year (which June wasn't quite), perpendicular alongside a beach, or in a strong collision of currents. As for bottom fishing, which they also failed at, lingcod and rockfish are underwater cliff dwellers, hiding in holes in the cliff facing out, waiting for prey to swim by so they can dart out and attack. Most of the bottom fish like the explosion of life found in the kelp beds and strong currents, which Vancouver and his men would have likely avoided. Kelp always indicates a rocky reef or shallow water, and strong currents would have been a hassle to anchor in, even for boats of the size they had. Unable to take advantage of what truly was a bountiful area, Vancouver and his men eventually went to their fail-safe plan, which was trading with the Natives. An utterly uneven commerce had been established, the Europeans preying on the First Nations' love of anything metal, often trading near-worthless brass buttons, nails and other shiny trinkets for dozens of fresh salmon and bushels of berries.

That night we feasted on the freshest food in the world. I was hooked. At my persistent urging, we fished and fished and fished. Russell showed me all the best spots and methods to catch the fish of Desolation Sound—secrets that would one day fill the bellies of my drunk friends.

If we weren't fishing, I would still try and tag along with Russell everywhere he went. There were certain times he didn't want me following him into the forest, and it wasn't until years later that I realized it was because he didn't want me to see his marijuana patch. I was blissfully unaware of how stoned Russell was much of the time. Only now does it make sense why it took Russell several hours to do some of the simplest tasks around our cabin when Dad wasn't around, like screw in the toilet paper dispenser, which is still crooked. He did, however, allow me to tag along with him to Lund a few times. Once, while Russell and I were walking together down the Lund boardwalk, we came face to face with my high school friend Nick Thomas, who was stopping by Lund for supplies while on a salmon-fishing trip with his family in the area. I didn't know Nick that well at the time, but over the next school year he would become my closest friend, and just a few years later we would embark on a seventeen-year career together in a successful rock 'n' roll band. Nick was a West Vancouver preppy skateboarder, and was shocked to see a mega-library-nerd like me wandering around a coastal backwater town with a lanky, bearded, dirt-encrusted hippie with a knife in his belt and an eagle feather in his headband. Nick's first question to me when I saw him in school in September was, "Who *was* that guy?!" I grinned proudly from ear to ear, pushed my glasses up from the end of my nose and launched into the story. Nick asked plenty of questions, mostly about the fishing. A few summers later, he was one of the only childhood friends I ever invited up to the cabin. He loved it, fishing from dawn till dusk.

Russell and I really hit it off, and I looked forward to seeing him more and more with each summer visit to the Sound. He slowly drew me out of my insecure shell, convincing me that the world around me wasn't going to bite. He taught me practicality in knots and knives, ambition and idealism, intellectualism and philosophical thought. Russell's motto for Desolation Sound was "There is always something to see." Day or night, it always seemed to be true. He graduated me from checkers to chess, and introduced me to such for better or worse life-altering books like *Catcher in the Rye, On the Road* and *To Kill a Mockingbird*.

Russell also opened up my passion for rock 'n' roll. My parents always had music around, but beyond our beloved Beach Boys, Elvis, Billy Joel and ABBA cassettes, and a random scattering of folk, classical, and teen heartthrobs of the late fifties and early sixties, Mom and Dad's passion and knowledge for music didn't run all that deep. Dad didn't even like the Beatles; he considered them responsible for the hippie movement he loathed so much. When I bought *Abbey Road* on cassette from the rotating metal cassette wheel beside the cash register at the Lund General Store, the idea was to try and integrate it into the road-trip rotation right in between the Beach Boys and Billy Joel. Dad would bark with protest, saying the music was "total crap" and that John Lennon was a "loony." Mom would chime in that she always thought Paul McCartney was cute, and that it was awful when John Lennon was killed, but confessed to never having been a Beatles fan either. Out popped "Maxwell's Silver Hammer," in slid "Surfin' USA."

Luckily, as straitlaced as Russell may have been in the eras of first- and second-wave rock 'n' roll, he was still a rebel without a cause compared to my parents. Growing up in northern Alberta in the late fifties and early sixties, he would lie awake at night listening to the new sounds of rock 'n' roll on the radio, and remembered it all. He recalled endless trivia about those early days of rock that I retained much better than anything taught to me in grade eight math. Out of Dad's earshot, Russell told me that Elvis was a phony; Chuck Berry was the *real* deal. He introduced me to countless artists that I would scribble onto scraps of paper and track down once I got back to the city: Bill Haley, Buddy Holly, Johnny Ray, Wanda Jackson, Jerry Lee Lewis, the Coasters, Link Wray, Eddie Cochran, Gene Vincent . . . Russell set the hook of rock 'n' roll so deeply within me that music would soon become my life, and would be the driving force that would eventually lead me far away from him, Desolation Sound and my family for over a decade. I shared my new found passion for rock 'n' roll with my pal Nick, who was already being introduced to great music by his older sister. On one late August weekend when Nick had come up for a weekend of fishing at the cabin, we sat together in our little boat, lines in the water, and decided then and there to form our own band as soon as we returned to high school that fall. We called ourselves the One-Eyed Jacks, named after Dad's favourite western of all time starring Marlon Brando and Karl Malden. The first songs we learned were "C'mon Everybody" by Eddie Cochran, "Gloria" by Them and "Keep on Dancin'" by the Gentrys. Very suddenly, the last place I wanted to be was Desolation Sound, so far away from the rock 'n' roll action. I wanted to be downtown at the record stores with Nick and the rest of my new bandmates, searching through the bins for deeper and darker sounds.

My parents would insist that I come with them to the cabin, but I began to complain with teenage indignation. I'd whine and plead with them to allow me to stay behind so I wouldn't miss the Hard Rock Miners concert, or the Violent Femmes, or Shadowy Men on a Shadowy Planet. Eventually I steadfastly refused to return to the Sound. I grew distant and insolent, complaining that Desolation Sound was ridiculously boring, that there was nothing for me there. I was officially morphing into a selfish, snot-nosed, punk rocker who sneered at the world like my heroes Holden Caulfield, Jerry Lee Lewis and the Gruesomes. It hurt my parents, but they allowed me my self-centred artistic expression, to their extreme credit. And so I left the cabin, my family, Russell Letawsky and Desolation Sound behind.

That burning love of rock 'n' roll eventually led me into a long career in my second and final band as the lead singer of The Smugglers, a group that combined rock 'n' roll with a Canadian coastal mythology, both in image and in song. The band released eight full-length albums with such titles as *Selling the Sizzle*, *Wet Pants Club* and *Mutiny in Stereo* on independent record companies from around the world (some incredibly obscure, like 1+2 Records in Japan, and some more notable like Mint Records in Canada and Lookout! Records in the US). We toured extensively throughout Canada, the US, Europe, Japan, Australia and New Zealand. We had a couple of very minor indie-rock hits ("Especially You," "Rosie," and "Vancouver BC"), while enjoying an incredibly low budget but fast-paced, jet-setting, visceral lifestyle. The trial-and-error, do-it-yourself knowledge and experience that I gathered from my life in rock 'n' roll led directly to my career as a music journalist at CBC Radio.

The promotional photo for The Smugglers' last album, *Mutiny in Stereo*, left to right: Grant Lawrence, Nick Thomas, Beez, Graham Watson and Dave Carswell.

Before my total sabbatical from the Sound, one of the proudest moments of my young music career came during my last summer trip for what would be many years. I was able to personally hand Russell a copy of *At Marineland*, a vinyl copy of The Smugglers' very first album, which included our amped-up, out-of-tune cover of the Coasters' 1959 B-side classic "That Is Rock 'n' Roll"—a song Russell and I used to listen to on my portable cassette player during those warm summer nights in the Sound. Of course he had no way of actually listening to the record, but he beamed with pride, holding it high with both of his dirt-encrusted hands, staring at the cover, flipping it over, his tanned, bearded face showing off his warm smile. He took the album back to his little shack in the cove and propped it up on his shelf alongside all of his prized books. When I headed back to Vancouver at the end of that weekend, Russell waved to me as our little boat gained speed leaving the cove. I looked back and waved at Russell standing on the narrow deck of his shack for what would prove to be the last time.

13
Take Me to the Riot

Every summer my parents would invite me back to the cabin and every summer I would refuse to go. "Too busy, touring, recording . . . " I would state with self-importance. It hurt them. I was rudely rejecting what they had hoped would become a Lawrence family legacy, something I would embrace and cherish. Dad eventually stopped bringing up Desolation Sound altogether, but Mom would always try. "But you loved it up there so much," she would say.

"So what?" I'd snap back. "I'm way too busy and it's too far away. I can't go back there, okay? It *sucks*." The truth was I was an egotistical, irresponsible, morally corrupt, immature and insensitive teenager who thought the world revolved around me. I wanted nothing to do with my dorky family, let alone our cabin. I wanted to finally be *cool*, like Lou Reed in the Velvet Underground or Scott McCaughey in the Young Fresh

Fellows. I wanted to trade in my Coke-bottle science-teacher glasses, the massive lenses of which covered over half of my face, and replace them with John Lennon granny glasses and Bob Dylan Ray-Ban shades. I wanted to write songs, record albums, tour with my band and see the world. When I wasn't doing that, I wanted to get drunk and party with my friends in the city. Of course, I still lived at home, and I was broke.

Since my parents were up in Desolation Sound so much in the warmer months, when I wasn't touring I was somehow entrusted with our family home in West Vancouver. Many times unbeknownst to my parents it became the de facto, parentless, party house. One summer, when the band had an unusual amount of time off, the parties were frequent and growing in size by the week. My parents were blissfully unaware and I was confident that I could clean up any mess so they wouldn't notice a thing. I'm not really sure what happened that one particular hot July night, but what started out as a small summer bash turned into one of those massive, out-of-control house parties that people read about in the paper every once in a while. Teens streamed in from all over the city . . . word somehow travelled so fast that groups of kids in the hundreds were charging down our driveway, a scene that resembled a cross between *Braveheart* and *Degrassi Junior High*. Soon our house, yard and street were jam-packed with partying teens. It was officially an out-of-control house party.

The police showed up in force, found me and said they needed my permission to clear the house. If I didn't give them that permission, I would be staring at a fine in the thousands. It was probably a bluff, but I was scared, so I gave them the green light. The police blitzkrieged the property, chasing screaming, drunken teenagers throughout my childhood home, over the couches, down the stairs, through the halls and out into the yard. Several groups of teens resisted, fighting back against the cops. A complete melee ensued. Police dogs were unleashed and billy clubs were swung. A small group of my closest friends watched in horror from our upstairs window as a bourgeois battle royale raged between the cops and the West Vancouver teen-elite. In the chaos, a cute Smugglers groupie flung herself up against me, begging me to keep her "safe from the cops." And so, like Nero fiddling while Rome burned, I made out with her in the laundry room as the teen riot ensued outside.

Eventually, after about an hour of mayhem, calm came back to a beer-can littered Bellevue Avenue. My neighbours slowly emerged from their homes like villagers who had survived a Viking raid. They were livid. Wreckage and debris was strewn up and down the block. Amazingly, the only damage sustained to the Lawrence family home was a solitary broken window, and my family wouldn't be back for two weeks . . . I could clean up the street and fix the window. By the time my parents were back, most of the neighbours would have forgotten about it or be on summer vacation themselves. I was soaked in sweat, fresh from an awkward teenage make-out session, and freaked right out, but in the clear. Unfortunately, those cops had really cracked some heads. Several kids had been whacked with billy clubs and some were even attacked and bitten by a police dog. The media got hold of the story like a German shepherd on a teenage butt cheek and wouldn't let go.

Meanwhile, a couple of days later amid the secluded serenity of Desolation Sound, my parents and sister decided to take a day trip into Lund. They stopped by the Lund General Store where Mom bought a few Jiffy-markered-up groceries. Heather grabbed the latest *Archie Digest* and Dad picked up a daily *Province* newspaper. He glanced at the cover, and then folded the paper under his arm. Twenty feet from the general store Dad stopped in his tracks, his face contorted into a grimace. "What's wrong?" Mom asked. Slowly, Dad unfolded the newspaper and stared incredulously at the front cover of the provincial paper: emblazoned across the top of the page in bold, black letters was the headline: BELLEVUE BASH CRASHED. Beneath it was a full-colour picture of a teenaged girl showing a police dog's teeth marks in her bruised and bloody thigh. Filling out the picture behind her was the beach in front of our West Vancouver family home.

"Jesus effing Christ!" They were on the next ferry home, cutting short their vacation by two weeks. I was in more trouble than I had ever been in my life, my parents screaming at me that I wouldn't have a choice but to go with them the next time they went to the cabin. I screamed back in stupidity that I would never go back, that I hated the place and that I had a music career to uphold. My still-bookish, nerdy and innocent little sister Heather was caught in the middle, flinching as the various doors of our house slammed loudly all around her.

July 24, 1991 Classifieds 986-6222 Office, Editorial 985-2131 Display Advertising 980-0511 Distribution 986-1337 72 pages 25¢

Bellevue bash crashed

Teens bitten by WV police dog in melee

By Michael Becker
News Reporter

Vancouver, B.C. Tuesday, July 23, 1991

THE Province

50 cents
60 cents minimum outside Lower Mainland

JACKPOT Lotto 649 $2.2 MILLION EST.

LOTTO

Sunny Page 52

'Police dog bit my leg'

West Vancouver's Holly Kleben, 15, is nursing wounds she says were inflicted by a police dog that accompanied officers called to remove uninvited guests from a Sunday night beachfront house party. Police will say only that it took 10 officers two hours to stop arriving guests before they could begin to move in on the crowd. See Story, Page 5.

Staff photo by Arlen Redekop

The coincidence of an unfortunate newspaper headline and a visit to Lund gave my parents reason to cut short their vacation that summer.

PART TWO

"Solitude is painful in youth but delicious in maturity."

– Albert Einstein

14
Somewhere Else

As Captain Vancouver and his crew scrupulously mapped the myriad waterways of Desolation Sound in the summer of 1792, the consistently negative eighteenth-century descriptors used by the captain also eloquently managed to summarize the feelings of a twentieth-century teenage brat: "Dull . . . uninteresting . . . awful . . . dreary . . . forlorn . . . gloomy . . . unpleasant . . . rude . . . dismal . . . inhospitable . . . desolate . . . " Captain Vancouver was slipping between insecure temper tantrums and depression due to a mixed onslaught of the terrible weather, the tedium of their task, the insubordination of his crew and being so utterly cut off from Britain, having received no correspondence or direction from his superiors for the two-plus years they had been at sea. He desperately wanted to match or beat the earlier explorative triumphs of his hero and mentor Captain Cook by making the major breakthrough discovery of the Northwest Passage. Surrounded by towering mountains and deep, narrow inlets, Vancouver the explorer felt claustrophobic and extremely irritated that he simply couldn't see much of anything, thereby getting at the very least a proper lay of the land.

While I sat stewing in a suburb of the very city named after that aggravated explorer, I could relate. I had a burning sensation to seek out my own glory. I wanted to experience the world's exotic ports of call, maybe not from the bridge of a schooner, but from behind the wheel of a tour van — the threat of scurvy probably equal in both situations. The Smugglers ended up touring all over the map non-stop for a dozen years, especially, purposefully, in the summer months. The tours were sordid, wild, hedonistic adventures that lived up to every euphoric high and frustrating low that we had ever imagined in rock 'n' roll. We found those exotic ports of call in the sweaty, smoky, booze-and-drug-soaked nightclubs of Toronto, New York, Paris, Tokyo, Montreal, Hamburg, San Francisco, Auckland, Halifax, Osaka, New Orleans, Rome, Melbourne and thousands of towns in between. Desolation Sound was the furthest destination from my mind.

Much changed for the Lawrence family in the meantime. I was vaguely aware that my family continued to make the trip throughout the warmer months of the year. Eventually, my sister went through a similar, much milder rejection of the cabin in her teen years, and so my parents began to regrettably make the trek without either of their kids. To my surprise, I learned that Mom had even gone to the cabin by herself a few times, something I never would have expected. But with Dad often too busy with work, she'd go unabated in her pink sweater, knee socks, nail polish and pedal pushers, managing the boat and getting to the cabin totally on her own. Russell was there to help her on her arrival. Mom kept a "Desolation Sound

Diary" for many years, mostly lists of groceries and supplies we needed, along with accounts of the weather and various recipes. She would every so often add personal notes, as she did on the occasion of her first solo trip to the Sound:

> July 22: Caught the 9:30 a.m. ferry after saying goodbye to Heather and Dad (Grant is away with his band). I am in a bit of a state of shock to be alone but I'm looking at this as an adventure. While lining up for the ferry, a family with two kids about nine and six years old are sitting in the car beside me, and I feel sad about how quickly you are growing up, Grant and Heather, and how many of the vacations to the cabin your father has missed.

> Aug 1: I certainly proved last week that I can be alone. I thoroughly enjoyed it and am glad I had the opportunity. Russell has been very helpful with the boat and the gas. Lots of tanning, reading, relaxing—a perfect holiday.

My dorky little sister Heather caught me by surprise by growing up into a beautiful, confident woman, instilled with the many values bestowed upon her from her *Little House on the Prairie* books and TV series. She married her high school sweetheart at a young age and quickly and happily became repeatedly pregnant with three children, just like Ma Ingalls. Heather's new family situation didn't bode well for regular Desolation Sound visits. The cabin had never been kid-proofed, so bringing a baby to the cabin would have seemed reckless.

It wasn't until The Smugglers finally started to wind down our touring schedule that I even contemplated going back to our cabin in the Sound, and it wasn't my idea. Even though Mom had never given up on me, it was at the persistent behest of my best friend and bandmate, Nick Thomas. An avid fisherman and outdoorsman, he would often ask about the cabin and I would blow it off. "It takes way too long to get up there," I'd snap back. "Don't you remember? Two ferries and then my family's stupid, crappy little boat, the same boat from when we were kids!"

"That's a cool boat," Nick would answer quietly.

"You have a short memory. It's not worth it, and there's no way I'm going up there and hanging out with my parents for an entire weekend." Nick wouldn't let up. He suggested that I approach my parents about going up on our own, getting a group of our friends together to make a weekend out of it. Eventually, reluctantly, I caved. One night while having dinner with Mom and Dad, I quietly and somewhat humbly gulped down the courage to ask them if I could take some pals up to the cabin for a weekend. They nearly fell out of their chairs. "You want to go back to the cabin?" Dad asked, more of a statement that a question, his shock tinged with a hint of cynicism.

"Yeah . . . thinking about it." It would have been completely within their rights to remind me of every insult I had thrown at the place throughout my teenage years ("stupid" . . . "prison" . . . "hell" . . . "shithole") and told me I didn't deserve a weekend on my own. My attitude toward the cabin, and by extension my family, really hadn't changed all that much. Even though I was definitely an adult, and the band was essentially over and done with, I still clung to a false sense of rock 'n' roll cool. We sat at the table in silence, my eyes on my roast beef. Mom jumped in, breaking the tension between Dad and me. "I think it'd be great if you took your friends up there; that would be wonderful, you'll love it!" Dad scoffed loudly.

Dad had never embraced my career as an "international rock 'n' roll singer," likely because in the early years he often ended up footing the bill, realizing well after the band had left for a six-week North American tour, for instance, that I had booked the gigs from our home phone, running up a huge bill with phone calls to places like Tuscaloosa, Hoboken, Drumheller, Fort Smith, Albuquerque and Charlottetown with no means of paying it off. The band would return penniless, having failed to draw large crowds in any of those early ports of call, and fights would ensue. Dad would yell about economics and responsibility, I would yell back about art and dreams. More doors would slam, Mom would mediate and my sister would cringe.

Up at the cabin, Dad would talk into the night with Russell, sharing his fears with him that I was on a fast track to Loserville. "He barely scraped through high school, and chose a rock band over university. He's never going to amount to anything without a university degree."

Russell repeatedly attempted to calm Dad down. "Relax! He's just finding his way, man. Everything will work out in the end. Look how I turned out."

Dad stared at Russell incredulously. When he realized he was being serious, Dad barked back, "You're a welfare recipient squatting in a dank shack in the middle of nowhere!"

"And I love it! Mind if I grab another beer?"

Mom was the go-between in my and Dad's impasse. She pushed hard for my weekend with friends to go ahead. Weeks later, a plan was hatched for the upcoming Canada Day long weekend. Mom suggested she stay at home, sending Dad and me to travel up a day or two beforehand to get the place running, hopefully rekindling a father-son bond in the process. Then Dad would head home the day my guests arrived. Dad was against allowing my friends and me to have the cabin to ourselves, likely still feeling burned by the teen-party riot of years earlier, but somehow Mom convinced him. Dad and I left Vancouver on a warm morning in late June, barely saying a word to each other as we sat side by side in the car. I tried hard not to show it, but every kilometre of the return trip was a totally unexpected nostalgic rush of childhood memories from the cobwebbed corners of my rock 'n' roll-rattled brain. I felt the long-forgotten anticipation in the first ferry lineup at Horseshoe Bay, where vacationers tapped their steering wheels nervously, knowing that life was simply *better* in the direction they were headed. Once the ferry entered sunny Howe Sound, a collective tension lifted from the shoulders of every passenger bound for their own pocket of paradise.

The hairpin turns of the Sunshine Coast still turned my stomach, but years of van touring with The Smugglers had cured me of carsickness. We wound past the familiar coastal towns of Gibsons, Roberts Creek, Sechelt and Halfmoon Bay, and down into Earl's Cove for the next ferry crossing. Still smaller and slower, that ferry brought us to the upper Sunshine Coast, where we twisted our way up through Saltery Bay, Powell River and the Sliammon First Nation reserve (speed limit 30 km/h). The snake of cars on the highway ever thinned as we drove north, until we were finally the only car, rolling down the hill toward the Okeover government wharf, the back door of Desolation Sound. When we made the final turn and the trees parted, that view of ultimate serenity unfurled before me like Heaven's Gate: oceanic nature supreme, those millions of twinkling diamonds scattered across the placid waters of the sun-drenched Sound. I felt a surge of emotion rush up my throat and flush my face. What the hell was wrong with me? Why had I forsaken it for so many years? Is such rejection the wide and wandering walkabout that so many of us must take in our lives to realize what we truly hold dear? Dad's road took him to Perth, Australia. Russell's wayward journey took him to a skyscraper in Toronto. For me, it was a few too many years in a rock band.

The wharf was a lot bigger than it had been a dozen or so years ago, and a lot busier. I remembered that our little aluminum skiff was once one of the few "pleasure craft" lashed to the dock back then . . . now the pleasure boats far outnumbered the oyster skiffs and workboats. It seemed that modern technology had finally reached the wharf as well. Right beside the top of the gangplank sat a battered and heavily used BC Tel payphone that I had never seen before. It had been installed only a few years earlier, and before cellphones became ubiquitous, it was the sole and primary communications outlet for residents and tourists to connect to the rest of the outside world. We unloaded our car and climbed into the boat without much being said.

The boat rocked back and forth under our weight, and I had to steady myself, having long lost my sea legs. We both plunked ourselves down on that salty aluminum bench seat and Dad fired up the outboard. Its guttural roar sounded like the bark of a friendly dog excited to greet us, as Dad and I skimmed out into the inlet on a perfectly calm afternoon. By now I couldn't hide it any longer; I was grinning ear to ear. Dad saw it, but remained stoic, his increasingly common mood as he grew older. The warm salt air whipped through our hair: the feeling of freedom. My head was on a swivel, remembering every little island and cove, marvelling at the eagles and ravens overhead. Every piece of nature was exactly as it was, as if no time had passed. It wasn't until we were in sight of the cabins that I noticed the changes. Man moves much faster than nature.

So many new cabins had sprung up on our rocky spine of the Sound that I barely recognized the place. Thankfully, most were still separated by natural barriers such as rock outcrops, cliffs, ravines or lagoons along the shoreline, protecting privacy and maintaining Dad's original design ideals. At the first sharp point of land we came to, just around the corner from our cabin, a huge new house literally hung off the cliff, like a diver ready to jump. Dad shouted over the outboard that it had been built by a friendly lawyer from Vancouver named Darrell. A little farther along was an angular house in the trees, owned by "Bernard the German." Dad described him as an ox of a man with a big, black handlebar moustache, who had built his cabin single-handedly, hauling up every piece of wood and brick and every appliance up the hill on his back. Deep in the bay there was a cabin that still housed an original "first wave" owner: Mike the retired bus driver. His two-storey cabin was perched high on a sunny cliff ledge. An incredibly tough guy and the packrat of the inlet, Mike had all sorts of tidal treasures on the rocks in front of his cabin. Across the bay from our place, there were more new neighbours. Lorenzo, an older, heavyset, heavy-smoking bachelor, had bought the Reverend Jim Davies' old cabin and loved it. And there was Prawn Pete, a lanky, retired outdoorsman who often delighted neighbours by bringing them fresh-caught prawns, then annoyed them by driving golf balls at the seals in the bay, convinced that they were eating too many of the salmon he was trying to catch. Then there was Candy, a friendly, funny, bachelorette arts-school teacher from the States. Everyone called her "Handy Candy."

One of the Sound's great characters, the charming, gregarious and hilarious Handy Candy, who could "fix anything but dinner." She once received an unwelcome Godfather-like surprise when plunking down in the cockpit of that very kayak.

I had already heard much about the new neighbours from Mom, but none more so than Handy Candy. They loved her. She was a lightning bolt of artistic, feminine energy that had never been present in the Sound. Handy Candy was tall and slender, with spiky, short-cropped blonde hair and funky, wire-framed glasses, often spending the summer wearing nothing but a one-piece blue bathing suit and a pair of flip-flops. She first fell in love with the Sound years earlier while on kayaking adventures with her then-husband. She witnessed our cabins slowly get constructed, which confused her because she thought they were in the Desolation Sound Provincial Marine Park. When she found out our land was privately owned, she knew she had to have a cabin of her own. So upon the collapse of her twenty-five-year marriage, Candy bought an almost-collapsed old cabin that had been taken over by squirrels. With the help of local carpenter Jim Nailer, she slowly rebuilt it with an artist's flair and lovingly christened the sparkling results "Camp Candy."

According to my parents, Handy Candy's arrival changed everything. For years prior, the cabins at Desolation Sound were filled with Canadians who, for the most part, kept to themselves. Because the vertical shoreline prevented many neighbours from walking to each other's cabins, summers would come and go with next-door neighbours sometimes never even seeing or talking to each other. Before Candy, neighbourhood aesthetics were almost non-existent; tidiness meant throwing all the empty beer cans into one big pile. On the flipside, Camp Candy was immaculate.

Handy Candy was an extremely social, attractive and gregarious soul, and made a point of motoring around in her pretty little blue boat, the *Tinkertoy*, to introduce herself to everyone. Soon she was introducing neighbours to neighbours who had never met over the course of twenty years or more. It was Dad who pointed out that it took a friendly, bathing-suit-clad American to unite a group of reserved Canadians. Handy

Candy single-handedly turned a scattering of cabins in the wilderness into a community in record time. And while her intentions were always good, she was outspoken and opinionated. She didn't back down or get intimidated by the mostly male neighbours surrounding her. She also wouldn't hesitate for a second to speak up if she saw room for improvement on neighbouring properties. Some took it the wrong way. Some thought a woman shouldn't be telling a man what to do.

In a retaliatory move that seemed torn from the pages of *The Godfather*, Desolation Sound–style, a neighbour decided to let Candy know that some of her unsolicited advice was unwelcome. One morning Candy was preparing to go for a paddle in her kayak. She pulled it down to the seashore and balanced the boat in shallow water, plunked herself into the cockpit and then let out a painful scream. Jumping back onto shore, she looked down and shrieked again. Lying in rigor mortis on the kayak's seat was a bloated, bug-eyed, quillback rockfish that had been caught and placed there for her to sit on, the sharp quills of the fish's dorsal fin pointing up. She never found out who pulled the prank or exactly what message that person was trying to send. Nonetheless, it didn't have the desired effect. Candy remained as opinionated as ever.

Candy earned the nickname "Handy Candy" from her ability to successfully tinker with just about anything. She just wasn't that *domestic*. For years she handed out business cards to neighbours that read, "Handy Candy — I'll Fix Anything But Dinner!" And she could. Fridges, propane tanks, rotten decks — she could fix it all. Another favourite Handy Candy phrase was "We're burnin' daylight!" if she were to ever catch you sleeping past 9 a.m. To visitors she'd shout, "Enjoy the place but we'll have to cut out your tongues before you leave," ever fearful of too many people finding out about our rocky paradise.

*

Dad cut the motor in front of our cabin, the boat's momentum sliding us atop the thick kelp bed floating on the surface just offshore. We came to a stop with a soft, familiar thud against our rocks. I carefully stepped out of the skiff onto the granite outcrop. Feeling the rough contour of the rock under the soles of my Converse sneakers caused a spiritual tingle up through my body. I took a deep breath, filling my lungs with memories of summers spent . . . the pungent scent of the slippery seaweed exposed at mid-tide, the thick moss clinging to the moisture of rain three days earlier and the cabin itself. The weather had aged its exterior. The deck was now the same shade as the rocks, but the inside remained an untouched museum of my childhood. It still smelled like a sauna upon entry, the cedar walls warmed by the sunlight through the French windows.

Dad sat back and watched me walk through the cabin slowly, through each room, remembering objects and wall hangings and tiny imperfect details the minute I set eyes on them. The games-and-puzzles shelf seemed trapped in time: stacked pell-mell on top of each other were well-worn boxes of *Trivial Pursuit: Genus Edition*, *Twenty Questions*, *Scrabble*, *Risk*, *Boggle*, *Monopoly* and other not-so-classic games such as *Pass Out* (an adult drinking game) and *Name Burst!*, a celebrity naming-game from the 1980s filled with of-the-moment monikers such as J.R. Ewing, Kelly McGillis, Oliver North, Gary Hart and Shamu. We had puzzles featuring the Smurfs, E.T. and Asterix. My embarrassing outboard motor posters and Heather's *Archie* cutouts were still pinned to our bedroom wall. It was all exactly the same.

From out on the deck I looked down into the cove. Russell's little wooden shack was still sitting down at the forest's edge, just as it had been when I last saw it. There was just one difference: no Russell. A few years earlier he had met a woman, and finally decided he'd had enough of living in the woods. He moved into a little house on the road to Lund, managing to slip through the grip of what had killed many others who spent too much time alone year-round in Desolation Sound.

15
Going Bush

I was prepared for Russell to be absent from the Sound. Though he tired of life in the wilderness, he was far more successful at the isolated, bare-bones lifestyle than many. He never lost his marbles from spending too much time alone in the cove, otherwise known as cabin fever or "going bush." Anyone who has ever spent an entire year in Desolation Sound, or lived anywhere for an extended time alone in the woods, knows that glorious, social summers can quickly turn into winters of terrifying isolation. It was never a secret that the winters in the Sound were treacherous. Human error usually played the starring villainous role, weather the supporting, in so many deaths during the dark season: the shooting of Gus Bloom, the plane-crash death of his son William, the drowning of a hippie from the Desolation Sound commune. All of those deaths were sudden and dramatic. Going bush was the creeping killer of Desolation Sound.

The dark time of the year is the dangerous time of the year. This is about as much sunshine as one can expect for weeks on end in the gloomy months of winter, some poorly exposed pockets of the Sound barely catching a ray of the low winter sunshine if at all. Nasty weather is a key contributor to "going bush."

The effects of going bush in Desolation Sound have arguably affected visitors for hundreds of years. Captain Vancouver's repeated descriptions of the Sound and elsewhere off the grey, sodden and intricate shores of British Columbia, especially his feelings of isolation from his crew, have been cited by various historians as contributing factors in his mental unravelling and eventual inglorious death. Mike Shuttler, the original Caucasian settler and hermit philosopher who was loved by many, eventually had to be removed from his Prideaux Haven homestead when it was reported to the authorities that he had begun greeting winter visitors with a shotgun. Anyone spending prolonged isolation in the wilderness risked the downward mental spiral of going bush. From all the stories I have heard and read on this dark subject, there seem to be five common stages that occur in almost every case.

Stage one of going bush is extreme loneliness . . . Loneliness felt in the pit of your heart; the desperate need for human companionship, wishing there was someone else to talk to, to relate to, someone to spend time with, someone to share thoughts and conversations with, and someone to love.

Stage two of going bush is the onset of depression . . . A crippling realization that you are in fact alone and there is likely no one coming. You will have to make do by yourself. You can lie in bed as days and nights blend, or shake it off by getting in the boat and going into town, talking a mile-a-minute once you finally reach the warmth of the Lund Pub. But in the winter in Desolation Sound, the days are grey and short, the nights long and black. The rains arrive in October and don't fade away until March, with only a few hours of light and little sunshine. Winds howl and storms rage, turning the inlets into life-threatening tempests, sometimes so stormy that taking a boat trip into Lund or Powell River is an impossibility that can last days or weeks at a time.

Stage three of going bush is resentment . . . Anger that no one is coming to visit, that everyone has forgotten you, forsaken you, doesn't care about you. Well fuck 'em. The entire rotten human race can go straight to hell. Everyone you can think of you curse, over and over. You write their names down in lists — the names of the hated — into your notebook until the pencil breaks through the page, which is then torn up and thrown into the fire. Then you do it again, plotting revenge.

Stage four of going bush is paranoia . . . Paranoia that if another human being is spotted anywhere close to you, whether in a plane, on a boat or, worst-case scenario, on foot, that human being is out to get you, meaning you harm in some way, watching your every move, plotting your imminent capture, arrest or death. The paranoid delusion of this stage often leads to the fifth and final stage of going bush.

Stage five of going bush is death . . . Death by suicide — not giving those in phantom or real pursuit the satisfaction of capturing you — or being killed by authorities responding to complaints that someone up beyond the end of the road had gone bush and was becoming a potential danger to themselves and others.

Throughout British Columbia's young history, there are plenty of stories of solitary figures going bush: shooting at passing aircraft; murdering innocent civilians who happen upon their camp, trap line, homestead or gold claim; murdering police officers attempting to capture them; or killing themselves. In Desolation Sound, one of the first truly dramatic and violent cases of a settler going bush occurred in the winter of 1921, just two years after the shooting death of homesteader Gus Bloom. The headline in the Vancouver daily newspaper read: "Shot Dead by Lunatic: Man Lost in Bush Goes Insane and Is Terrorizing Upcoast Village."

By the time Alexander Johnson, a Swedish immigrant living in Desolation Sound, went on his shooting rampage in December of 1921, he was well into stage four of going bush, and on a fast track to stage five. Alex lived occasionally with another male friend on the south shore of Okeover Inlet, which in the winter is even darker and wetter than the rest of the Sound, shrouded in the clammy winter shadow of a steep hillside. Over the course of more than a year, Alex Johnson slowly went insane to violent proportions. By the time he hit stage four, he was inexplicably convinced that he was being hunted down by his former friends. Much of the last six months of his life was spent hunting alone in the woods, avoiding other people. He rarely ever left his cabin without several loaded firearms.

Johnson's occasional roommate was a Swede named Frank Gustafson, a fisherman who was gone for long stretches of time. Upon his returns, Frank would be understandably concerned with Johnson's erratic behaviour. While Johnson seemed to trust Gustafson, he would repeatedly tell him that others they knew were coming to murder him any day. Johnson's former best friend in the area was a popular, good-natured Italian immigrant named Raffaele "Ralph" D'Angio. At Gustafson's behest, D'Angio agreed to visit Johnson after a hunting trip to try and convince him that he meant him no ill will. On the frigid, dim winter morning of December 15, 1921, Ralph D'Angio slogged down the muddy trail to Alex and Frank's cabin, entering through the front door. Frank was in a side room making coffee and tending to the morning fire while Alex was still in bed. Ralph called out to Alex, who upon seeing Ralph, jumped out of his bed and grabbed two guns from the bedside table. With barely a word exchanged, Alex Johnson starting blasting at point-blank range. His first shot hit Ralph D'Angio in the head. Frank Gustafson saw Ralph put his hand to his head, and then crumple over when the next shot hit him. Frank panicked and wrestled to get out of the back door, finally forcing it open. Clad in only his long johns and bare feet, he escaped into the woods as he heard another shot ring out from the cabin, then heard Alex Johnson yell out in Swedish: "There's a lot more I got to do before I die!"

Gustafson ran barefoot through the rugged winter terrain for ten minutes without looking back until he reached the nearest neighbours, warning them that Johnson had gone mad and was armed with at least five guns. At the same time, Johnson went out the front door of the cabin and stomped down the trail with a gun in each hand, shooting at anyone he saw. Neighbours fled their homes into the forest, or hid in their root cellars shaking with fear and cold. Some reported their houses being shot at five or six times. Alex Johnson's reign of terror would last throughout the day and into the night, keeping many residents hidden in the woods and exposed to the winter elements.

Word eventually reached Lund and the next morning a telegram came through at the police detachment in Powell River. It stated the emergency situation in a few basic words, pleading for help, signed "Lund Citizens." By noon, an armed posse left for Lund led by Constable W.H. Hadley, the same guy who had tracked down Oskar Roos two years earlier. When the constable and his posse arrived, they learned from panicked neighbours that Alex Johnson had barricaded himself in his cabin with plenty of ammunition, threatening to shoot anyone who came near (Hadley had heard that threat before). Unlike the Oskar Roos manhunt when Hadley was stonewalled by the locals trying to protect the popular bootlegger, this time the Swedes came out in force, many frightened that Johnson had turned to seemingly random violence. Hadley and his posse of eight deputies and several armed locals trekked the six kilometres along the frostbit coast of Okeover Inlet to Johnson's cabin, surrounding it.

From behind the safety of a giant tree trunk, Hadley called out to Johnson to surrender. There was no smoke coming from the chimney and the only sound the posse could hear coming from the cabin was a dog's mournful howl. They slowly crept forward, guns drawn at the ready. Still not hearing anything but the bawling dog, Hadley made a dash for the cabin, pinning himself against the outside log wall between the front door and the window. With one eye he gingerly peeked inside and saw the feet of a man sprawled on the floor. Calling his posse forward, they broke down the barricaded door and crowded into the dark shack, guns drawn. When their eyes adjusted to the light, the locals in the posse identified the man on

TERROR OF LUND ENDS OWN LIFE

Alex. Johnson Found Dead at Threshold of His Homestead.

Killed Ralph Deangio, Who Was Paying Visit to Shack.

Then Went on Warpath Armed With Five Guns, Says Eye-witness.

Had Been Acting Strangely For Past Year, Declare Residents.

PARK RESERVOIR BONE DRY

The Vancouver Daily Province, December 17, 1921.

the floor as Alex Johnson, his sad dog standing sentinel over his dead body. A few feet away lay Ralph D'Angio. G.H. Bay from the *Vancouver Daily Province* reported on the murder-suicide:

> It was a gruesome sight that greeted Constable Hadley and his posse who had set out to capture the madman. With his rifle lying beside him, Johnson was stretched out at the door of his homestead with the lower part of his face completely shot-away.

Johnson had managed to shoot himself three times in committing suicide, including the presumably fatal blow to the face. On the table beside his bed, the constable found a long suicide note scrawled in Swedish, beginning with "Please write and tell my folks. I had to act quick," followed by unintelligible, paranoid ramblings and accusations that his best friends were trying to kill him. Alex Johnson's descent into madness was certainly in keeping with the advanced stages of going bush, brought on by long stretches of physical and psychological isolation in an unforgiving landscape during the darkest days of the year. Modern health officials likely would have diagnosed Alex Johnson as a paranoid schizophrenic in desperate need of stabilizing medication. G.H. Bay, however, drew a different conclusion, reflective of the thinking of the day:

> Moonshine, or the moon itself, is ascribed the cause of the double tragedy. An empty bottle was found beside Johnson's bunk. On the night of the shooting, one of the finest full moons that ever shone shed its placid beams upon Lund. The supposed effect of the moon on lunatics is well known.

During the inquest, Frank Gustafson testified that Alexander Johnson didn't drink. Johnson's official death certificate lists his cause of death as "rifle wound, self-inflected, while temporarily insane." The D'Angio family remained in the Okeover Inlet area for many years. Down the hill toward the Okeover government wharf there is a road that branches off to the right named D'Angio Road.

Mark Vonnegut, the son of none other than American novelist Kurt Vonnegut, also fell into the trappings of going bush while trying to live out a utopian hippie commune dream just south of Desolation Sound, on a farm near Powell Lake in the late sixties and early seventies. His goal was to seek out "liberation, enlightenment, and salvation" in the Canadian wilderness. Instead he found himself slipping into a violent and psychotic parallel universe he couldn't control. Due to the effects of isolation and incredible amounts of very potent dope, Vonnegut was diagnosed with schizophrenia and committed to a mental hospital in Vancouver. Vonnegut thankfully made a full recovery, and in 1975 published a book about his ordeal entitled *The Eden Express: A Memoir of Insanity*. In the afterword of a subsequent edition, Vonnegut, now a doctor, says today his condition would have probably been diagnosed as manic depression.

Jeff Shuyster was a successful oyster farmer in Desolation Sound and a much-loved local character. He worked tirelessly on his oyster beaches to create a viable business, earning himself the nickname "The Oyster Baron of Okeover Inlet." Originally from Montreal, where he was a teenage track star, Jeff maintained his physical fitness throughout his life by constantly exercising. He'd often run overland from his oyster lease to Lund and back again, over extremely rugged terrain. He once entered himself in Powell River 15K race but when he arrived, he realized that he had forgotten his running shoes, so he ran the entire race in his rubber boots. He came in second place. He was tall, bespectacled and often pretty filthy. He wore jeans shorts that weren't cut-offs . . . the lower half of the pants had simply worn away from oil, battery acid and dirt, and his afro-like mop of black hair often had sticks and seaweed protruding from it. He played the saxophone, was a math whiz, wrote for the local periodical *The Lund Barnacle* and had a dog named Kip, after Kenyan runner Kipchoge Keino. Jeff and Kip's diet existed primarily of raw oysters from his beach, keeping them both lean and healthy. Russell considered Jeff one of his best friends and affectionately called him "Pig Pen" whenever he ran into him at the Lund Pub.

Jeff spent long stretches of time alone in the Sound. Like Alex Johnson, Jeff also lived on the dark side of the inlet that barely saw any sunlight during the winter months. Jeff had managed to cheat death several times, including almost drowning in a winter storm and being pulled to safety by a Coast Guard helicopter, then suffering the after-effects of hypothermia after refusing medical treatment. Shortly afterward, he narrowly escaped from his house when it was burning down. Within days the entire inlet showed up to rebuild his home, proving his popularity with just about everybody. Jeff Shuyster was the last person anyone thought would fall to the trappings of going bush. But over time, the oyster market steadily declined while costs continued to rise. Russell had already noted that Jeff was careful with his money. When Jeff would visit the Lund Pub, the Oyster Baron would purposefully have in his pocket the exact change for one beer, down to the penny. If someone wanted to buy him another he'd drink it, but he wouldn't spend another cent of his own beyond paying for that one beer.

Oyster prices continued to drop, along with Jeff's profits. No matter how hard he worked, Jeff couldn't get ahead, and it slowly drove him mad. It was a question of his own self-worth, which meant everything to Jeff. He said at the time with his trademark dark humour: "Shellfish farmers hate being in the red." The oyster market never rebounded, and tragically neither did Jeff. He eventually slipped into a dark depression, kept to himself, was in and out of hospital, and when seen by others he exhibited frightening behaviour that was way out of character. He was reported missing on a dreary, wet day in December and was found by the RCMP dog team a day later. He had committed suicide by hanging himself in the woods behind his home, just days before his fifty-second birthday. Jeffrey Shuster, the Oyster Baron of Okeover Inlet, is remembered by two plaques: one at the Okeover government wharf and another along the boardwalk in Lund.

Thankfully, Russell Letawsky never got beyond stage two of going bush. Many times our family would show up to the cabin in the spring after a long, dark winter and Russell would emerge from the woods, looking like he had grown to be a part of it. He would excitedly sit at our table and hold court for several hours straight, drinking beer after beer, asking and answering his own questions. Dad always explained to us what was going on with Russell — that he was just excited to see us –and none of us ever felt threatened in any way.

Russell's sound mind, physical strength and ever-pleasant disposition carried him through many a winter unscathed. When our family would show up after a long dark season he'd sit at our table, smoke his pipe and talk for hours.

For close to ten years in Desolation Sound, Russell somehow managed to stave off going bush year after year. Russell knew when it was time to leave. Unfortunately, his first foray of living "in town" didn't last too long. After ten years in the wilderness, Russell was challenged to start up a regular, new life all over again. Since his last job was at a photography studio back in Kamloops and he still had some camera equipment that hadn't been totally destroyed by dampness, he attempted to start up a business as a freelance photographer down the highway in Powell River.

One of Russell's first photography contracts was a biker wedding for a local motorcycle gang, and being his first gig, he really wanted to go full throttle. Maybe he was a little too eager to please. He was instructed to stand by the side of the road and take photos of the wedding procession of motorcycles as they roared down the highway just outside of town. Russell surveyed the site and decided to do one better, hauling his camera equipment up to the top of a bluff to capture the entire wedding procession—about fifty motorcycles—from an aerial perspective. He schlepped his gear up through the undergrowth to the top of the cliff that overlooked the road. He set up his tripod, attached his camera, and zoomed in on the crest of the hill. He soon heard the rumbling thunder of several dozen motorcycles. He leaned down and peered into the lens, focusing the camera, his finger at the ready. He could hear the motorcycles, loud, intimidating and guttural, but to his surprise, none crested the hill. Two bikers finally entered his camera lens, one wearing a flowing white gown. The problem was, he could only see their backs; they were coming from the wrong direction. Russell spun around and realized to his horror that the wedding procession was cresting the hill behind him.

Panicked, he tried to reposition the tripod and the camera as quickly as he could, snapping madly. He detached the camera from the stand, kicking it over, and started shooting everything he could. When he eventually developed the film he wound up with a bunch of blurry shots, highly debatable whether or not they were anything, let alone a wedding procession on motorcycles. He was pretty sure none of the blurs were the bride and groom—he had missed them entirely. Despite the rough start, Russell went on to successfully photograph many more weddings, even more biker weddings, all while living with various girlfriends on various pieces of land between Powell River and Lund.

I left my viewpoint on the deck and climbed down the rocks toward Russell's shack, yelling over my shoulder to inform Dad of my whereabouts. The cove's gravel beach crunched under my feet as I approached the dark windows and moss-covered roof. I climbed up the makeshift rock staircase and pushed open the door. With apprehension I stepped into the centre of the room. The shack was musty and stank of rot. Russell had left almost everything behind. Dad explained later that Russell always planned to return for the remainder of his things, but hadn't. The bookshelf above his bed was stuffed with his now-moulding books; musty blankets and pillows lay on a rotting mattress; and other shelves held rusting pots, pans and tin cans. It looked like he had taken his chess set, his rifle, his radio and his Smugglers album. Scattered across the uneven, well-worn floorboards was evidence of mice and other critters having had their way with the place. Besides the advanced toll of Mother Nature, the cabin was otherwise untouched and would remain so for several years, a fading remembrance of the hermit of Desolation Sound.

Back up at our cabin, Dad showed me everything there was to running the place—which was now fully equipped with running hot and cold water, plumbing, propane lamps, stove and fridge. Once I convinced him that I had the hang of it, we drove the boat back to the Okeover government wharf. For the first time ever I dropped *him* off, feeling guilty that I didn't deserve the trust my parents were bestowing upon me. Standing on the wharf together, Dad hugged me. "Be careful, be respectful of the neighbours and call me if you need anything."

"I will Dad, I promise. Thanks." He turned and walked up the wharf, leaving me alone in Desolation Sound for the first time ever. Once I was certain he was gone, I cracked a beer and waited for my friends to arrive. The sound of that cracked beer can was the beginning of a new era in my life that would bring a completely new appreciation and respect for Desolation Sound and the stories it contained.

16
Cloudy with a Chance of Drunk

My friends showed more blatant excitement when they arrived at the Okeover dock than I had shown a couple of days earlier, tearing down the hill at full speed in their cars, stereos cranked, horns blaring when they saw me. They considered it a great journey from the city — driving at top speed until they could drive no farther, drinking beer, playing hacky sack and suntanning at the ferries terminals I once found so cruelly boring. After surveying the scene with exclaims of "Holy shit," "Oh my god," and "Why didn't you tell us about this place?" they proceeded to load physically staggering amounts of beer into our tiny boat, sinking it lower and lower in the water with each case. They couldn't wait to motor north for a seventy-two-hour lost weekend — across the inlets, toward craggy mountains and a hungover unknown.

I began to invite more and more friends up to the Sound, this being one of the largest groups stuffing our cabin all at once. I'm on the far left, Nick is on the far right, Julie has her arm around Rory, Soraya is in the middle, crouching between two girls. This shot was taken at Snake Lake, which lives up to its name every time.

We were a tight group of friends who had remained so since high school. Nick was stocky and athletic, and his girlfriend Soraya looked like Cleopatra. Rory was a tall, lanky blond who was vocally left wing, and his hilarious, sexy brunette girlfriend Julie looked just like Veronica Lodge with freckles. And then there was the weekend's wild card gooseberry . . . our extremely loud, intense, punk-rock skinhead friend Roger, who had broken the cardinal rule of nicknames by giving himself one: "Roger the Dodger." He thought it was incredibly cool, though we thought it was incredibly stupid. It was a terrible nickname, as he was constantly getting nicked by the cops for all sorts of petty, drunken crimes. Roger the Dodger listened to his boom box louder, swore with the most vigour and partied harder than anyone we had ever met. Paradoxically, Roger was also a gourmet chef. And even though it was a cloudy day, Roger the Dodger was shirtless — his wiry, pale, near-skeletal frame completed by skin-tight black jeans; knee-high, tightly laced combat boots; black, wraparound shades; and a shiny shaved head. He heaved a massive cooler into the boat, which we hoped was filled with all sorts of culinary delights to tickle our palates all weekend long. That was until Roger the Dodger popped it open with a devil yell, revealing seventy-two ice-cold cans of Iron Horse extra-strong malt liquor beer, one beer for every hour of the weekend. Somewhere in heaven or hell, Oskar Roos was smiling.

After the boat was loaded with enough hooch to keep a frat party drunk for a month, Rory ran up the hill to park his car before we made the journey. Rory was oblivious to the fact that he was jogging up the same steep hill that brave young Constable Hadley had to climb when attempting to capture Oskar Roos eighty years earlier. The entire hillside behind the Okeover government wharf area was once the homestead of the infamous Roos. It was also on these shores where he kept the fishing trawler that also doubled as a moonshine delivery service and was the boat from which Gus Bloom was shot. After being found innocent in the Bloom shooting, Roos lived a long and colourful life in Desolation Sound, establishing Okeover Landing where he eventually opened a restaurant and oversaw the plans for the government wharf. He died in 1962 at age seventy-eight. He and his wife had five children. On their homestead overlooking the wharf now stands the Laughing Oyster seafood restaurant, a rustic, gourmet oasis that serves delicious meals to summer yachters. Directly behind the restaurant is a tall and arching cherry tree, planted by Roos a century earlier.

Not far from that same cherry tree, Rory hopped behind the wheel of his beat-up '84 Mazda. Just as he was about to turn the key, he felt a heavy impact from behind. A big, white pickup truck had backed up directly into Rory's car with a loud crunch. Rory had the impunity and righteousness of many young men in their twenties. Rory hopped out of his car, surveyed his crumpled rear bumper and lost it, raising his arms skyward with indignation. "What the hell was that, asshole?"

The driver's door of the big, white pickup opened slowly. A mountain of a man stepped out, with deep-set, dark eyes and a big, black handlebar moustache. From Dad's description, I realized that this alpha-giant must be Bernard the German, our next-door neighbour whom I still had yet to meet. I quietly slid a little farther down in our boat, still tied to the dock and loaded to the gunwales with friends and beer, all of us surveying the scene from one hundred feet away. Roger the Dodger perked up, sensing some fun: impending violence. I forced him back in his seat with a hand on his bare and bony shoulder. "Sorry about that, my friend . . . but take a look at that," said Bernard the German in a slow, deep and steady timbre, his accent a mix of German and Canadian hoser. He pointed up at a hand-painted sign directly above Rory's car: NO PARKING. THIS MEANS U. "I guess that means you, eh?" said Bernard. "Bit of a tight turnaround down here."

I had forgotten to warn my friends about "island time." Island time can exist anywhere off the grid, and is certainly not restricted to actual, you know, *islands*. Island time is a way of life, an end-of-the-road philosophy, a pace, a rhythm. If you're on island time, everything moves a whole lot slower than it does in the city. Almost in easygoing defiance of the rat race, nothing is ever that big of a deal. In Mexico, they call it *mañana*, meaning "tomorrow," as in that's when they'll get around to it. In the Yukon it's called "ish-time," as in there is no such thing as an exact time for anything, no punctuality. Things get done when they get done, shit happens and anger gets you absolutely nowhere in these types of places. Any open display of frustration or lack of patience toward a local marks you as a city slicker immediately, and can quickly freeze you out of the local community. Rory was not yet on island time.

Unfazed by the sheer size of the German, Rory spat back, "So that makes it okay to ram into my bumper, you dumb hick? You're lucky my car isn't worth fixing. Just watch where you're driving, you stupid, blind old fart." Bernard slowly turned around and looked at the rest of us stuffed into our boat at the dock waiting for Rory. Bernard's eyes pivoted back and set on Rory with a deep, dark glare. "Is that the Lawrences' boat you're in? Welcome to the neighbourhood, buddy." Bernard got back in his truck. Rory gulped. Dad had been gone for less than an hour and we had already shredded one of my promises, with several more to come.

We *putt-putted* away from the dock with about an inch of clearance between the gunwale of the boat and the surface of the ocean, going so slowly that no one bothered to wear a life jacket. "Fuck it, man!" shrieked Roger, pointing to the already growing pile of empty Iron Horse cans on the bottom of the boat, already ahead of his quota. "If we sink, we could always start bailing with those!" The sky was as iron-grey as Roger's empties, but it was dead calm without a trace of wind, so the boat ride was a safe one.

Upon arrival, all my pent-up fears of how my friends would receive our cabin were abated. Everyone loved our rustic getaway, which gave me a very different perspective on the old place. "Wait," I remember thinking to myself, "this place has appeal to people beyond my two parents, an appeal to people below the age of fifty?" In my teenage shallowness I was always put off by our cabin being so remote and inaccessible. I assumed it had no appeal. It was nowhere near a ski resort, or a lake. There was no electricity, no roads and no white sand beach, so why would anyone like it? It turned out those were the same reasons my friends were excited to be in Desolation Sound. Rory, a carpenter, loved the post-and-beam design. Nick, the fisherman, loved the immediate proximity to the ocean. The girls loved the sprawling deck space. Roger the Dodger loved being completely out of reach of any authority figure of any kind, celebrating by cranking NoMeansNo on his boom box.

Nick couldn't wait to go fishing, and had already used his time at the government wharf wisely. While we were loading the boat, he had reached into the water and pulled a small limpet shell (commonly known as a "Chinese hat" shell) from the dock pilings, skewering the tender meat under the seashell onto a small hook that he dropped in the water. As Rory argued with Bernard the German, Nick ignored us all, methodically bobbing the bait in the water until a shiner—a small perch with bright silver scales, not much bigger than a minnow—took the bait. Nick hauled it up effortlessly and threw it in his fishing bucket, with a plan to use it as bait to hook something larger.

Within an hour of arriving at the cabin, Nick, Rory, Roger the Dodger and I were back in the boat, leaving the girls to their *Hello* and *Star* magazines and deck chairs. We puttered out to the rocky point where our neighbours' newly built cabin hung off the cliff. We cracked another round of Iron Horse while Nick snagged the little shiner he caught onto the large and gruesome-looking barbed hook at the end of his "Codbuster" fishing lure, the same type I had used with Russell years earlier. As usual, we were fishing for "bottom fish": rockfish, lingcod and red snapper. Nick loved salmon fishing, but there were very few salmon left in our once-teeming inlet, having once spawned in the millions in a large river at the head of nearby Theodosia Inlet. In 1956, in an effort to generate more power for Powell River's pulp and paper mills, the river was dammed and mostly diverted to Powell Lake, effectively destroying a huge salmon run that had been in existence for thousands of years. Sliammon legend has it that the salmon run was once so massive that in the spawning months of the fall you could walk from one shore of the inlet to the other on the backs of the salmon. Recently, the Sliammon First Nation and a few other government bodies were successful in restoring the Theodosia River to its natural flow, but the salmon population has yet to rebound.

With a plop Nick dropped his hook into a kelp bed, letting the reel spool out with the weight of the lure, while we drifted with the swift current. This was a favourite fishing spot Russell had shown me a decade and a half earlier, where several currents collide like a busy city intersection. Russell explained that there is an explosion of life wherever ocean currents come together. Sure enough, seals cavorted nearby, chasing schools of surfacing herring, while seagulls glided overhead, looking for leftovers. Dark little perch darted through the underwater vines of kelp that spiny green crabs clung to. A bald eagle sat on a craggy treetop, sternly eyeing us, knowing that if we were to catch a little one and throw it back, it would be an easy dinner. In the two or three seconds that it took for a thrown-back little fish to regain the strength to swim, it would often remain on the surface, which was just enough time for the eagle to silently swoop down and snag it with outstretched talons.

Within ten minutes and two beers, Nick had a bite powerful enough to slam his fishing rod down on the gunwale of the boat, snapping us all to attention. Knowing that Roger the Dodger and Rory had never been ocean fishing before, Nick yelled out in dramatic, tour-guide fashion, "Get the net!" In all my fishing experiences in Desolation Sound, likely thanks to Russell's many hot spots, I have never been in a situation where we've waited more than ten minutes for a bite; sometimes the fish took the bait the instant we dropped the hook. Roger grabbed the net, as he and Rory both peered over the side of the boat with drunken anticipation, swearing quietly to each other. On his feet, Nick engaged an unseen fish in a herky-jerky five-minute battle, until finally a creature rose from the deep, dragged up by Nick's barbed Codbuster. Ten feet below, we were somewhat surprised to see that it was a fairly small, but obviously very tough lingcod, and were amazed that it had put up such a fight. Nick expressed dismay at its puny size. "Shit. That's a throw-back. Whoa! Look at that!"

This is exactly what a person looks like when a lingcod bites the hook. Rory's finding out just how much of a fight these predatory fish can give, while Nick looks on. I'm pretty sure this fish was dinner later that night.

Abruptly appearing out of the ocean's darkness, rising rapidly from the depths right behind the undersized lingcod, was a massive, tubular, bug-eyed, ugly monster of a fish. It was a much larger lingcod, one of the biggest Nick and I had ever seen. At least four feet in length, its head was the size of a watermelon, its body like a python. Its huge mouth was agape, showing off rows of ferociously jagged and uneven teeth. To the shock of us all, the monster lingcod rushed up behind the little lingcod Nick had hooked, and swallowed it whole, hook still attached. Now Nick had a far bigger fish to deal with. This time when he screamed, "Get the net!" it was in honest urgency. The powerful fish thrashed about on the surface, then disappeared under the boat, Nick scrambling around us to keep up with it.

Rory and Roger the Dodger leapt to their feet and let out a string of excited obscenities at the sight of this unexpected burst of underwater cannibalism, pumping their fists and high-fiving, causing the boat to rock dangerously, beer and salt water sloshing to and fro. Nick strained to hang on to the fish while I grabbed the net from Roger. All four of us were on our feet, yelling and swearing, ordering each other around, like cavemen discovering fire. I pushed Roger and Rory aside and dipped the net into the brine, managing to get it over the ling's giant head and most of its body, but he was too big, too strong, and too slippery . . . I was staring right into its face, its eyes as big as golf balls. I could see the smaller lingcod in its gaping mouth, and the head of the shiner in the smaller lingcod's mouth: a food chain of life and death before my eyes.

I tried to lift the net and the big fish into the air, but it thrashed and splashed its way out of the trappings. This caused Roger the Dodger and Rory to let out another deafening round of abusive swearing directed at the fish — "You slippery motherfucker!" — while Nick leaned back, forehead veins pulsating like Dirty Harry, trying to keep the line taut. "Hurry . . . up . . . and . . . net . . . him . . . you . . . idiot . . . " Nick grunted through gritted teeth, his face turning red. "The hook is set in the smaller lingcod. If the big one coughs it up we'll lose him."

"Try and lift him out of the water," I shrieked back, "and I'll get the net under him!" Grimacing, Nick reeled the fish in further, lifting its heavy sleek form out of the ocean and up into the air. Its deep green scales were decorated with black patterns like the spots of a jaguar. "HOLY MOTHER OF FUCK!" screamed Roger the Dodger. As sure as Nick had predicted, the big fish knew it was in a death struggle; its instincts said "screw this." It coughed up the hooked lingcod in mid-air, then snapped its body up, twisting into a dive, ready to plunge back to the depths. But Russell had taught me well, and even though we had never dealt with a fish this big, I followed its movement just quickly enough to catch it headfirst in the mesh trap. Primal screams of triumph rose from the tiny boat.

The ling was heavy, which plunged the net back into the water, but I held on tight and dragged it back to the side of the boat. Together Nick and I hauled it up, out of the water and into the bottom of the boat. It was like lifting a soaked toddler. The huge ling slapped and flipped its body from side to side, sending empty beer cans rattling against the inner sides of the boat. Roger and Rory, swearing and muttering with a mixture of fear and delight, scrambled to get out of its way, the boat still rocking from side to side. Nick meanwhile still had the little lingcod on the hook to deal with, miraculously still alive after having been swallowed whole by the monster fish. With a twist, Nick quickly removed the hook and threw the little lingcod back in the water. "Eagle!" Nick yelled, pointing up. The eagle that had been watching us the entire time came swooping down silently toward us, bright yellow talons outstretched like Nosferatu.

"FUCKING FUCK FUCK!" Roger the Dodger screamed, incredulous at the raw nature rapidly unfolding around him. The eagle plunged talons-first into the water, ten feet away from our mouths agape. Not naturally buoyant, the eagle couldn't stay in the water long, and was immediately flapping its muscular wings, six feet from tip to tip, to regain flight. When it did, its talons were clenched like fists . . . but empty. We looked down into the water. The little fish was gone. "It escaped! / Holy shit! / It made it! / Jesus Christ! / Beer me!" we all yelled at once.

The huge lingcod still snapped its body of pure muscle in the bottom of the boat, gills opening and closing like an accordion, gasping for water. The monster fish still had enough strength that it took Nick and Rory to pin it down while I walloped the remaining life out of it: three times, hard between the eyes with the wooden fish bonker, just as Russell had taught me. Roger yelled "YES!" between every strike. I felt instant remorse for taking the life of this innocent creature, but those feelings were quickly shoved aside as all the other guys celebrated the drunken man-rush of landing such a big fish. More beers were cracked, as the eagle glared down upon us from his treetop, frowning with what I was certain was a look of disgust.

We were all stunned and invigorated from the food chain that had unfolded in the past two hours: Nick hooking out the meat of a tiny seashell, which captured the three-inch shiner, which caught the tough little lingcod, which landed us the monster. The way we figured it, the big winner was the little lingcod, which in the space of minutes had lived through being hooked, swallowed whole, spat out, handled by a human, dodged an eagle's talons, and got away with its minnow meal to boot. The beer kept flowing, and our yelling turned into dirty jokes and drunken stories and gales of maniacal laughter from Roger. We drifted with the current under the grey skies and got drunk. By the time we finally returned to the cabin, we had a big fish in the cooler, and an entire fishing net full of empty cans of Iron Horse.

What we hadn't realized was that sound carries over still water like a loud conversation in a library. Every one of my neighbours new and old had been privy to every foul syllable we had shouted and every lurid story we had told, in crystal-clear desolate sound, serving as my reintroduction to the neighbourhood after so many years away. We sat on the deck triumphantly, sharing with the girls our incredible fish tale. After a while we heard a boat approaching. We could see a hulking man in a small aluminum skiff motoring toward us. "Uh oh . . . " I said. "That's Bernard the German."

"Oh shit," said Rory quietly.

"What the hell does that big Kraut want?" asked Roger the Dodger, crushing an empty can in his fist, eager to cap off his day with a beating.

"Chill out guys, he's my next-door neighbour," I said, certain he was coming by to complain about our noise and language. Bernard cut his engine and let his boat drift. He rose to his feet, holding a metal barrel with a rope attached to it.

"Sounds like you had quite the fishin' adventure!" he yelled. He didn't give us a chance to reply. "No hard feelings about the . . . incident . . . at the dock this afternoon, eh?" With that, he threw the barrel into the ocean. It immediately sank like a sack of rocks, the rope spiralling out after it. He hung onto the other end and tied a small buoy to it, then threw that up onto shore. He fired up his boat and left, heading back to his cabin without another word or gesture. We all looked at each other, dumbfounded.

"Maybe it's a crab trap?" suggested Nick.

"It could be a bucket of oysters," I said.

"Maybe it's a fuckin' bomb," hissed Roger.

Once Bernard's boat was out of sight, we bounded down to the rocks. Nick grabbed the float and the rope and gave it a tug. "Pull it up, man!" Roger yelled, his drunken curiosity running wild. To our surprise and delight, what Bernard had sunk was a weighted keg of Bavarian Pilsner beer. Bernard was using the twenty feet of ocean depth for natural refrigeration. We threw the keg back down for another couple of hours until it was nice and frosty. We had a hell of a candle-lit party that night, feasting on freshly seared lingcod prepared by Roger the Dodger and complemented by cold Bavarian beer. And we were sure to raise a toast to the tough little lingcod, to Bernard the German, to fresh food and friends, and to Canada Day.

It was the first of many long, lost weekends over many years spent with friends at the cabin, though Roger the Dodger's invitation would soon be revoked for several reasons. It was also the first of many encounters with Bernard the German. When that Canada Day long weekend was over, and we motored back across the Sound toward the dock on a gloriously sunny July day, I felt an unfamiliar tugging in my soul. I didn't want to leave. Just like that, I had fallen back in love with a wild place filled with dangerous beauty and salt air. I could feel one long chapter of my life closing, and another creaking open. I had been down in the dumps about The Smugglers winding to a close, but being in Desolation Sound made me think not of the fleeting glory of rock 'n' roll, but rather of the claustrophobia of soiled clubs painted black, stinky vans and nine-hour flights. I started planning my next trip up to the cabin before we arrived at the wharf.

Rory Brown and Nick Thomas, best friends and embracers of living large in Desolation Sound. Nick and his wife, Soraya, always prepare a seafood feast from the ocean's bounty and here Rory and Nick fool around with the pincers of a boiled red rock crab.

The mighty giant of Desolation Sound, Bernard the German, his moustache in full force. Bernard is pictured here in a rare moment of rest on the deck he built, with his faithful dog, The Dude, at his side.

17
Hangover Days

"Fish and visitors stink after three days."
– Benjamin Franklin

Over the next few summers my trips to Desolation Sound became more and more frequent. I began to make the trip at every available opportunity, sometimes sharing the experience with a widening circle of friends – some from work, some from out of town, sometimes a girlfriend. Nick and Soraya and Julie and Rory's trips became an annual event we all looked forward to. I took most of my visitors into Lund, and was shocked at the changes the little port had gone through in my absence. It seemed brighter and friendlier. Ever since the town was founded in 1885, Lund had always been a tiny, tough, blue-collar port that in recent decades had experienced a wild clash of cultures every summer when the hippies, kayakers and wealthy tourists showed up. Few if any local entrepreneurs had ever taken advantage of the rather obvious niche market.

Upon returning, I found out that the historic Lund Hotel had slipped into bankruptcy and decay. It even shut its doors for a short time, until a Powell River businessman partnered with the Sliammon First Nation to buy it. And so 125 years after the Sliammon were kicked off one of their ancient village sites by the Indian Act of 1876, the Sliammon band now found themselves part-owners of the hotel, pub, restaurant, general store and gas dock that were built by the very Europeans their ancestors were forced to make way for. Although the irony may be bittersweet, the hotel was saved from neglect, fully restored and turned back into a thriving business.

I also learned that an enterprising woman named Nancy Bouchard was largely responsible for bringing Lund into modern times as well, when she opened Nancy's Bakery, a tiny, upscale, artisan eatery. It was an immediate hit the with yachters and the Savary Island crowd, many of them desperate for any place in Lund that sold fresh, healthy food in a environment where a fistfight wasn't imminent. Many of the locals grew to love Nancy's, too. Even the most hardened Lundoners acknowledged it was a long-overdue and modern alternative to the rowdy pub, the touristy hotel restaurant and the processed foods of the general store. Burly bikers started hanging out at Nancy's, opting for an espresso and a cookie rather than a beer and a brawl. Eventually, Nancy's Bakery expanded into a large, beautifully built, post-and-beam building overlooking the harbour. Nancy Bouchard helped bring Lund into the twenty-first century and gave the little town what it had long needed: a loving, classy touch that brought everyone together in relative harmony. The bakery's giant cinnamon buns have become the stuff of legends, so much so that Nancy has earned herself the nickname, "The Cinnamama from Lund, Land of the Rising Bun."

Popping up around Nancy's tidy business initiative and the newly reopened hotel were several other nice little shops that we took the time to explore, all of them helping transform Lund from crusty to quaint: a sweater store, a kayak rental shop, a book nook, an adventure tour company, an art gallery, sculpture shop and a gazebo that hosted weddings, parties, anything. Lund was even finally celebrating itself with various events such as a shellfish festival, a solstice parade and a holiday every summer called "Lund Dayz" (though in typically dysfunctional-yet-lovable Lund fashion, "Lund Dayz" was actually only one day). The town also took the initiative to at last formally mark the end of Pacific Coast Highway 101, replacing the faded, hand-painted sign with a large, stone obelisk that read "Mile 0." Lund, and most definitely Nancy's Bakery, quickly became a must-stop whenever friends came to visit.

My friends and I were also learning what a rough and tough place Desolation Sound still was and always will be. Anyone who has ever spent any time in the Sound, be it a long weekend or a lifetime, faces many hazards on a daily and nightly basis. In the forest there are predators large and small: bears, wolves and cougars at one end of the scale; wasps, hornets and ticks at the other. On the gravel beaches and in the tidal pools there are box-cutter sharp oyster shells and barnacles, potentially paralytic red tide in shellfish, and the stinging tentacles of the crimson-red lion's mane jellyfish, the largest jellyfish in the world.

Out on the ocean there is the constant threat of storms, hypothermia and drowning. But the fear that pervades most people's consciousness time and time again is the all-encompassing disaster of fire. In Desolation Sound water surrounds everyone, yet fire is a repeat offender when it comes to sending dreams up in smoke. In 1918 a fire destroyed the Lund Hotel, which was subsequently rebuilt as the building that remains to this day. In 1923 a devastating lightning-caused forest fire swept across the mainland of the Sound, wiping out entire mountainsides of trees stretching down the inlets. Panicked settlers told stories of the hillsides glowing red in the night, hot cinders and ash crossing the inlets and falling on their cabins, which they continually doused with salt water. They could do nothing but protect their own properties until the forest fire burned itself out. In the 1960s the cabin owned by Oskar Roos burnt to the ground, right down to the root cellar—the evidence of which can still be seen by a charred scar on one side of the old cherry tree that stands behind the Laughing Oyster Restaurant. In recent years several oyster farmers have dealt with cabin fires that destroyed their dwellings in minutes. There have been fire-suicides, arsons and sometimes even boat fires, which often set off a string of spectacular, toxic explosions when the flames lick fuel tanks.

Roger the Dodger returned a few more times, but as violent skinheads are wont to do, he rather quickly wore out his welcome. Desolation Sound is an inherently quiet place, and Roger the Dodger was an inherently loud person. Once, on a lovely summer afternoon, Roger challenged Nick's precocious six-year-old daughter, Maddy, to a game of chess. Roger eventually realized through his drunken haze that he wasn't smarter than a first grader, and was about to take a hard check. When little Maddy strategically picked up her black knight for the checkmate deathblow, instead of admitting defeat to the wily little girl, Roger the Dodger jumped to his feet and kicked over the chessboard with his combat boot, sending chess pieces scattering off the edge of the deck to the rocks and ocean below. He then craned his shaved head to the heavens, balled both fists and let out a deafening "MOTHERFUCKER!," which echoed and bounced across the Sound like a shotgun blast, sending flocks of birds to the air and seals to the surface. Little Maddy was stunned, wide-eyed and silent, and had the word burned into her memory. Nick and Soraya were not amused.

Another summer, Roger the Dodger brought up an actual girlfriend, to the surprise of us all. There wasn't a whole lot of privacy in our cabin with just two bedrooms, so we all had to share space. One night during an extremely hot stretch, there were upward of ten guests sprawled around the cabin, sound asleep. I was nestled in a lower bunk, while Roger and his girlfriend were asleep on a double mattress on the floor. Three or four other people were also asleep in the room. In the jet-black darkness of a drunken sleep, I was jolted awake by the most frightening word anyone can ever utter in the Sound, let alone scream at the top of his or her lungs . . . "FIRE!!!"

I sat bolt upright, slamming my forehead into the beams of the upper bunk. I was out of the bed in a second, immediately stumbling over sleeping bodies. Racing through my head all at once was the amount of children in the cabin (four), exactly where they were (the other bedroom), and the proximity of the hose (the deck) and the fire extinguishers (the kitchen and living room). There was instant chaos in the cabin; those who weren't awakened by the scream were awakened by my plundering over top of them. Children broke into loud wails, adults groaned. I finally found a flashlight. Racing out of the bedroom, I slammed into Nick in the hallway. We swung our flashlight beams around the cabin in a panic. All was dark, nothing was out of order and nothing was on fire. Back in the bedroom, we shone our lights down on Roger the Dodger and his girlfriend. They were both sitting up. Roger was cursing and rubbing his eyes. She was visibly confused, disoriented and embarrassed.

Through a quick, expletive-laden explanation from Roger, we were informed that Roger's girlfriend was in fact a loud "sleep-talker" who suffered from frequent "night terrors," routinely yelling random, frightening words throughout the night. Roger the Dodger had forgotten to mention this tidbit of information. Sure enough, the following nights featured several encores of ear-piercing, sleep-shattering screams of "FIRE!" followed by "MURDER!" and "RAPE!" By the end of that weekend, I had a fire extinguisher, bear spray and a machete in my bunk. My nerves were a wreck, my eyes bloodshot, my forehead bloodied. Sadly it would not be the last time "FIRE!" would be heard in our neighbourhood.

The Okeover government wharf, looking out into a hungover unknown. My skinhead friend Roger once skidded backward into a phone booth with his muscle car on this wharf. Roger and the car were fine, but the phone booth took a plunge to a watery grave.

When I dropped off Roger the Dodger and his girlfriend at the dock, the Dodger wasn't quite done. After loading up his ridiculous, jacked-up muscle car at the head of the Okeover government wharf, we said a terse goodbye as he and his girlfriend slid through the windows, *Dukes of Hazzard*–style, into the bucket seats. Always the showman, Roger the Dodger revved up the engine for a dramatic, rubber-burning, squealing exit up the wharf to the road, but what he didn't realize was that he had left his car in reverse after backing down the wharf. I dove out of the way as his Mercury Montego squealed backward toward the gangplank leading to the dock and boats below. Roger swung the steering wheel, narrowly missing the gangplank and instead peeling straight for Desolation Sound's one and only working phone booth.

Everyone used that phone booth, and on busy long weekends in the summer, there were even lineups. Neighbours got to know each other as they chatted patiently while waiting for their turns to talk to the outside world. We all knew that phone-booth number off by heart: 604-483-2939. On every surface of the phone booth were hand-written, carved and scratched notes and numbers of everyone and everybody who had ever used the phone booth. It was in that phone booth through various calls through the summers that I had found out my sister was pregnant, that my grandfather had passed away, and that I had landed a job at the CBC. And I subsequently filed countless live summer reports for CBC Radio from that very phone.

And now Roger the Dodger's car was screaming toward this monument at top speed, in reverse. The car's rear bumper smashed into it with a sickening munching of metal, bringing the Montego to a stop, but ripping the phone booth from its moorings, forcing the entire thing to splinter through the red-painted, heavy wooden guardrail. The phone booth teetered on the edge of the wharf before flipping upside down and plunging twenty feet, hitting the ocean below with a mighty splash, bobbing for a moment and then disappearing under the surface, leaving only a trail of bubbles in its wake.

Roger the Dodger and his girlfriend slid out of the car and Roger immediately burst into shrieks. "Holy shit, man! What the fuck?! That phone booth bent my chrome!!" Then he burst into maniacal laughter, surveying his barely bent bumper. Miraculously, the phone booth was empty at the time of impact and we were the only people at the wharf. I hustled him and his girlfriend (who could now add "PHONE BOOTH!" to her repertoire) back into their car and told them to beat it.

The phone company took months to arrive with a replacement booth. After recovering from our shock, confusion and mourning over our drowned phone booth, Roger the Dodger's inadvertent and violent act forced many of us to enter the cell-phone age. At low tide, we could peer over the edge of the wharf and see the phone booth lying face up in its watery grave, its BC Tel logo slowly being covered up by seaweed and algae. By the time the phone booth was finally replaced, things had changed for good. No more numbers or messages were scrawled and scratched onto the new phone booth, and no one chatted while waiting in line to use it, because now everyone had a phone in his or her pocket. Roger the Dodger was never invited to the cabin again.

18
Welcome to the Night Sky

"Any paradise worth the name can sustain all flaws in creation and remain undiminished and untarnished."

—Henry Miller, Big Sur

As the years passed, as soon as the weather was warm I was practically living in the cabin while my parents, growing older, spent less and less time there. With my sister busy with her young family and my parents staying home, I had the place to myself for long stretches of the summer. I was chronically single, so if friends or family weren't around I wouldn't hesitate to make the trip alone. Through many mistakes, I was becoming almost adept at keeping the cabin functioning, feeding myself from the sea's ever-giving bounty, and slowly becoming more and more comfortable both on the water and in it. Possibly for the first time in my life, I was even becoming somewhat *rugged* in appearance. I grew up extremely self-conscious of ever removing my shirt in any public situation for fear of anyone catching a glimpse of my skinny, concave chest, but now I was pulling off my shirt all the time to jump in the ocean. It felt liberating to feel the sun on my shoulders.

Desolation Sound is a physically demanding place, and I was constantly moving, lifting, hauling, chopping, paddling, pulling, swimming, climbing and hiking. I grew tougher, my shoulders filled out, my knees felt stronger, my hair grew longer, a beard filled my face and all the time spent out on the water turned my skin brown. I was also usually encrusted with the dirt of the forest, the oil of the boat and the salt of the ocean. My cumbersome glasses were long gone, replaced by versatile contact lenses that I could even swim with. My hair stuck out in every direction from the wind and salt, which I tried to contain with my once-white Winnipeg Jets cap. I knew I was starting to become accepted when the locals stopped totally ignoring me at the government wharf. I looked just filthy enough to be able to convincingly curse the red tide with an oyster farmer while quaffing a can of Black Label or turn around and chat knowingly about the best entrees available at the Laughing Oyster with yachtsmen over a gin and tonic.

I purchased a small kayak, naming it *Little Blue*, and paddled it everywhere, seeing the Sound for the first time up close and in silence, in comparison with the skiff with its loud and polluting outboard motor. I learned to snorkel along the reefs, and found the warmest waters to swim in. Parts of Desolation Sound boast the most temperate ocean water north of the Gulf of Mexico, one of the reasons the area was deemed park-worthy in 1973. A study by BC Parks explains this phenomenon:

Three very important factors influence the movement of the sea water in such a manner as to create the warmest water on the British Columbia coast during the summer months. Firstly, the maze of islands restricts the colder Pacific waters with those of the Strait of Georgia. Secondly, the tidal currents flowing around Vancouver Island meet in this area. Thirdly, the warming effect of incoming tides flowing over sun-baked tidal flats and out flowing water from shallow lakes and lagoons together create the phenomena of effectively raising the water surface temperature in Desolation Sound to 27 degrees Celsius.

Kayaking *Little Blue* through the placid waters of Kahkaykay Bay, in search of a good place to snorkel. This little kayak brought me down to a whole new level of appreciation for the nature and tranquility of Desolation Sound.

The warm salt water of the inlets felt like the fountain of youth. I would swim several times a day and I was having the time of my life. I was alone, but never by myself for very long. I was getting to know my human neighbours much more than I ever thought I would. Even though it often felt like I was partying with the cast of *Cocoon*, we were all becoming good friends. We were united in our love for the land and the ocean, believing that contrary to Captain Vancouver's original assessment, we had indeed found paradise.

Handy Candy's humour, kindness, and extreme handiness was invaluable as I learned the myriad tricks of keeping a wilderness cabin from falling over, catching fire or exploding. There was Rick, an eccentric English professor who tried to live life to the fullest and was consequently always suffering some type of injury: a swollen knee, a broken collarbone, a twisted ankle. Rick would often shout the mantra of the Sisters of Perpetual Indulgence, his favourite obscure lesbian nun sect. "Deny thyself nothing!" he'd scream, fist in the air, when he roared by in his boat. There was "Harpoon" Jack and his wife, Pat, who had both gone to high school in Winnipeg with the godfather of grunge, Neil Young. Harpoon was the drummer in an early incarnation of Neil Young's first band, the Squires. Harpoon and Pat had remained good friends with Neil and always had plenty of backstage stories to share with us over a heated game of crokinole.

There was Angela, a nutty British bird who was perpetually tipsy and charming like a character from a 1940s movie. She'd often teeter on the edge of the cliff on her property, one hand loosely gripping a bottle of apple cider. Her convincing end-of-the-road appearance was betrayed only by her perfectly upper-crust British accent, and her use of phrases such as "By Jove! Would you just look at those lovely little cherry blossoms.

They're as graceful as a Japanese poem!" There was Lorenzo, the swingin', smokin' bachelor who hosted the neighbourhood happy hour every night.

And there was Murray and Martha, a couple that was constantly bickering and constantly building something, saws whirring and hammers pounding, yet no improvements to their cabin were ever noticed. The local joke was that one day they would, with great ceremony, reveal a perfectly detailed, to-scale re-creation of Michelango's statue of David, carved out of a single piece of driftwood. Murray and Martha hated the sunshine, so they built their cabin in the darkest, dampest corner lot they could find. If ever they were caught in direct sunlight, they'd shield their face and scurry into the shade like lepers.

There was Darrell and Anita, the friendly lawyer and his wife who defied gravity by constructing a cabin hanging over the water from a cliff on the point. There was Jeremy, a freedom-seeker and adventurer who dreamed of sailing his trimaran from Desolation Sound to Mexico. And there was Bulgarian George, well into his seventies, who was the Sound's oldest summer resident. He was spry, wise and incredibly interesting to sit and chat with on a hot afternoon. Of course there was also Bernard the German, along with his wife, Patricia, and granddaughter, Bernadine (who was named after Bernard). Bernard the German was the big bear of the neighbourhood. He was more often teddy than grizzly, though he certainly knew how to growl. He and I formed an unlikely friendship, and in many ways Bernard the German filled the void that Russell's absence had created. That we bonded while removing the last of Russell's remains from Desolation Sound was bittersweet.

Russell's shack was never really waterproof, and over years of neglect it had become rotten and condemnable. The owners of the lot Russell was "caretaking" never did show up to build, but asked Bernard the German and a few other neighbours to please tear Russell's shack down and burn the contents, if only to clean their property up and bring it back to its natural state. Bernard the German showed up one morning, knocking on our cabin door. "Mornin' buddy," he said in his slow hoser drawl as I answered the door in a pair of boxer shorts. "Your next-door neighbours want that old shack of Russell Letawsky's torn down. I'm gonna do it in a few days and I could use your help."

I was still wary of Bernard, not really sure what he thought of me, nor was I sure what I thought of him. He was nothing like me, a huge blue-collar ox staring down at me with deep-set eyes over that black handlebar moustache. His news didn't endear him to me. I couldn't bear the thought of destroying my friend and mentor's home; I had always hoped and even assumed that Russell would return. I was defiant. "Wha . . . ? You can't do that . . . That's Russell's *home*! That's . . . a historic building!"

Bernard the German let out a low chuckle. "He's history, all right. That dude ain't coming back, and that ain't no home. He's been gone for years, there's nothing salvageable in there, its rotten right through and it has to go. I'll be tearing it down in two days." Without another word he turned and left me standing there, looking down at Russell's shack, and then at the wide back of Bernard the German as he thumped down the stairs to his boat.

That afternoon I crossed the gravel beach of the cove and climbed up to Russell's shack. I pushed open the door that hung on just one rusty hinge. Various kids visiting our cabin over recent summers had rooted through most of Russell's leftovers and strewn them about, making a nasty mess worse. I stepped into the middle of the room, the wood-plank floor feeling soft under my feet, and looked around, trying to convince myself that the dank chamber was worth saving. And suddenly where there was floor under me, there was none. Like a trap door in an opera house stage, the floor planks gave way, collapsing under my weight, rotten right through. I let out a panicked scream to no one, dropping through the floor. I threw my arms out to the side to stop from falling all the way through onto the rocks and empty bottles and cans several feet below. My chin was just above the floor, my legs kicking at the air. I heaved myself forward, getting my torso up and onto the filthy floor of the shack. I managed to get a knee up, then hoisted the rest of my body to relative safety. Scraped, shocked, but otherwise unharmed, I inched along on my stomach through the rotten muck until I reached the door and came to my feet on solid rock.

I was covered head to toe in mould, mud, algae and trash. Maybe it was time for the shack to go. As promised, two days later a crew of a few men led by Bernard showed up armed with sledgehammers, chainsaws and a can of gasoline. Within an hour, the shack had been flattened and set ablaze. I stared out of our French windows as they destroyed Russell Letawsky's home. After the shack had burned and the fire was smouldering, the crew left, leaving only Bernard the German down in the cove, staring at a mound of unburnable wet trash that was previously hidden by the shack. It seemed that over the course of the decade that the hermit Russell Letawsky called the cove home, he didn't care much for garbage removal, instead opting to simply throw any debris under the cabin. Now with the shack gone, it all lay in plain, rotting sight.

Donning a pair of thick rubber gloves, Bernard the German started stuffing the trash into garbage bags while I watched from above, forehead against the window, arms crossed. Then it started to rain. Then it started to pour. Then it got Biblical. Bernard never looked up, and kept stuffing the bags. I grabbed my raincoat, pulled on my rubber boots and Winnipeg Jets cap, grabbed a handful of garbage bags and a pair of gloves and stepped out into sheets of rain. I scrambled down the cliff and crossed the beach. Bernard stood up tall and stretched when he heard me coming. "Nice of you to show up," he said with a sarcastic grin, rain water dripping off the ends of his moustache. "Your buddy Russell left a hell of a fuckin' mess here."

It was true. We worked for the next two days in the rain, stuffing garbage bag after garbage bag with Russell's remnants: hundreds of rusted pipe tobacco canisters, rotting tarps, broken glass, soiled clothing, an unbelievable amount of odd wool socks, random outboard motor parts, and stubby beer bottles and cans of every description, mostly brands that no longer existed in BC like Old Vienna, Schooner and BEER, causing frequent moments of pause to "remember when" between Bernard the German and me as the rain poured down. When we finally heaved the last of the garbage bags onto the bow of Bernard's skiff to haul to the dump, the rain finally subsided after three long days. We sat down on the rocks and cracked a couple of Bernard's potent homebrews and exhaled. Almost every scrap of evidence proving Russell had lived in the cove was now gone, and I expressed to Bernard that he needed to be remembered. "After cleanin' up two dozen bags of that hippie's leftover shit, you want to remember him?"

"Yeah I do. This cove has never had a name. I want to call it Russell Cove." Bernard let out a burst of deep laughter.

"Sure. Whatever, man, in the memory of Russell Letawsky, we hereby christen this spot Russell Cove." We both took a long swig and sat in silence looking out at the water. Bernard turned to me and put his huge paw on my shoulder. "I'm sure Russell would appreciate that gesture, kid." A couple days later I nailed up a sign to a big fir tree that said, *Welcome to Russell Cove* to make it unofficially official.

And so, on that soaking weekend, I made another unlikely bond. I proved to Bernard the German that I could get my hands dirty and work alongside him. He was the blue-collar giant and I was the softie from the city, but we got along well and made each other laugh. His official stamp of approval came shortly after the Russell Cove cleanup, when he gave me a gift I have hung onto tightly ever since: a glistening, razor-sharp, wood-handled machete. "If you're gonna be spending a lot of time out here, you'll be needing that." I accepted the blade with beaming pride.

Like Russell, Bernard grew up in northern Alberta. He was born into a large German-immigrant family. He was a child of the sixties, and was always a giant, even at a young age. He and his friends had embraced the hippie counterculture movement, which made Bernard pretty much the most physically gigantic hippie in all of Edmonton, with the thickest German accent. In the late 1960s, like many teenagers around North America, Bernard and his pals got swept up in summer road-tripping, and took a VW bus over the Rocky Mountains and down to Vancouver's hippie haven of West Fourth Avenue. In 1969 they heard about a free Rolling Stones concert happening just outside of San Francisco and pointed the van south. They missed the notorious Altamont by two days, but kept going to Haight-Ashbury in San Francisco. There, Bernard and his teenage pals from Edmonton found themselves a couple of years late for the real "summer of love" action, instead arriving in the winter pall just days after the shocking brutality of Altamont, where four people had died, including one homicide. But drugs were everywhere in San Francisco, and they tried everything that was offered to them, whether it was a doobie, a line or a needle. They had the time of their lives, but the freedom of '69 would eventually come back to trouble the big friendly German.

When Bernard returned to Canada he lived hard and fast for several years, eventually marrying and settling down in Vancouver. Looking for some recreational real estate and a retirement home, he saw an ad for a lot in Desolation Sound and bought in. Bernard had an incredible passion for the Sound that was more raw and visceral than Russell's philosophical outlook. Bernard had a few favourite sayings. Whenever he saw something of beauty that moved him, like a surfacing sea lion (one the Sound's largest and most graceful mammals, often longer than our skiff), or a pair of soaring eagles, he'd point and say in his slow, low German-hoser timbre, "That . . . is . . . fuckin' . . . awesome," emphasizing every word. Bernard the German said this phrase with such honest conviction that his enthusiasm was infectious. Bernard's other observation that always seemed to be true about Desolation Sound was, "The weather's always nicest when you have to fuckin' leave." We had some great times.

When Bernard and I would return from collecting our prawn traps out near the Strait, Lorenzo never failed to wave us into his place for happy hour on his deck. All the neighbours spent a lot of time on Lorenzo's deck. Lorenzo loved the Sound too, but for different reasons than many of us. He wasn't what anyone would consider *outdoorsy.* He never fished, he never swam and he rarely got dirt under his fingernails, but he loved to sit in the sun, have a drink, smoke a cigarette and entertain. Lorenzo *loved* to entertain. Handy Candy was usually already there, two or three gin and tonics down. She always said she'd be stopping at one or two cocktails but never really did, often repeating the maxim, "One or two drinks at the most! Three I'm under the table, four I'm under the host!" Then she'd gulp down another and shout, "Ah, the hell with it, drink all you want! The mosquitoes will just suck it back out of ya!" Lorenzo kept her drinks flowing, usually payment for the repair of a propane leak or a rotten floorboard. An impromptu dinner usually followed, as Lorenzo loved to cook, we all loved to eat and we were all usually too drunk to feed ourselves. It was a near-nightly exercise in relaxation.

Sometimes I would paddle home from these happy dinners in my kayak, *Little Blue*, late at night, the world so beautifully still. Crickets chirped up a symphony; in the distance I could hear rushing water from far-off creeks and waterfalls. Occasional gleaming animal eyes from shore caught my flashlight beam, probably a family of otters or raccoons cracking open shellfish at low tide. From the woods there was the occasional *hoot-hoot-hoo* of an owl, or the *whoosh* of a nighthawk dive-bombing prey. If the moon was new and the sky particularly dark, each dip of *Little Blue*'s paddle would ignite an underwater fireworks display, the rare and spectacular phosphorescence phenomenon — tiny plankton that literally came alight like aquatic fireflies when the ocean's still surface was disturbed ever so slightly.

Often I would turn out my light and stretch out my legs on *Little Blue*'s narrow bow. I'd crack a beer and just drift in our bay, listening to the night, while staring up at the infinite stars. It was a feeling of serenity untouched. As I stared into the open night sky so far away from the city, I couldn't help but calmly contemplate the vast depth and beauty of the universe, and the nature that surrounded me. I thought of my neighbours who were becoming unlikely but good friends: Lorenzo, Handy Candy and Bernard the German. I thought of Russell, and wondered where he was and what he was doing. I thought of my family and friends, loneliness, togetherness, how much I savoured the Sound, and I thought of how much I disagreed with Captain Vancouver's aesthetic observations, but thanked him anyway for giving it the name Desolation Sound that kept so many away on description alone. Handy Candy always remarked on how lucky we were to be the stewards of this special place.

Rory's homemade wooden kayak floats in the crystal waters of Russell Cove, so clear that it looks like the boat is hovering on air.

19
When Animals (Don't) Attack

I was perpetually curious as to just how the assortment of people that ended up in Desolation Sound ever found the place, from Captain Vancouver all the way to Handy Candy. Some sought glory, some work, some escape and some even salvation. Some saw ads in the paper, some stumbled across it, some heard about it through word of mouth and one cool Bulgarian dude read and dreamt about Desolation Sound from behind the Iron Curtain. One of the most popular books ever written about Desolation Sound and the characters therein is the West Coast boat-cruising classic *The Curve of Time,* by M. Wylie Blanchet, published posthumously in 1961. The book chronicles the poetic adventures of a single mother and her brood of five children and a dog exploring BC's southern inner coast by boat, summer after summer, during the 1920s and '30s. One of their favourite spots was Desolation Sound.

Their adventures with cougars, bears, whales, Native villages, tidal rapids and summer storms has been published and republished at least eleven times since 1961, distributed all over the world and remains one of the top-selling BC books of all time. Many a cruising yacht or dusty cabin has a copy on the shelf, and the humble narrative has empowered many to make the trek to see the Sound, which is how Bulgarian George arrived.

Capi Blanchet and her children spent many summers in the 1920s and '30s cruising in Desolation Sound—and inspired many to follow in their wake. Left to right, David, Capi, Peter and Joan Blanchet during one of their summer expeditions.

Bulgarian George would roar around the Sound at top speed in his second-hand oyster skiff turned pleasure boat that looked like a cross between a dumpster and a landing craft from D-Day. Bulgarian George's face was often expressionless, his eyes hidden by black, wraparound shades, his tanned face framed by a shaggy white beard and a full head of white hair. He looked like a cross between Santa Claus and Leonard Cohen.

Bulgarian George was the oldest and probably the smartest person in Desolation Sound. Not only was he a retired scientist, but also a university professor, mountaineer and classical pianist. He had even pulled off the unthinkable . . . somehow he had managed to haul a full upright piano across the Sound, up the rocks and into his cabin. And though he was well into his seventies, he also had a ping-pong table and was still an expert rock climber. Whenever I showed up to visit he always offered me a firm handshake and a drink: water or red wine were the only options. I never drank wine, but when I asked him where his water came from, he pointed upward. "Roof," he grunted in his stoic Bulgarian accent. I took a peek at his twenty-five-year-old moss-covered roof and accepted the wine.

One of my first questions to George was how he ever discovered Desolation Sound. After a long pause, he indulged me. As a young man growing up behind the Iron Curtain, he loved reading the few adventure books from the West that managed to be translated and make it to his local library. One of his favourites was M. Wylie Blanchet's *The Curve of Time*. George eventually left Bulgaria, emigrating to the United States, where he became a professor at several American universities. Upon retirement, he and his wife, who barely spoke any English, pondered finding their own place in the wilderness and his thoughts returned to *The Curve of Time*. He looked it up on the Internet, bought a copy, and found he loved Blanchet's natural, adventuresome prose just as much as he did the first time. His next step was to find a Canadian real-estate website and search "Desolation Sound." A small ad for a cabin came up, listing the price and one line: "At the gateway to Desolation Sound." He bought the cabin sight-unseen. And so there I sat with Bulgarian George on the deck of that cabin, sharing a bottle of red wine.

On one of those gorgeous afternoons paddling *Little Blue* over to Bulgarian George's for an afternoon chat, I took a detour through a chain of tiny islets while looking for a new place to snorkel. The tide was rising over the giant granite slabs of shoreline rock, warmed by a solid day of sunshine. The tidal waters heated up as they crested the rocks, creating near-tropical temperatures and perfect conditions. I pulled *Little Blue* up onto the shore of the small, deserted island the First Nations used many years ago for their burial boxes. The island had a foreboding quality, but its shoreline was pristine and perfect for swimming and snorkelling. I had carefully circled the tiny island in the kayak to make sure no other boats were pulled up and no one was on it, so I could doff my shirt and shorts and snorkel *au naturel*. After twenty minutes of observing a particularly beautiful underwater garden in clear green water, alive with sea anemones, perch, crabs, sea cucumbers, eels, kelp and starfish, I pulled myself out of the water and flopped down naked on the warm, flat rocks, drying off by the warmth of the sun and the heat of the granite. I cracked a cold beer, took a few sips and drifted off to sleep.

I couldn't have been under for more than a few minutes when I was awakened by the sound of a sharp crack coming from the woods directly behind me. My eyelids popped open, revealing a brilliant blue sky overhead. Did I really hear that, or was I dreaming? My body tensed as my mind thought of the ghosts of the island's past, angry that I was desecrating their purgatory with my naked body upon their shore. I had the horrible feeling I was being watched. Shaking the visions of angry spirits from my head, my imagination raced to a more likely reality and harkened back to the stories the Cougar Lady of Okeover Inlet would tell in my childhood. On rainy days in the Sound, the Cougar Lady would allow my sister and me to warm up in her cabin while our parents loaded the boat or the car, depending on what direction we were heading.

My routine after snorkelling the reefs: drifting off to sleep on the warm granite rocks. Little did I know what was lurking in the forest directly behind me.

Over biscuits and tea she used to wax on in her refined British accent about her Golden Rule of Survival for when she was alone picking apples in her orchard, or harvesting clams down on her beach: "Never turn your back on the woods, children. Cougars attack from behind."

Nancy Crowther shot her first cougar in 1930, when she was thirteen years old. At the time, she and her mother were looking after her father, who was rapidly going blind. Nancy and her father were returning from the general store in Lund one day along their trail when they came across a dead deer not far from their cabin. Mr. Crowther recognized it as a fresh cougar kill. He explained to Nancy that they needed to kill the cougar or it would come after their goats. Nancy and her near-blind father hid themselves downwind from the cougar kill for close to two hours, Nancy petrified it would leap out from behind them. Eventually, the cougar returned to the carcass, and Mr. Crowther handed Nancy his .22-calibre rifle. Nervously she steadied the rifle, aimed for the head and killed the cougar with one shot.

"It was a lucky shot," she told the Victoria *Times Colonist* many years later in 1964. "You can shoot a .22-calibre at close range into a cougar's head and the slug won't even penetrate the skull. About the only place to shoot a cougar for a sure kill is right in the centre of the neck. It snaps the spine and kills it instantly." At the time of the interview she had upgraded her weaponry to a much more powerful .303-calibre rifle, the same one with which she greeted our family on first foray to Desolation Sound. Each time Nancy killed a cougar, she carved a notch into the wooden butt end of the gun. At the time of the newspaper interview there were eleven notches. Before she died, she would double that number, also shooting at bears and wolves that came after her animals.

We sat cross-legged and wide-eyed before the Cougar Lady. She leaned forward and explained in a hushed tone that a cougar is a silent, stealth hunter, always sneaking up on its prey, some prey often bigger than the cougar itself. She told us that full-grown cougars needed the daily equivalent of a deer to satiate their appetite, and would settle for goats, sheep, pets . . . or humans, especially children. When a cougar attacks, it pounces from behind with incredible force, snapping its powerful jaws around the victim's neck to sink its huge teeth into the prey's spine. The cougar had the same goal as Nancy — snap the spine as quickly as possible, rendering the prey immobile and unable to fight back. Nancy called the cougar "the ghost of the forest." My sister and I would be frozen in fear, hanging on the Cougar Lady's every word.

Decades later, there I lay, naked and alone, my back to the woods on an island undoubtedly filled with spirits, and possibly something deadly. My ears pricked to the slight crackle of dry salal leaves, like the crumpling of Christmas wrapping paper, not twenty feet behind me. I hopped to my feet and spun around, staring into the thick green forest. It rose up straight in front of me, dense. Nothing moved. Another sound, closer . . . distinct movement, the lightest crunch of twigs on the forest floor . . . I slowly backed closer to the shoreline, stepping into the water. *Little Blue,* my bathing suit and paddle, were at least one hundred feet away down the rocky shore. I didn't take my eyes off the green foliage where I thought I last heard a sound. Several stressful moments later, the shrubbery parted ever so slightly. I strained to see. To my sheer terror I realized that just a predator's leap away from me, I could see a smooth patch of tawny brown fur, the exact colour of a cougar's back. My teeth began to chatter.

After the rigour of the Cougar Lady's warnings wore off enough to allow physical movement, my sister and I would glance around behind us, scanning her living room, just in case. For thirty years her words stuck with me. After the word "fire," the word "cougar" was the source of one of my deepest fears when alone in the Sound, and one I was often able to suppress by staying close to the water. Now the ill-fated warnings seemed to be coming true before my eyes.

I backed into the water until I was knee-deep. The ocean suddenly felt much colder than it had just a few minutes before, my teeth rattling like a typewriter at full tilt. I waited for the hunter to move, to attack and to show itself, yet it remained completely still. My heart pounded like the tom-toms on DOA's *Hardcore '81* album as I tried to assess my situation. It was likely waiting for me to run for it, and then it would pounce, sinking its teeth into the back of my neck, its claws lancing into my naked torso, shredding my flesh like Jell-O. I would be found mauled and half-eaten, just feet from my kayak, naked as the day I was born. That's if they would ever find me at all. The rising tide would take away *Little Blue* and who knows what the other critters from land, air and sea would do with the rest of me.

But . . . why wasn't it attacking? Could this mighty predator of the forest, the top of the food chain, be frightened of me? I decided to accelerate the situation, to be the aggressor, to at least attempt to end the standoff and bring the beast into the open or save my skin by either startling it or scaring it away. Standing waist-high in the water, I held my freshly cracked Black Label beer in one hand. In the other, my $75 mask and snorkel set. I threw the snorkel set. It landed in the bushes with a crash a few feet directly in front of the patch of fur. There was movement. I braced myself, backing farther into the water, up to my chest. I took what might have been my life's last gulp of beer. I slid another step back and braced myself, the water up to my neck, only my beer and my face above the water line.

Rising from the dense greenery like twin periscopes from a sniper's nest were two large, wide ears, nearly a foot long, pointing straight up. Then two big, soft, brown inquisitive eyes arose to peer at me over the bushes; after that, a black, wet nose, and a slim jaw that delicately moved back and forth, chewing quietly on leaves. It was a beautiful black-tailed deer, unflinchingly staring at me with a now barely interested expression.

"Ughhhhhh!!!" I grunted aloud, smacking the surface of the water with my free hand. My heart deflated and my muscles relaxed as I waded back to shore. The next chug of beer never tasted so good. I stood there, dripping on the warm rocks, still shaken and feeling ever so not the coastal mountain man, imagining the Cougar Lady's certain disgust at my foolishness and cowardice. The deer stepped lightly out of the woods with all the grace and poise I lacked. Its delicate cloven hooves made contact with the shoreline granite slab, sounding like high heels on a marble floor. The deer came completely free of the forest just a few feet away from me, as if to reveal itself and say, "No need to fear, naked fool." It was an immaculate, peaceful creature. After our brief eye contact, the deer ignored me. It daintily walked away along the shoreline, pausing every time a tasty leaf took its fancy.

When I eventually paddled over to Bulgarian George's that afternoon, shorts back on, I shared the story with him over a couple of glasses of Shiraz. In the retelling I managed to shake myself up again over what could have been. It was then that Bulgarian George gave me a sage piece of advice that I would never forget. He firmly placed his tanned hand on my shoulder and said in his thick low accent, "Grant, the only thing worse than the cougar attack . . . is spending your summer worrying . . . about the cougar attack." He paused for a moment. "And besides, if it was a cougar, you'd have never heard a thing." When he lifted his hand, it was as if he had exorcised the fear that the Cougar Lady had instilled within me so many years ago. Feeling the effects of the wine I squinted and stared at him in the sunlight and realized George the Bulgarian was right. What the hell did I have to be afraid of? I made a pledge to suppress my fear of animal attacks and embrace Desolation Sound's treed wilderness beyond the shoreline without hysteria.

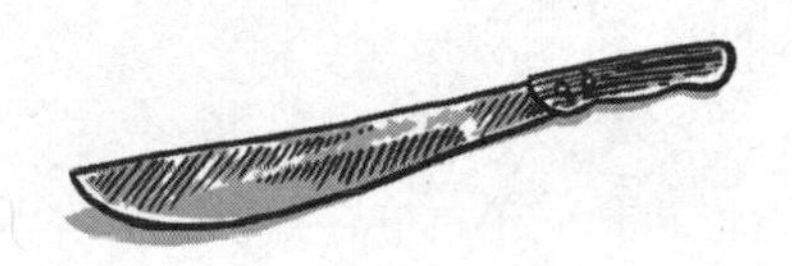

20
My Sword Hand's Anger

One of my only regrets about our cabin was that unless you really loved the ocean, there wasn't much to do once you got there besides sit on the deck and drink beer — not that there was anything wrong with that. We were bunkered by steep cliffs on either side, and there wasn't really anywhere to just . . . go for a walk, or a hike, without partaking in some K2-like rock climbing. The woods behind the cabin were dense brush, with few but the First Nations, loggers and occasional marijuana farmer ever penetrating very deeply. Captain Vancouver and his men hardly explored any of Desolation Sound beyond the immediate shoreline, one midshipman describing what he saw as "bounded by steep, lofty mountains, covered by an impenetrable forest, chiefly of pine." It was actually several species of coniferous trees, but whatever, I agreed with the impenetrable part.

After several summers in the Sound, this was how I began greeting most of my guests. Photo taken in the freshwater cedar grotto in Kahkaykay Bay.

Shortly after my newfound Bulgarian George-instilled philosophical courage, and in need of a project, I came to the conclusion that my friends and visitors should really be able to give their legs a good stretch. One sizzling summer day I decided that I would take up the challenge of cutting a swath into that so-called impenetrable forest directly behind the cabin—lions and bears be damned. My plan was to blaze a trail from our back door in Russell Cove overland through the deep dark woods to Isabel Bay, all within the Desolation Sound Marine Park grounds. A two-hour-long hike, there and back again. There was a pioneer ghost story intertwined with Isabel Bay, which would make for interesting conversation on the hikes with guests.

With quiet resolve I put down my beer can and tossed aside *Tintin and the Blue Lotus*. I pulled on an old pair of Dad's jeans and a long-sleeved shirt. I armed myself with my new machete and my old jackknife. As I was heading out the door, I grabbed an axe for fallen trees, a compass, a chocolate bar and a couple more cold ones. Weighted down with weaponry, I began to hack a hole in the forest. Saying there wasn't anything back there wasn't totally true. Twenty years earlier, when Dad and Russell had dug our first well and run plastic water lines to the backs of all the newly built cabins, they created a network of trails through the forest. The problem was that ever since Russell had left, no one maintained them with any regularity and they had become completely overgrown and nearly impassable. So really, as long as I could find the traces of their paths, my project was more a major cleanup than a blaze. That first day I made it about one hundred feet beyond our back door before I staggered back, sore, disoriented, sweat-soaked and exhausted. The only wildlife I had seen was a nest of some fifty slithering garter snakes, the sight of which caused me to leap two feet in the air with a cowardly shriek.

I returned to the woods undaunted. Each day for a week I hacked and whacked with the machete, forest greenery flying to and fro. I ached from exhaustion but to my nostalgic delight, I eventually came across the worn and rotten signs Russell had created so many years earlier, even finding my faded BEAR COUNTRY sign, untouched but for the vines wrapped around it. I worked from morning till sunset, possessed. I stopped shaving, ate little and stayed off the ocean and out of the sun, completely focused on the ever-lengthening trail. Through salal, huckleberry and sword fern I slashed, knocking over deadwood, sawing through fallen trees, heaving heavy rocks, pulling up vines and cutting back overhanging branches. Slowly but surely, by the end of each day the trail wound its way through and through and through an otherwise silent cathedral of moss and trees. Finally, on the eighth day of bone-aching bushwhacking, I traversed a high, rocky ridge. Looking down between the thick trunks of towering old-growth cedar and fir that dated back eight hundred years, I caught a glimpse of the sheltered waters of Isabel Bay, the surface shimmering from a slight breeze. I felt a shiver up my spine, remembering the pioneer tragedy that had occurred on its otherwise idyllic shores.

Enticed by overseas advertising of a fruitful frontier, in 1927 Arthur Jones, his wife Helen and their ten children made the incredible cross-Atlantic continental trek from their native England to take up residency in the remote little bay I looked down upon. Unlike many of the Scandinavian settlers, the Joneses had very little experience with the great outdoors. In England, Arthur was a stenographer and an accountant, trades that did little good when battling the forces of raw nature. His Swedish neighbours up and down the inlet described Arthur as somewhat of a headstrong English snob, and a very strict husband and father. Within a year of settling in the secluded Isabel Bay, the family was broke and destitute, forcing Jones to take a job at a logging company across the inlet. That didn't go well. In May 1928, the boss accused Jones of lying and Jones responded by slapping the boss across the face. Jones was not only fired but formally charged with assault. Loggers held Arthur Jones captive until the Powell River police boat could come and get him, arresting him and hauling him away without Jones being able to go home to let his family know what was going on. No one at the logging camp bothered to inform Mrs. Jones and the family.

Arthur Jones was taken to Powell River and found guilty of assault. He faced either two months in the notorious Oakalla Prison, or a $20 fine. Arthur only had $15 on him and was outraged when sent by police launch to Vancouver to serve the time. All the while, Mrs. Jones and the ten children had no idea what had happened to their patriarch until finally, three weeks after his disappearance, Mrs. Jones and her eldest daughter,

Madge, rowed to Okeover, the nearest settlement. Fourteen-year old Madge was then sent on her own to hike six hours to Powell River to discover that her father had been thrown in prison and had another five weeks to serve. An extremely bitter Arthur Jones returned from prison to his family in Isabel Bay after serving the two months, only to find that his family hadn't been able to properly attend to the garden for lack of fences that he was supposed to build that spring. The vegetable garden, including a crop of potatoes that was supposed to get them through the winter, had been totally devoured by deer.

Arthur flew into a rage, first at his seemingly incompetent eleven-member family, and then at the Powell River police, filing a formal complaint of police misconduct. That didn't go over well either. The Powell River police answered the complaint by throwing the defiant Arthur Jones back in jail, and then motored up to Isabel Bay to inspect the property. They found it overrun with skinny children and an exhausted mother, so they seized two kids the police deemed malnourished and took them to the hospital for examinations. To his extreme indignation, Arthur Jones was formally charged with child abuse, found guilty and sentenced to a year in jail or an insurmountable fine of $500.

Her family broke and starving, a desperate Mrs. Jones wrote a letter to the BC Attorney General begging for mercy. Helen Jones' letter was first published in Heather Harbord's *Desolation Sound: A History*:

> If Mr. Jones has erred at all, it was in being too anxious to get a home made here for the children . . . Do you think it had been any pleasure to Mr. Jones or myself to sacrifice every kind of social intercourse, who have always been used to it, to come to a place like this and try to start a home out of stumps and rocks? Mr. Jones worked from daylight till dark every day he was home and what has he got for it.

Mrs. Jones mailed the letter with her very last stamp. Not much was known of the Jones family for the next year, except that somehow they survived the winter without Arthur, likely on some kind of government assistance. Arthur came home from prison the following year a hardened, resentful man, yet unbelievably they managed to have *another* child, bringing the grand total to eleven children and two parents—this on the eve of the Great Depression, a decade in which the entire population of Desolation Sound suffered mightily.

Down the inlet, the soon-to-be Cougar Lady, Nancy Crowther, and her parents had settled into their homestead the same year the Joneses arrived. The Crowthers were experiencing their own dismal situation, but at least they had fewer mouths to feed. In an interview with journalist Murray Kennedy, Nancy remembers the 1930s as "a terrible time." Families like the Crowthers and the Joneses were so poor "we couldn't afford shoes, so we wrapped cloth around our feet . . . to walk on barnacles. We made dresses out of curtains and flour sacks." Nancy also remembered a couple of "starving children" who were taken to the hospital. These were likely the Jones children seized by the police. Nancy and her parents were able to survive on clams and goat's milk. At some point during the bleak 1930s it appeared that Arthur and Helen Jones separated, Helen taking the children with her to Powell River. The scant remaining records show that Arthur Jones remained at Isabel Bay, unemployed since his arrests.

The brutal realities of the non-existent economy coupled with wilderness survival came crashing down on Arthur Jones one final time in the winter of 1939, when he torched the family home, himself within it. As the flames engulfed the house and a thick column of smoke rose over the inlet, he shot himself in the head, bringing to an end twelve misguided years of

Desolation Sound misery for Arthur Jones. His death certificate lists the incident as "suicide" by "burning of house," the result of the fire being "complete incineration" of his body. He was fifty years old. The Jones family mostly remained in the Powell River area, though Helen eventually moved to Vancouver where she died in 1952. One of the little islands that dot Isabel Bay is called Madge, named after the girl who travelled all the way to town to find out what had become of her father.

I could see Madge Island from the bluff where I stood sweating. With my finish line in sight and my machete glinting in the emerging sun, I continued to hack through the waist-high salal and cedar boughs, pushing toward the Isabel Bay shoreline. I could smell the seaweed and hear the birds. Ecstatic at the thought of finishing something beyond a case of Black Label, I pulled my sweat-soaked shirt off over my head, readying myself to toss my forest weaponry aside and take a victory plunge into Isabel Bay. I plowed through the final ten feet with reckless abandon, spider webs sticking to my face, the branches and thorns scratching and cutting at my arms, the wildwood not wanting to let me out without a fight.

I burst through the forest wall into the bright sunlight, sopping wet, bleeding and triumphant, the Isabel Bay–Russell Cove trail complete. The sun felt euphoric upon my heaving bare shoulders. My delirium was quickly tempered when I realized that I had emerged very close to the Jones' original homestead. Unlike other old homesteads in Desolation Sound, a lot of evidence of the Jones' time in Desolation Sound can still be seen, including several overgrown garden terraces propped up by rock walls and a gigantic, leafy walnut tree. Beside it was a flat, overgrown clearing, presumably where the house stood. Next to it was a little freshwater creek. Walking softly through the homestead, I tried hard to imagined it overrun with eleven skinny children who were, hopefully at one time or another, happy.

I walked back to the edge of shoreline overlooking Madge Island and was about to drop my drawers and jump into the Bay's inviting waters, when I once again felt the creepy sensation that I wasn't alone. I sensed movement off to my left along the shore. This time, my pants remained on. Squinting in the sun I spied two long, thin fibreglass sea kayaks balanced up on the rocks like teeter-totters, just fifty feet down the shore, their lead lines tied to overhanging cedar boughs. A young couple emerged onto the rocks in the typical tourist kayaking uniform: Gortex water shorts, tank tops, sun hats and strap-on sandals. Both squinted in my direction. I gave a friendly wave of the machete. The man slowly raised his arm and returned what looked like an undecided acknowledgment. Having been without guests for over a week and giddy from my trailblazing breakthrough, I was eager to share my success of the day, so I made my way across the rocks toward them.

When our young family had first arrived in Desolation Sound a few decades earlier, kayaks were rare. For hundreds of years, the only self-propelled boats in the Sound were the First Nations dugout canoes, followed by the Europeans in their rowboats. For our first few years in the Sound all we had was our leaky blue rowboat, in which we made our first trip across the inlet. For many years, Russell paddled the only kayak that I saw in the Sound with any regularity. He had somehow come to possess a long, dark green, two-man kayak. He would sit in the rear cockpit while his big shaggy mutt Loop would sit obediently in the front cockpit, and Russell would paddle them to and from the Okeover government wharf when the weather was agreeable. Russell's kayak was such an anomaly back then, especially with a big dog in the front seat, that they would often have to stop and pose for pictures snapped by passing yachters while he and Loop bobbed dangerously in their wake.

When ecotourism eventually boomed across the western world, Desolation Sound became an internationally sought-after, world-class kayaking destination. Because it was the largest marine park on the west coast of Canada and boat-access only, kayakers could skim into areas of the pristine park that the yachters and sailboats couldn't reach, essentially having large portions of the park completely to themselves and their kayaks. Taking advantage of the kayaking tourism trade was Powell River Sea Kayak. The guides always informed vacationers bound for the Sound that there were no roads, hardly any trails, very few permanent residents and that passage was only done on the water. Once the kayakers found a shoreline campsite within the park, they could be totally alone for days or weeks on end, should they choose to be so. And yet abruptly before this kayaking couple in this haunted bay was a shirtless, bearded, machete-wielding man headed straight for them.

I lacked any and all self-awareness that my caveman-like presence might have been a source of alarm for the kayakers, even though the body language of both kayakers was guarded at best. They were turned into each other, holding one another, their furrowed brows facing a filthy, armed bushman with a maniacal grin, emerging from endless, uninhabited bush. "Hi!" I yelled excitedly, now right in front of them.

"Hello . . . " replied the man in a reserved tone.

"How's it going? You camping?"

"Are you all right? You're bleeding . . . " said the woman, gesturing to my arms with her eyes.

"I didn't even notice that. I'm fine. Where are you from?"

"We're . . . from Victoria," replied the man, now shielding the woman with his body, seemingly prepared to take the first blow of the machete. "Where are . . . you from?"

"I live in downtown Vancouver, but I've been out here a while. It took me a week just to get to here, and this particular place kind of spooks me a little." As the words tumbled from my mouth, my adrenalin began to fade, and my awareness began to focus. My cuts started to hurt, my eyes relaxed, and I saw two nervous people in front of me. "Uh, I actually have a cabin in the next bay, around the other side of the peninsula, or about an hour or so straight through that bush. I just finished a trail from there to here that took me a week to blaze and I'm spent."

With that somewhat rational explanation, the tourists exhaled just a little bit. I put the machete aside to complete the gesture. After a few more minutes of chit-chat, I accepted their invitation of an ocean-chilled beer and a sit-down in their camp, which consisted of a small nylon tent on a patch of moss, drying clothes strung up in an arbutus tree, a small Coleman stove and a little transistor radio. Their names were Carl and Jenna. This was their first time in Desolation Sound, and they were impressed by its grandeur and surprised by its remoteness. "What do you mean that this place spooks you?" asked Carl.

"Uh . . . well . . . do you like pioneer stories?" Against possible better judgment, I told them the story of Arthur Jones and his fiery suicide that had occurred just a few feet from where they camped. Their look of unease crept back across their faces, so I decided to drop the always-reliable CBC credibility biscuit in their basket. "Well, I noticed you have a radio there," gesturing to it with my empty beer can. "I'm actually a music journalist with CBC Radio and I host a radio show every Saturday night. We're in repeats for the summer but you can still hear me Saturday on 105.7 FM at 10 p.m. if you want."

They looked relieved, but still slightly skeptical. Jenna, possibly just being polite, said she thought she might have heard me on the radio before. I rose to my feet to leave and insisted they tune in on Saturday night. I also extended an invitation to stop by the cabin, via trail or kayak, for snacks, a drink or just to use a real toilet. They politely assured me they would do so on all counts if they had the time. I thanked them for the beer and the Band-Aid, did a quick and clothed victory plunge and gave them a final wave of the machete before I proudly disappeared back into the forest on my fresh new trail.

A few nights later I was alone in the cabin zoning out while doing the dishes. I remembered it was Saturday night so I reached over and flipped on the radio to hear which repeat of my show they were playing, but couldn't find the frequency. I froze, dropping a plate in the sink with a sudsy splash. I stared at the radio as I realized my mistake. My weekly Saturday-night radio show aired on the CBC Radio *Two* network, which could not be heard in Desolation Sound because its signal wasn't strong enough. I *knew* that, I've always known that, all my neighbours knew that, my parents knew that, my friends knew that; how could I have forgotten that major detail? My thoughts raced to poor Carl and Jenna, huddled in their tent in the *Blair Witch* darkness of Isabel Bay, the Arthur Jones ghost story fresh in their heads, trustfully tuning in at 10 p.m. to 105.7 FM to prove all their worrying about me was for naught, only to hear horrifying static, wondering if they had had a conversation with a ghost or a madman, at any moment expecting me to slice through their tent with my machete, shirtless, bearded and screaming, "SO HOW DO YOU LIKE MY RADIO SHOW!??"

A week later, I bumped into Carl and Jenna on a supply run at the Okeover government wharf, the floating crossroads of our corner of the Sound. It was an awkward meeting at best. While Jenna parked their car, I parlayed with Carl over a couple beers, still cold from the Lund General Store's walk-in cooler, the black Jiffy-marker price staining my hand with ink. They had indeed tried to listen to my radio show, they had indeed heard static and had indeed experienced deeper suspicion and a restless night, breaking camp early the next morning. I told Carl that I felt awful, doing my very best to level his concern with the offer of a second can of beer. I stopped the first oyster farmer I recognized and had him repeatedly verify my role at CBC. Carl and I shared another nervous laugh. "See?" I said. "Just my dumb mistake."

Jenna appeared at the top of the gangplank and gave me a hard stare, arms crossed. Looking up at her with a wave and a smile that were not returned, I asked Carl where they'd be camping over the next few nights. "Uh . . . Lover's Beach," he answered with hesitation.

"You're kidding" I replied. "That's even closer to my cabin than Isabel Bay! Look, let me make this up to you. I really insist that you must come by for drinks one of the evenings this week. . . . Please, I'd love to have you. French doors, tall flagpole, looks like a superintendent's lodge; you can't miss it."

Jenna's arms were still folded across her chest and she hadn't budged from the top of the gangplank. "Uh . . . all right," Carl answered. "We'll talk it over once we get settled but that would be nice."

"Awesome! So I'll see you in a couple of days—don't bring a thing, we're minimalist up here!"

With that, I hopped into my skiff, revved up the outboard and took off, looking back with a friendly "cheers" of my raised beer can.

Two or three days passed without a sign of Carl and Jenna's kayaks. The calendar tends to blur during the summer in the Sound, and I lost track of the days as I continued on with my daily routine of . . . not much. A few evenings later, Lorenzo invited me over for dinner to meet a few of his friends visiting from the States. I was still without visitors of my own so I was happy to join them, but I hadn't showered or shaved in about a week, so Lorenzo's invitation seemed like a good excuse to do both.

The solar-heated hot water of the cabin's shower stall poured down on me in ecstasy as I scrubbed off a week's worth of dirt and salt. The tingly feeling of the soap, fresh water and steam rejuvenated my skin. I stepped out of the shower and towelled off, then tossed the towel aside to lather up and shave. Without any electricity, in the fading light of the day, I had trouble seeing exactly what I was shaving in the bathroom, so I took my little shaving mirror and tried shaving in the kitchen sink. I still couldn't see properly, so I moved toward the window. The sun was starting to set and the light inside the cabin was getting too dim to really see what I was doing, so I stepped out onto the deck, fully naked but for a thick white beard of shaving cream, a razor in one hand, and a small circular shaving mirror in the other.

Standing on our deck at the top of the staircase twenty feet away from me were the kayakers Carl and Jenna. They stared directly at me, mouths agape. I stared back. The space between us filled with tension. I saw their eyes leave my face and trace my naked, dripping body downwards to my shrivelled manhood. Jenna's expression curdled. I looked down, too, and was reminded that I was indeed totally naked. I quickly positioned the shaving mirror to cover my southern exposure.

There are no doorbells or intercoms in Desolation Sound. When dropping by someone's cabin, even if invited, it's been century-old recommended etiquette to, at the very least, "give a yell." A Desolation Sound cabin is a private place, where people unwind, seeking solace and relaxation in whatever state they please. In Desolation Sound over the years, it was downright unsafe to not give a yell first, as you never knew what people might do should they be suddenly surprised or unexpectedly set upon.

None of us said a word. I tried a faint, pathetic smile. After a few more seconds of silence, Jenna slowly reached out for Carl's hand, and with a slight tug they both went back down the stairs out of view. Unsure of what to do, I waited another twenty seconds and then called after them. "Hello! Hellooooo?" They had reached their kayaks pulled up on the rocks. "Hey!" I called out, as if the last thirty seconds never existed. "You made it! Come on up!" I said, gesturing with the razor, keeping the mirror tight against my crotch. They slid their kayaks into the water. "I was just getting ready to go out but you should come up and take a look!" I called down. "At the cabin, I mean. I forgot you were coming over!"

I never saw Jenna's face again as she climbed into the cockpit of her kayak and throttled her paddle. Carl glanced up, gave me a palms-up what-can-I-do look, and sat down in his kayak. They paddled away, leaving me standing at the edge of the deck, the mirror and razor at my sides, shaving cream dripping from my chin. "Come by tomorrow for breakfast!"

Not looking back, Jenna loosened her grip on her paddle long enough to give me the finger, not even missing a stroke.

If I had only been wearing this sweater when I came upon the camping kayakers, maybe they would have been convinced that I was a legit CBC Radio host, instead of a bleeding, shirtless, machete-wielding psychopath.

21
Purple Haze

When my pals Nick and Rory finally arrived a week later to relieve my solitude for a weekend of action in the Sound, the first thing they wanted to do was give the brand-new Russell Cove–Isabel Bay trail a try. I was eager for someone other than me to navigate it, so we made a plan that they would walk the trail to the other side where I would pick them up in the skiff. I hadn't quite finished replacing all of Russell's old route-marker signs, but I was sure that Nick and Rory could figure it out. Rory was very savvy in the woods, having grown up in the banger wilds of Prince George, BC, and Nick was pretty tough too, much more so than me. They took off, disappearing into the forest in shorts, T-shirts, flip-flops and a couple of small backpacks, while I cracked a beer and relaxed on the deck, knowing I wouldn't have to go get them for a while.

After about an hour and a half of suntanning and finishing off *Tintin and the Seven Crystal Balls,* I ambled down to the boat and puttered over in the direction of Isabel Bay to pick them up. When I rounded the point into the natural harbour, I was mildly surprised to not see them waiting onshore. I thought I had given them plenty of time to walk the trail and have a victory swim, but they were nowhere to be seen. I guess I should have replaced those signs. Nick and Rory completely missed their first big turn. They kept moving north when they should have been walking east, and were soon bushwhacking, pushing forward through brambles and thick spider webs, commenting to each other on what a lousy job I had done on the new "trail." Eventually, they realized their mistake.

"This can't be the trail, there's no way Lawrence would ever venture through this shit," said Nick, pulling cobwebs out of his hair and brushing his bare arms for spiders. Rory, always up for an adventure, was willing to press on. "We're almost entirely surrounded by water, I'm sure we'll come to the shoreline soon, one way or the other. Let's just keep moving." Within twenty minutes they were ankle-deep in a mosquito-infested bog, surrounded by leafy skunk cabbage plants and their bright yellow swamp lantern flowers, and bulrushes taller than they were. The rich, black mud sucked their flip-flops off their feet as they stumbled to escape the swarming bugs. "Fuck this," shouted Nick. "We need to get to higher ground."

Stepping up and over a fallen tree, they brushed aside some thorns and cedar boughs and felt firm soil beneath their feet. Rory pushed forward and stepped into a small clearing lit up by streaming sunlight. Nick caught up, and they both glanced up to feel the sunshine on their grubby faces. Halfway across the clearing Rory froze in his tracks, holding Nick back with a hand to his chest. "What??" said Nick, glancing around.

Rory turned slowly toward Nick with a sly grin on his face. He reached over to the stalk of a nearby plant, shook it a little, and pointed up. Nick took another look skyward. Lofting lazily in the sunshine just a few feet above their heads was the telltale, infamous silhouette of a green and leafy tropical plant that was definitely not native to the British Columbian rainforest. To their amazement they both quickly realized they were standing quite literally in the dead centre of a grove of towering, fully mature, seven-foot-plus marijuana plants.

Throughout the forest on all sides of the Sound, there are rumoured to be plenty of marijuana patches. Some are said to be tended to, and some are long forgotten, growing wild amid the ferns and cedar trees. Some were planted in the very centre of little islands in the middle of the inlets that people rarely set foot upon. Some say a few of the leased oyster farms in the Sound were mere fronts for the real crop found thirty feet or three hundred metres into the woods. The RCMP conducted occasional aerial searches in helicopters and float planes, looking for suspicious clearings, and have been seen at the Okeover wharf hauling garbage bags full of pot plants (also known as "Desolation Dope") from a police boat into a van to supposedly be incinerated.

For the entire time that Russell lived in the Sound, he had a modest marijuana patch. It was located on a sunny bluff just a few hundred feet behind our cabin, probably on our property, but neither I nor any of my family members ever even knew it was there, nor would any of us have known better if we had brushed by the tropical plant. Dad was vehemently against pot, considering it a hippie crutch for a lazy, slippery-slope loser lifestyle. I knew that he had never tried it, or even knew what it smelled like. One time when The Smugglers were practising in the basement of our family home, we lit an incense stick one of the guys had bought at a corner store. Within minutes he burst into the room accusing us of hot-boxing the family basement. He would have been royally pissed if he knew Russell was cultivating an illegal marijuana crop near our cabin. To Russell's credit, though he was often drunk, stoned or both, as a child I was never the wiser, thinking he was simply just one of the most happy, mellow, snackin' dudes around.

On one occasion, when our family wasn't at the cabin, an RCMP helicopter appeared out of nowhere, buzzing like a Jurassic mosquito low over Russell Cove, searching for grow-ops. Russell was back at the well doing some maintenance, and ducked into a thicket of alder when the chopper was directly overhead in a bright blue sky, causing the trees to bend and the branches and leaves to flap wildly from the downward thrust of the chopper's blades. Russell knew that if his patch was discovered, he could avoid detection by disappearing into the forest.

The chopper circled above Russell three times, but missed his relatively small marijuana garden. Later that afternoon, he heard the helicopter again, higher this time. He stepped out of his shack and looked up to see it pass over, its lower racks stuffed with garbage bags. Someone else's crop had been seized. Russell kept watching the helicopter as it flew out over the inlet, and then to his surprise he saw something large, round and green drop from the chopper to the calm ocean below. Russell whistled for his mutt, Loop, and the two of them jumped into Russell's leaky skiff and putted out to investigate, Russell hoping no one else had seen what he had just seen. When he reached the bag it was half-submerged below the surface of the water. He scooped it out and tore at the plastic. Sure enough, it was a bag stuffed with fully mature, leafy dope with plenty of scintillating buds ready for harvesting—a huge sack of pot inadvertently delivered to his doorstep by none other the Royal Canadian Mounted Police.

Eventually, after too many successful aerial raids, the farmers got wise and planted their crops so far back in the woods that no one would ever find them . . . unless it was by complete chance, just as Nick and Rory had done on their lost hike.

And for all the love and harmony that existed out in the open Sound, back in the woods where the larger marijuana plants grew the farmers were rumoured to guard their crops with the paranoid ferocity of a miner over a gold claim. It took time, skill, hard work, luck, perfect growing conditions and plenty of secrecy to successfully harvest a potent outdoor marijuana crop. Accusations and violent altercations over discovered and raided patches were common in Lund and Powell River. In fact, recent studies have shown a strong link between heavy marijuana intake and paranoid schizophrenia, or "going bush," as it's referred to in Desolation Sound.

None of this mattered to Nick and Rory. They quickly surveyed the crop and counted at least forty towering, mature plants, well past the flowering stage. These plants were ready to be cut, dried and smoked. Some had been very recently harvested, cut off cleanly at the stock. There were plenty of fresh footprints in the soft dirt. Glancing around nervously for the farmer (or farmers), Rory and Nick looked at each other with anxious excitement. "What do you think?" Nick whispered to Rory.

"I say we grab some," Rory whispered back. "Just a bit, and then we get out of here."

Just a bit turned into a free-for-all that would make Cheech and Chong blush, both Nick and Rory snapping off as many stalks as they could stuff into their knapsacks. Once they could barely zip them closed, they broke into a clambering dash through the forest to get as far away from the clearing as quickly as they could. They weren't sure in what direction they were racing, but soon they were headed down a steep incline. After a few minutes they stopped to get their bearing, panting, hands on their knees. "We should just keep heading down this hill," Rory suggested.

"Are you sure?" asked Nick. Rory drew in a breath, but was cut off by a loud crack up the hill from where they had come.

It was the only answer they needed. Though it could have been a squirrel, a deer or just deadfall, their nerves were on a heightened edge; they looked at each other with fear in their eyes, both possibly remembering certain scenes from *Deliverance*, and took off in a wild careen down the forest hill.

In the meantime, I was slowly motoring up and down the coastline of Isabel Bay, near the trail mouth and the designated pickup spot we had arranged, just in front of Madge Island. I started to think they had overshot the trail completely, and might emerge on the tiny isthmus of very private property in historic Portage Cove. The Portage Cove isthmus was another ancient First Nations site, connecting Desolation Sound's largest peninsula to the mainland with one thin strip of dry land. For centuries, the First Nations used the cove both as a shortcut canoe portage from the outer Sound to their village in Kahkaykay, and as a huge clam garden. It would take less than ten minutes to carry a canoe from one side of the isthmus to the other, yet hours to paddle the long way around, so it was a heavily used thoroughfare. Then the federal Indian Act was imposed, the Natives got the boot, the isthmus was sectioned off and a notorious American settler named Joe Copeland bought the lot, shutting down the portage for good.

Joe Copeland was a bugler in the American Civil War, enlisted with the southern Confederates fighting against his dad, who was a colonel for the Yankees. After the South lost the war, like many Confederate soldiers, he drifted west, where he heard rumours that one of his ex-army pals named Jesse James was looking for recruits for an outlaw gang. The legend goes that Joe Copeland joined Jesse James' notorious band of thieves, robbing banks, stagecoaches and trains across the American west. Joe eventually eluded capture by sneaking into Canada. In Vancouver he stole a rowboat and rowed it north up the coast, all the way to Desolation Sound, where he purchased the Portage Cove isthmus from the government. Over the years Joe Copeland grew increasingly eccentric, often greeting passing boats while perched out on the rocks in his tattered grey Confederate uniform, blowing on his bugle. And he never went anywhere without a German Luger pistol in his belt. Copeland eventually sold his property and died in the 1930s. The Copeland Islands Provincial Marine Park, just northwest of Lund, is named after him.

Through the decades various owners continued to block trespassing of any kind on the natural portage, first the Natives in their canoes, then years later the influx of tourists in their kayaks. The current owners were no different, and when I motored over to see if Rory and Nick had unluckily emerged there, I was greeted with multiple, large NO TRESPASSING and PRIVATE PROPERTY signs. Powering slowly back up the shoreline to Isabel Bay, I thought I heard something above the sputtering of the engine. Turning around, I saw them. About a half-kilometre down the shore toward Portage Cove, Nick and Rory were standing on the edge of a cliff, waving their arms and jumping up and down. I revved up the skiff and sped over as they scraped and slid down the rocks to meet me. They were filthy, covered in mud, their hair filled with brambles, their clothes sweat-stained. "What the hell is going on?" I yelled once I was in shouting distance.

"Don't stop!" Rory shouted back. "Keep the motor running!" Both of them hopped onto the bow and plundered into the boat. "Drive! Go! Go!" Nick exclaimed breathlessly. As soon as we were around the other side of the point, I cut the engine and demanded an explanation. Like an episode of *Danger Bay* meets *Up in Smoke,* Nick and Rory unzipped their knapsacks and held up their leafy treasure, both of them exploding into laughter. It took me a few seconds to realize what they were showing me. "Is that . . . marijuana?" I asked incredulously.

Still panting, still laughing, they both excitedly recounted their escapade. I freaked out, immediately glancing around us, scanning the shoreline. "Are you insane?" I whispered loudly. "You *raided* a grow op? You could have been shot for that! The people around here who grow that shit are crazy!!"

"So we assumed!" replied Rory, still laughing and panting. "Don't worry, they won't miss it, they have a whole forest of the stuff growing back there." I gunned the engine and got us back to the cabin as quickly as possible. I wouldn't touch the stuff but, needless to say, after drying out the plants to the best of our ability, the rest of that weekend was one deep, long purple haze for Nick and Rory, and free of any psychotic reactions. In the weeks following, I made sure I uttered not a word to a living soul at the Okeover wharf about the discovery of the Desolation dope, and even kept our skiff out of sight for a few days for fear it had been spotted near the grow op. As I was quickly learning, the only thing that travels faster than boats over the waters of Desolation Sound is gossip.

Rory and Nick went from being up the creek to up in smoke when they found a large marijuana grow op after getting lost on a hike through the dense woods of Desolation Sound Marine Park.

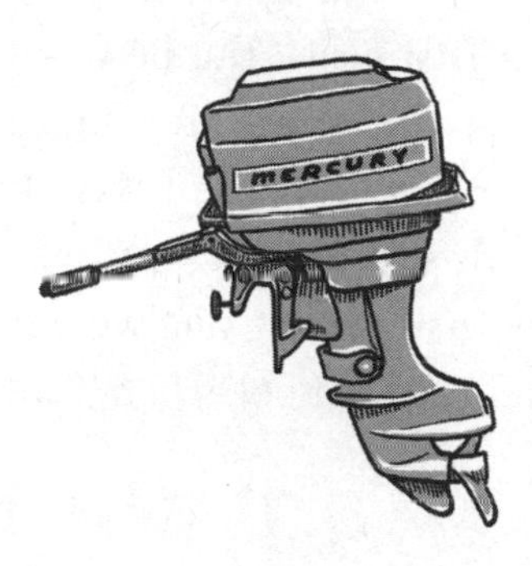

22
Stormy High

My family had been zipping to and from the government wharf in the same twelve-foot tin can of a boat through sunshine, wind, rain and storm for over twenty years. It had begun to leak along the seams of the hull and the outboard motor was becoming less reliable, routinely sounding like a garburator with a fork stuck in it. Running the little boat was still a breeze in perfect weather, but a summer storm could make July look like January for three days straight. The rain came in hard from the southeast straight up the inlet, which pelted our cabin windows. The waves crashed against the rocks and the winds howled, which caused our Canadian flag to flap like a matador's cape and our old wooden "Lawrences" sign hanging off our front eaves to creak back and forth with loud complaint, a telltale sign we were in for a bad three-day blow.

The weather in Desolation Sound made all the difference. Be there with a storm whipping through the inlets, socking the clouds against the mountains, rain pouring down and Desolation Sound can be so dark and depressing that you'll never want to return, just as both Captain Vancouver and I experienced on our first visits. But be there when the sun is out and it's a picture-perfect postcard with sunshine and high-pressure systems that could blissfully last days and weeks on end. The southeasterly storms battered Captain Vancouver and his men when they first arrived, and were one of the leading causes for the Captain's foul mood when he bestowed the name upon the place:

> This afforded not a single prospect that was pleasing to the eye, the smallest recreation on shore, nor animal or vegetable food, excepting a very scanty proportion of those eatables already described, and which of the adjacent country was soon exhausted, after our arrival. Nor did our exploring parties meet with a more abundant supply, whence the place obtained the name *DESOLATION SOUND.*

The weather that summer was unseasonably bad and Vancouver's crew were constantly battling the exhausting southeasterly gales. The surveying parties were forced to row through treacherous waves, soaking themselves in cold rain and salt water under grey skies and whipping winds. The 170-person crew was miserable. They desperately dreamt of returning to the exotic ports of call like Hawaii, Tahiti and what would become Australia, where gorgeous and friendly Natives frolicked naked under the swaying palm trees of paradise.

Occasionally my friends would have bad luck with summer weather, visiting our cabin when every living thing seemed to just disappear, everyone and everything seeking shelter from the storm. Many of the massive yachts cruising the Sound would wait out the storms (which usually lasted for three days like clockwork) in the serene waters of Kahkaykay Bay just around the point from our cabin. On one torrentially rainy, cold and stormy weekend, Rory and Nick, unabated by the weather, paddled a couple of kayaks over to the biggest yacht they could find, glistening like a mother pearl in the downpour. A crew-member swabbing the deck leaned over the side to greet the two soaked kayakers in toques and Gortex, the only souls out on the water in such foul weather. "Pardon me," Rory shouted up through the rain in his most refined British accent. "Would you have any Grey Poupon?"

Once, and only once, we had a West Vancouver Scout leader ask to use our cabin as a weekend wilderness retreat for his young troop. We warned him of the ruggedness of the Sound but he assured us that he was an experienced mariner and outdoorsman, and that they would be arriving in his recently purchased yacht. The troop shoved off from the tony West Vancouver Yacht Club and cruised up the inner coast. They arrived just before dark as a weak southeasterly storm was rolling in, the Scout leader tying up the yacht to our mooring line, eager for a snug night of s'mores, songs and knot-tying exercises.

When the troop woke up the next morning the storm had broken, the water was dead calm and the sun was peeking over the eastern ridge. One of the Scouts timidly asked their still-snoozing leader if he had moved his yacht. Sure enough, when the Scout leader leapt from his sleeping bag and looked down into Russell Cove, the yacht had vanished from its mooring. The Scout leader let out an anguished squeal. Not considering for a second the winds and waves during the night, the Scout leader was absolutely certain that some local, drunken scallywag must have stolen it, and had likely left it wrecked somewhere on the rocks. They could be stranded! He immediately summoned the troop into action, half of them scouring the shoreline in one direction, the rest in the other, while he paced the deck, fuming and flummoxed.

Hindered by sheer granite cliffs, the troops couldn't go very far, returning minutes later without a sighting. The Scout leader took to the shoreline himself, cliffs be damned, bound for Handy Candy's place. He woke her up with his panicked shouts, and together they climbed into the *Tinkertoy* and motored across the inlet, eliciting the help of another neighbour, the friendly lawyer Darrell. Darrell, doubting anyone would steal a yacht, suggested they head toward the mouth of the inlet in the direction of the tidal current.

At the same time, several kilometres down the Sound, a local caretaker named Rhonda was peering out her kitchen window while making her morning coffee. True to Russell's old Desolation Sound motto of "there is always something to see," Rhonda squinted in the morning light, focusing on the peculiar sight of a luxury yacht floating backward down the inlet, silently being drawn out to the Strait of Georgia with the tide. Rhonda pulled on her boots and mackinaw, hopped into her skiff and motored out to it. She pulled alongside and yelled, "Anybody aboard? Hello? Hello onboard!" No one answered. She attached a line from her stern to the yacht's bow line, which was dragging in the water, and towed it back to shore, securing it to her dock. She climbed aboard. The boat was empty, with no signs of life or mischief.

Within minutes, the search party had arrived, roaring up to Rhonda's dock in the *Tinkertoy*. "That's my boat!" shouted the Scout leader, on his feet and pointing.

"It was floating backwards down the inlet!" Rhonda barked back. Candy pulled the *Tinkertoy* alongside the yacht and the

Scout leader scrambled aboard, hastily checking it over from bow to stern. Candy and Darrell knew Rhonda and her wild red hair from the Okeover government wharf, and explained who the Scout leader was. Somewhat satisfied that everything was in order, the Scout leader turned to Rhonda with a furrowed brow and an outstretched index finger: "Woman! Did you steal this boat?"

"Man, I already told you. It was floating ass-backward down the inlet, dragging its bow line." She looked over at Candy and Darrell. "Aren't Scout leaders supposed to know how to tie knots and 'be prepared' and all that shit?"

It was miraculous that the fibreglass boat was without a scratch, as it easily could have been dashed on the rocks. Instead it drifted unscathed throughout the inlets, floating some five kilometres. The Scout leader began to untie the yacht from Rhonda's dock. Rhonda put her rubber boot firmly down on the rope the Scout leader was working on. "What about my salvage fee?" asked Rhonda.

It's common practice on the coast that if anything of any value is found on the water or the beach and the original owner is to come calling, the salvager should receive a negotiated fee. The suspicious Scout leader was in no mood for any reward. He urgently wanted to get back to his troop and out of the Sound as quickly as possible.

"Salvage fee?! I should think not!" With the palms of his hands the Scout leader felt his short-short khaki Scout pant pockets front and back, then his khaki Scout shirt breast pockets. Then he searched them again, and then again more thoroughly and urgently. Unfortunately, in his haste the Scout leader forgot the keys to the yacht back at the cabin, meaning the yacht was in for another tow, this time behind the *Tinkertoy*. Rhonda untied the boat and tossed the rope over to him. "That was a half-hitch by the way," she shouted mockingly. As they towed the yacht very slowly back to the waiting Scout troop, they left Rhonda standing at the end of her dock, hands on her hips, thoroughly unimpressed with the entire affair. Upon hearing the story, Dad made sure to get Rhonda a bottle of red wine and a large coil of rope as a reward. Dad's nickname for her ever since has been "Help Me Rhonda."

The storms kicked everyone's ass at one time or another, and were constantly underestimated by visitors. On another stormy occasion when I wasn't at the cabin, my sister Heather had come up to stay with her husband, Matt, their kids, Paige, Tanner and Avery, and their tiny chihuahua, Lily-Shepard. On the morning of their departure from the cabin to go back to the city, the sea was grey and mean. It was the beginning of another blow-up, much bigger than what the Scout troop faced, a storm that would turn peaceful seas into a raging tempest within minutes. Heather recognized this weather pattern from traumatic journeys as a child in the very same tiny aluminum boat into which she was about to load her own family. She had no choice but to hurry everyone to pack up and get moving.

By the time they were ready to leave, whitecaps were cresting in the cove and the winds were gaining a nasty velocity. Soon the sky blackened and the rain came, as they desperately shimmied down the cliff into our inappropriate boat to make their escape. Once everyone was huddled in the open boat, try as he might, Matt couldn't get the relic outboard to start. The wind was taking control, blowing them closer and closer to the rocks in the cove. The outboard sputtered to life just in time, like the *Millennium Falcon* in a minefield, steering them into the deeper water seconds before they would have smacked into the jagged rocks and been swamped by the pounding waves.

By the time they motored into the inlet, the storm had whipped itself into a full gale. Heavy black waves crashed above them, tossing the boat around like a bathtub toy. There wasn't a single other boat on the water of any size. Matt steered from the stern's back bench, Lily-Shepard the whimpering, bug-eyed chihuahua cradled in his arms. Heather, Paige and Avery were on the middle bench, while seven-year-old Tanner was in the very front taking the full brunt of every wave.

Heather told me later that it was as if someone was constantly dumping buckets of cold water onto their heads. Heather and Matt would have just enough time to wipe the stinging salt from their eyes, get a glimpse of where they were and then get dumped on again. Within ten minutes of beginning their pounding voyage, their clothes were soaked. The kids were shivering and screaming, while Heather was hanging on tightly to four-year-old Avery, terrified he would be swept overboard as the waves slammed the boat with spine-altering force. Ten-year-old Paige was on the other side of Heather, clinging to her soaked sweater, screaming that they were all going to drown. Tanner was taking the worst of it, sitting hunched over with his back to the relentless torrent, taking each soaking silently and stoically. Somehow they managed to make it across the inlet in six-foot swells, then hugged the shoreline, trying to get as close as possible in case the boat capsized.

They had made it about halfway to the wharf, fighting a losing, sopping battle with the storm every inch of the way, when Heather began to truly panic about the safety of the children and the buoyancy of our tired old skiff. Icy ocean water rapidly filled the bottom of the boat, sloshing around their feet and luggage. Matt handed out bailing buckets and anyone who could started to bail frantically. Heather scanned the shoreline and suddenly remembered that somewhere off to the right, through the rain and wind and waves, was a sheltered little bay where Dad would launch our little blue rowboat when we were kids. Heather had no idea if the Cougar Lady still lived there or if she was even still alive, but it was worth a shot just to take shelter. Heather screamed at Matt over the gale to steer them in the direction of the Cougar Lady's bay, and that the children had to get to shore immediately. Matt yelled back that they were almost at the Okeover wharf—he yelled something else but he was cut off when a rogue wall of grey water smashed into the boat, momentarily submerging them all. That was enough to convince Matt to alter their course.

They eventually found the entrance of the cove, which offered them a slight reprieve from the gale. They steered toward a little dock bobbing in the chuck, Matt grabbing ahold of it when they got close enough. They dragged the sobbing children out of the boat, little Avery now blue, shoeless and shaking. Lily-Shepard was essentially a comatose, lifeless rag, having gone from *Beverly Hills Chihuahua* to Desolation Sound drowned rat in mere minutes. After a brief discussion, Matt made the questionable decision to continue on to the Okeover wharf to get the car so he could drive down the old dirt road to the cove and pick up Heather and the kids.

Once again the outboard motor wouldn't start and once again he was almost thrown upon the rocks before it came to life. Heather was still huddled on the dock with her bawling kids and the whining dog when a woman appeared at the top of the dock, calling down to them. It turns out that Heather had come ashore a few doors down from the Cougar Lady's cabin but this kind stranger still invited them all into her shack to warm up by the fire and have some hot chocolate while they waited for Matt to pick them up — just as the Cougar Lady used to do for Heather and me after a treacherous crossing when we were kids. The woman found them some dry clothes she was planning to donate to charity. Heather and the kids became that charity. Heather found a bulky green sweater with strange stains all over one side, very similar to the sweater I remember her wearing every day of grade eight. Paige found a pair of neon shorts and a Kokanee beer tanktop. Tanner slipped into a woollen poncho covered in dog hair with a hole cut in the top for his head. Little Avery found some grease-marked coveralls that had been cut off at the arms and legs, so on his four-year-old body they met the bottom of his bare feet and his elbows, a sort of Caillou-meets-Cooter look.

When Matt finally pulled in to the Okeover wharf, the boat was full of water. He crawled out onto the wooden dock floats dressed in a dripping green garbage bag he had pulled from their supplies. Those who were waiting out the storm at the wharf couldn't believe that this soaked, wretched, plastic-clad Gollum in a tiny skiff had made it through the gale-force storm, by far the worst in recent memory. After Matt picked up Heather and the kids, they cranked the heat and the Sharon Lois and Bram and punched it to Lund for coffee and food. When they stepped into Nancy's Bakery every head turned, but by then their pitiful motley crew had a sense of giddiness from the *terra firma* beneath their feet and what they had just been through. It had taken Heather thirty years, but she finally felt (and looked) like a true Lundoner.

23

Big Buck$, Terror of the Inlet

Mom freaked out when she heard the tale that threatened the very lives of her daughter and grandchildren, and after years of suppression she loudly demanded that we finally get a "proper boat." One with a real engine, padded seats, a windshield and her ever-consistent deal-breaker: a roof. Dad was reluctant, still blindly seeing nothing wrong with the leaky little skiff. "What's a little rough weather?" he would say. "It's nothing we haven't been through before." But when Heather, Mom and I offered to pool our money for the purchase of a new Lawrence family boat, Dad stepped up as the patriarch, promising an upgrade the following year. Somewhat true to his word, depending on varying definitions of "upgrade," next summer he hauled a very used, seventeen-foot, faded blue fibreglass speedboat with an old ninety-horsepower outboard up to Desolation Sound. He had bought it on Craigslist for $5,000, rusty, buckling trailer included.

The mighty ***Big Buck$*** and her ninety-horsepower outboard opened up the rest of Desolation Sound in ways our little skiff never could, often infuriating kayakers when we'd roar into the Polynesian-like waterways of the Curme Islands.

It was our chirpy neighbour Handy Candy who named it, the first time she saw it tied up at the wharf. "*That's* your new boat? *That's* the boat your dad bought? Well," she said with obvious sarcasm, "you're just gonna have to call it *Big Bucks* in honour of such an impressive purchase! And make sure the 's' is a big dollar sign!" And so *Big Buck$* was christened. In turn, our little skiff, which we kept and had never been given a name, was naturally and rightfully christened *Lil' Buck$*. Although *Big Buck$* was definitely a beater, with its deep-vee hull and its powerful, guttural engine it was light years faster and safer than our tiny skiff, which we had endured for so many years. Because of its power, speed and ability to take on almost any weather, *Big Buck$* opened up the entire Sound to our family and friends in ways *Lil' Buck$* never could. Soon we were exploring far-off regions of Desolation that were completely new to us, like the Curme Islands, a tiny archipelago of five or six gorgeous little islands with saltwater channels just big enough to motor in *Big Buck$* at a dead-slow speed. We'd often spend the day, annoying the kayakers with the mere presence of *Big Buck$*. We'd swim the easy length between islands in clear water of bath-like temperatures and dry ourselves on protected, sun-drenched rock shelves.

On other days we'd speed across the Sound to visit the rustic cliffside village of Refuge Cove, where well-worn wooden boardwalks along the rocks connected all the buildings like in Robert Altman's *Popeye*. In Refuge Cove we'd fill up the guzzling *Big Buck$* with gas, grab a bite to eat at the floating Boat Stop Café and walk up the gangplank to visit the historic Refuge Cove General Store, picking up ice cream for the kids and beer and snacks for us. Heading north from Refuge Cove, we'd roar into Teakerne Arm where Captain Vancouver sat anchored and depressed during his survey of the Sound. We'd head north to Cassel Falls, a waterfall that cascades down one hundred feet into the ocean from Cassel Lake above. We could motor *Big Buck$* so close that we could feel the mist of the falls on our faces. Farther north still, we would occasionally slice through the glassy waters of Pendrell Sound, a deep inlet known for its bottle-green, serenely warm waters. Jumping off the boat into water four-hundred feet deep, twenty-seven degrees Celsius and filled with harmless white jellyfish was shockingly joyous. Were we still in British Columbia?

The next generation: Nick and Soraya's daughter, Alia, holds hands with Rory and Julie's son, Arlo, on the dock at Refuge Cove, one of our favourite destinations in Desolation Sound. Note this generation's life jackets.

We'd also rumble into the tranquil popular anchorage of Prideaux Haven, a geographical wonder of saltwater canals that wandered through small islands with shorelines of smooth, flat granite rocks sloping gently into the placid water, nary a jagged barnacle to be seen. The ideal location is likely why it was chosen for a homestead by Desolation Sound's first settler and hermit philosopher, Mike Shuttler, he of the knife wound across his face. A century before Scarface Mike called it home, Captain Vancouver's mapping crews rowed through the inviting waters of Prideaux Haven, where they found what they thought was an abandoned First Nations village. They pulled their boats up on shore to look around, finding the remains of a settlement that was likely three-hundred to five-hundred persons strong. All that was left were the posts and slats where the buildings used to exist, troughs for sewage, mounds of discarded clamshells and scattered debris. If Vancouver or his men needed any other reasons to dislike Desolation Sound, they found it here. When a few of the sailors started poking through a heap of leftover clothing, they were the victims of a surprise attack by an unlikely opponent. Captain Vancouver's account of the incident is one of the few moments where he shows a sense of humour:

> Whilst examining these abandoned dwellings . . . our gentlemen were suddenly assailed by an unexpected numerous enemy, whose legions made so furious an attack upon each of their persons, that unable to vanquish their foes, or to sustain the conflict, they rushed up to their necks in water. This . . . however, proved ineffectual; nor was it till after all their clothes were boiled, that they were disengaged from an immense horde of fleas, which they had disturbed by examining too minutely the filthy garments and apparel of the late inhabitants.

The incident was a cause for much-needed levity back on the ships . . . world-exploring, courageous British Naval officers and crew, many of whom had survived conflict, war, Native uprisings and disease, put fast on their heels by an army of fleas.

The Prideaux Haven "Flea Village," as it was so named, likely wasn't abandoned. The First Nations who lived there had probably relocated to another location for the summer, deconstructing the wooden walls and roofs of the longhouses and smaller living quarters at the Prideaux Haven village, loading it all into canoes and rebuilding somewhere else. The remaining struts and posts that Captain Vancouver's men had found would have made it easy for the Natives to rebuild when they returned to the Prideaux Haven location. Vancouver's men were routinely grossed out by the living standards of the coast Natives, in particular describing the Prideaux Haven village as having "an astonishing Quality of Filth and Dirt with a very offensive Smell." Truth be told, their pride and mood was likely affected by being vanquished by bugs, because the squalid conditions below deck on their ships couldn't have been much better. Two hundred years later, "Flea Village" had returned to a wall of trees along the shoreline as we'd roar by it and other exotic locations at top speed, to the scorn of kayakers and yachters alike. Soon, Candy had altered our beat-up boat's nickname to "*Big Buck$*, Terror of the Inlet."

Much to the disgust of our immediate neighbours, Nick, Rory and I soon realized that besides carrying us to far-reaching corners of the Sound, *Big Buck$* could also be used for obnoxious recreational activities such as "tubing": tying one end of a long rope to an inflated inner tube, the other end to the back of *Big Buck$* and being pulled very fast up and down the inlets. Unfortunately we didn't have a proper inner tube, so we borrowed Nick's daughter Maddy's large, green inflatable turtle, tying the rope around its neck. It worked just as well. We'd speed around our bay giving turtle-tubing rides to anyone who dared.

There's a headbanger named Terry smoking a cigarette and hanging on for dear life to that inflatable turtle as they both go for a wild ride courtesy of *Big Buck$*. Didn't end well.

One eager participant was an incredible specimen of headbanger named Terry who was visiting a neighbouring cabin. His look was classic summer banger: cut-off, frayed and faded short-short jean-shorts (or "jorts" as he called them), a proud, scraggly mullet and oversized white runners with the tongues hanging out. Like most bangers, he loved the outdoors, as long as he had several dozen D-batteries for his boom box and several dozen cold beers in an easy-access cooler. He was perpetually shirtless, showing off the dark brown, sunscreen-free tan on his sinewy, hairless frame. Terry always had a beer in one hand and his boom box in the other, tuned loudly to the Powell River classic rock station.

Terry loved visiting Desolation Sound. Over the ear-bleeding party-rock sounds of Steve Miller's "Jungle Love" or ZZ Top's "Legs," he would often shout his favourite mantra: "Look at all the fuckin' beauty!" I always marvelled that a hesher like Terry, who drove a forklift by day and won air-guitar contests by night, could clearly see what Captain Vancouver could not. Maybe if George Vancouver listened to Rush, drank fourteen beers a day, wasn't under the suffocating pressure of an imperial empire and had showed up when it was sunny, he would have shared Terry's unbridled passion for the Sound.

When it was his turn, Terry excitedly hopped on the turtle, lit a fresh cigarette, and yelled for us to "Jus' fuckin' give'r!" I pressed down hard on the throttle and *Big Buck$* charged forward like an angry bull, tearing across the bay, Terry and the turtle at the end of the rope skimming along behind us, his mullet flap doodling gloriously. At first, as bangers are wont to do, Terry showed off a little, gripping the turtle around the neck with one hand, and with the other punching it repeatedly in its innocently smiling face, causing us to crack up every time we looked back. Terry starting yelling, but we couldn't hear him over the roar of the engine, so he began making hand signals, which we took to mean speed up, so we did. More hand signals followed, which we took to mean to take some tight turns.

On one particular arching bend, Terry and the turtle slid way off to the port side of *Big Buck$*, until Terry and the turtle were seemingly racing us side by side. Every muscle in Terry's torso flexed as he desperately hung onto the turtle; every muscle in his face flexed as his lips desperately hung onto his cigarette. We did a complete circle, heading straight for the sizable waves we had just created. Terry and the turtle pounded over top of them like a Mini Cooper down a flight of stairs, creating huge sprays, but he hung on tight. On the next turn, the waves were even bigger, colliding into one another in explosions of white-water. When the turtle hit the waves a second time, it popped straight up in the air, flipped upside down and tossed Terry like a rodeo clown. On all fours, Terry spun across the surface of the water as if he were Banger Jesus, completing four out-of-control cartwheels before finally plunging below the surface.

Frightened that I had taken it too far, I slowed *Big Buck$* and steered toward where Terry had gone under. He surfaced a few seconds later, doused cigarette still proudly between his lips. "Are you okay?" I shouted. Treading water, Terry yelled back, "Fuck yeah! It was a little rough on Jim and the twins but let's do 'er again!"

There was one boat that was faster and louder than *Big Buck$*. It was owned by a friend named Larry, whose personality very much mirrored his boat. He and his boat, fittingly called *The Larrytude*, would often visit/terrorize the Sound during the summer, bringing up several members of our beer-league hockey team, the Vancouver Flying Vees, for a booze-soaked weekend in the sun. His boat was big and slick, with massive, deafening twin outboard engines. Every summer, he would charge up from the city along the inner coast in record time. Like Rodney Dangerfield in *Caddyshack*, his boat would scream into our quiet bay at full throttle, often with a teammate water skiing behind, the music blaring, empty beer cans flying out of both sides amidst a stream of billowing pot smoke mixing with the engine's noxious exhaust.

Captain Vancouver's men were forced to navigate the "labyrinth" of Desolation Sound with a little more sobering caution than Larry. Vancouver described the inlet that led directly to our cabin as "a very narrow channel, rendered almost inaccessible by the number of sunken rocks and rock islets which it contained." It was true. Throughout the Sound there were innumerable hidden, rocky hazards only exposed at low tide, some of them earning names like Lion Rock, Sky Pilot Rock and Stacey Rock. All of them had claimed wrecks of boats large and small; locals and tourists alike had stories of smashing into one or more while trying to steer safely through the inlets in weather both blissful and brutal. It was a mariner's reality that

Larry didn't give a shit about, as he did most of his steering by staring at a computer screen mounted on his boat's dashboard, a Global Positioning System that veered him full speed around any unseen rock, shoal or reef so he could keep the full-volume booze party rockin' on autopilot. Roll over, Captain Vancouver.

Those hockey-team weekends that Larry captained became legendary debaucheries, weekends my neighbours learned to loathe. "Flowin' Rowan," "Bomber," "Oly," "Saleem the Dream," "Silver Screen," "Ball-Deep," "Lock-Eye" and "Cabo-Wabo" all made the trip up over the years to spend time at their goalie's cabin. We would inevitably get plastered, make loud predictions about the upcoming Flying Vees season and bitch about our teammates who weren't there, getting progressively louder and loutish with each round of beer. At night we'd try to entertain ourselves with games, though most of us could barely stand. On the first night we'd usually attempt to stagger through a game of Charades, but it would quickly break down into fits of hysteria when titles like *The Little Sperm Maid* and *Shaving Ryan's Privates* worked their way into the mix. On night two we'd pair off for a heated battle of *Trivial Pursuit: Genus Edition*. The difference between "exact answers" and "close answers" often led to near-fistfights . . . usually Larry versus anyone who challenged his vague, defiant answers backed up by drunken bluster. If things got a little too temperamental, Larry would step outside for a cigarette, smoking on the deck directly above our leaky propane tank.

Lovingly obnoxious though he and his boat might have been, Larry treasured *The Larrytude* and treated it with the utmost care and respect, something few humans interacting with Larry ever received. No matter how hard he partied at the cabin or how late it got, he would always find a kayak to paddle out to his anchored boat to sleep, making sure it didn't "Scout leader" away in the night. Larry was a bachelor, and a creature of habit. He had a daily morning ritual that he fulfilled whether he was at his bachelor pad in the city or on his boat in Desolation Sound. Each and every morning, he'd wake up, grab the morning paper, light a cigarette, sit on the can and take a long, therapeutic dump.

And so one morning after a blindingly drunken night in our cabin, he groggily woke up on his boat, having no idea how he even got there. He found an old newspaper, lit a cigarette, kicked off his ginch and simply hung his ass off the side of the boat in the sunshine, completely naked, taking his morning crap. On this particular morning, the rest of my teammates and I were inside the cabin shuffling around, nursing hangovers and making breakfast when one of the guys informed me of Larry's activities. I grabbed the binoculars and trained them on Larry's boat, and then on Larry's butt, to survey the soiled scene for myself. To my dismay, I also spied a tour group of kayaks from Powell River Sea Kayak, rounding the point. They were following the coastline, paddling straight in the direction of Larry's boat.

Larry was about halfway through the foul growth of his stinky tail when the flotilla unwittingly paddled to within twenty feet of him, rounding the side of his boat. When they were in full and sudden view of Larry's morning ritual, several of the tourists let out audible gasps and exclaims of disgust. Larry, noticing the group for the first time, turned his head slightly, took the cigarette butt out of his mouth and tossed it into the water with a hiss. He gave a friendly wave of his hand. "Morning, folks!" he shouted jovially. Then he turned and went back to reading the week-old newspaper. It gave new meaning to the expression "Watch out for floating logs."

24
Lorenzo's Inferno

"Be sure to stop by my place for a drink. Big, tall, green chimney, halfway up the inlet, you can't miss it!" That's what Lorenzo the swingin' bachelor of the Sound would tell everyone he met down at the Okeover government wharf. Everyone knew Lorenzo was generous, everyone knew he was kind, everyone knew he was fun and happy hour at Lorenzo's remained one of the neighbourhood's favourite nightly rituals. Lorenzo was a lifelong bachelor with a blue-collar background and white-collar tastes. Throughout his life he had travelled the world and liked the sunny, warmer spots best. Eventually he wanted a summer place of his own, closer to his apartment in Vancouver, and through a tip from a friend Lorenzo discovered a cabin for sale in Desolation Sound.

And it wasn't just any cabin. It was the Reverend Jim Davies' place. Reverend Jim had spent thousands of dollars rigging that cabin with all the comforts of home: electric lights, a dishwasher, washer/dryer and Jacuzzi tub, all powered by a wall of deep-cycle batteries, an array of solar panels and wind-turbine energy. It had more mod cons than all of the rest of our cabins combined. When Reverend Jim realized that he was getting too old to keep up the place, he decided to sell. All Lorenzo had to do was slap down the money and turn a key. Reverend Jim even left him chocolate and a bottle of wine on the pillow of the master king-size bed. That Lorenzo was able to stroll into the relative lap of luxury without so much as slamming his thumb under a hammer irked some of the other neighbours, because he never had to *work for it*. While many were still slaving away on cabins that never seemed complete, Lorenzo sat on his weatherproofed latex deck in shorts 'n' shades pouring out gin and tonics while reading the paper and listening to the BC Lions football game. Neighbours griped and gossiped.

Eventually, the gripes and mean-spirited jokes that were made behind his back were said to Lorenzo's face. People would tease him for not knowing where the gas tank on his boat was, or for not knowing how to pump water from the well. And on it went. Lorenzo spent ten years trying to shake his city-slicker reputation. He stopped asking for help and learned to do things himself. When a few of the neighbours persisted with their teasing, invitations to Lorenzo's famous happy hour and mealtime decreased, sometimes ceasing all together. Suddenly, these neighbours had to buy their own booze and food, and figure out some different way to spend the evening hours other than on Lorenzo's deck. They also had to find different methods to charge their cellphones and laptops, other than in Lorenzo's wall sockets.

Each year, Lorenzo would show up in the Sound around mid-March to open up his cabin for the season. He'd roll up the blinds and throw open the windows, sweep out a winter's worth of dust and air the place out. He'd check for mice and search the ceiling for water leaks. He'd clean the gutters of twigs and sweep all the leaves off the deck. He'd plant the seeds for his summer flowers, check for spring bulbs sprouting, and pull the deck furniture out from under the cabin. After a day or two he'd get to one of the dirtiest jobs of all: cleaning out his famous green chimney, which could been seen for miles around.

On a beautiful, crisp and breezy day, Lorenzo was on his hands and knees in front of his state-of-the-art, airtight fireplace, scooping out the previous year's ashes into a box. He had a fire the night before but the ashes were grey and cold. He ran his long chimney brush up the inside of the chimney and twisted the handle to open up the bristles of the brush. He scraped the black soot from the inner chimney bricks, letting fine clouds of black dust and hardened chips of ash and cinder fall and cover the hearth. Lorenzo swept everything into a box, which he put out on the deck to use later as garden and compost fertilizer. Over his shoulder Lorenzo heard his name, and turned to see his next-door neighbour Prawn Pete traversing the trail between their cabins. Prawn Pete asked Lorenzo if he wanted to accompany him on a hike into the forest to check on the well. Lorenzo was game, so he threw on his coveralls and his rubber boots and hit the trail with Pete.

At the same time across the bay, Bernard the German and some friends were sitting on the deck knocking back Bavarian homebrew. From his deck, Bernard had an eagle-eye view of the entire inlet. After a while, one of Bernard's friends asked about a plume of light brown smoke rising up from the direction of Lorenzo's place. Bernard suggested it was probably just Lorenzo burning off some brush on the beach, but he still reached for his binoculars to get a better look. Adjusting them into focus, it appeared that the smoke was coming from Lorenzo's deck. On his feet, Bernard moved to the edge of his deck railing and focused again. This time he saw the flames.

Within seconds Bernard had raced down to his boat and was speeding across the bay. By the time he arrived, two other neighbours were on the scene. Lorenzo's deck was engulfed in flames. Leaving the two neighbours to attempt to douse the flames with garden hoses and buckets of ocean water, Bernard stumbled over the rocky terrain to the back of the house where he turned off the huge propane tank that was fuelling some of Lorenzo's major appliances. Next Bernard crawled under the house and removed two smaller propane tanks. By the time he got back out, the fire had swallowed the entire front of the cabin, shattering the sliding glass doors of the deck in the intense heat.

All the while, Pete and Lorenzo were on their hike toward the well blissfully unaware of the unfolding nightmare. The two of them climbed a large bluff to check on the level of the water tanks. There they too had a view of the entire inlet. Pete saw the smoke first. "Geez, Lorenzo, that's an awful lot of smoke and it's coming from around your place."

"What the hell could that be?" wondered Lorenzo.

"We'd better get back there pronto and find out." Both knew something was potentially very wrong as they hurried back along the trail through the woods. Emerging on the shoreline, they saw the smoke had turned a dark black and was billowing up into the sky. They hurried along the rocks, rounded the point and came into the view of the cabin. It was an inferno. By this point, several neighbours had arrived by boat, and all were pitching in trying to simply control the fire and keep it from spreading to the forest and the surrounding cabins. Lorenzo's cabin was nothing but raging flames. It was gone. We had procured a neighbourhood firehose that could pump ocean water, but Lorenzo had recently been elected fire marshal and it was inside his cabin. While the neighbours struggled back and forth from the ocean to the fire, soaking the nearby trees with buckets of water, Lorenzo simply stood on the rocks in shock and silence as the cabin of his dreams burned to the ground before his eyes.

Within an hour, the cabin was levelled and the fire had all but burned itself out. Luckily, it burned straight down and, save for a few blackened tree trunks, the surrounding forest and neighbouring cabins were saved. The only remnant that stood amid the smouldering ash and toxic remains was Lorenzo's landmark green chimney, now black with soot, and his airtight fireplace, unnaturally six feet up in the air where his living-room floor used to be. Lorenzo lost everything but the clothes on his back. Even his wallet and keys to his boat and car were inside. It was later surmised that the ashes in the fireplace still contained embers of the night before that weren't completely extinguished. The breeze had brought the embers to life, igniting the box, which caught onto the deck. Lorenzo eventually made it down to his condo in Vancouver, and has been trying to get over his disaster ever since.

About a month after the fire, I made my first trek up to Desolation Sound that year. I knew that after opening up our cabin, I would have to go see the charred remains. As I quietly paddled over, I wished for the usual sight of Lorenzo emerging from his sliding-glass door, waving me up for a drink or a meal. Instead, his famous chimney stood like a tombstone over a grave of ash. I pulled myself out of the kayak and stood on the rocks below the cabin in a haunting silence broken only by a piece of aluminum siding, crumpled from the heat, warbling with every gust of wind.

I was stunned by the severity of Lorenzo's loss. Forget cougars, the permanency of this fiery violence was truly my deepest fear. I gingerly made my way to where the front of the house once stood, stepping over heat-shattered glass and bent black nails. A tiny flash of colour caught my eye. Taking a closer look, I realized that I was standing where Lorenzo's flower boxes used to be, his yearly explosion of colour. I leaned down and saw that tiny purple flowers had forced their way up through the layers of ash and destruction. I crouched down and touched the soft flower petals and shed a tear for what was. Our Desolation Sound neighbourhood would never be the same after Lorenzo's fire.

Lorenzo's famous green chimney stands like a tombstone over a grave of ash. Lorenzo's beloved cabin with all the mod cons burned straight to the ground within an hour.

25
Left and Leaving

As summer after summer came and went, wholesale changes began to occur in our Desolation Sound neighbourhood. The owners of the original cabins were now in their mid-sixties and seventies, and their aging bones were beginning to disagree with the rugged landscape. Add to that a seller's real-estate market with prices hitting all-time highs, and several long time neighbours decided to bug out. Faced with starting over from scratch, Lorenzo decided to collect the insurance money and sell his beloved property. I was upset to hear this news, foolishly hoping that the tough little flower in the wind was a premonition that Lorenzo *would* return and rebuild, and our happy hours, dinners on the deck, storytelling and gales of laughter would resume. Apparently money talks and metaphors walk. When I pressed him on the issue of staying and rebuilding, Lorenzo looked at me with sadness in his eyes. "Why should

I bother?" he sighed. "I'm a sixty-four-year-old bachelor. How many years will I get out of this place anyhow? I'm taking the money, Grant." He made a huge profit and relocated to a new development on Vancouver Island.

Another neighbour had fallen during the night, injuring his head, requiring the Coast Guard to fly him to Vancouver. Even Bernard the German, whom I thought was indestructible, had fallen ill. On our trips to the prawn traps he complained of feeling dizzy, and that his muscles ached much more than usual. I suggested he was possibly dehydrated, as all he ever seemed to drink was highly potent Bavarian homebrew. He grunted that I was probably right, and started drinking a lot more water, but it did nothing to stem his symptoms. Eventually, it was diagnosed that his body had been harbouring the Hepatitis C virus for many years, which had likely entered into his bloodstream from a shared needle in his hippie days. When the virus began to aggressively attack Bernard's liver, he realized he had more to see, so he suddenly sold his hand-crafted eagle's nest of a cabin and bought a sailboat to sail around the world. I was shocked and dismayed. My old buddies—my personal cast of *The Beachcombers* meets *Cocoon*—were disappearing.

On one of Bernard's last nights in the Sound, he was entertaining several friends visiting from Germany. They played in a genuine Bavarian Oktoberfest oompahpah band, and on that hazy evening they performed several songs on the accordion and trumpet on Bernard's deck, attracting a crowd of kayakers paused in the high tide, clapping politely after each song. The aquatic audience gave Bernard the idea that his neighbours would probably like the show, too. So he loaded the band onto his skiff, casually cruising our craggy coastline of cabins with traditional live Bavarian music wafting through the warm evening air across the water. Everyone came out and gave them a hearty wave, applause and thanks for the live musical treat. Bernard then slowly steered his boat into Kahkaykay Bay, winding his way between appreciative audiences in the yachts anchored for the night. Bernard and the band made one more round, the giant German with the black handlebar moustache waving and blowing a few kisses as he passed by. It was a fitting and final send-off for my pal Bernard the German.

The aging population was replaced by younger owners who renovated and rebuilt cabins that were larger and fancier than anything any of us had seen in thirty years in the Sound, some of the places so out of place and out of hand that they bore a closer resemblance to a hotel than to a cabin. I considered some of the new "cabins" monstrous eyesores completely unbefitting to our rustic, ramshackle neighbourhood. It was Mom who astutely pointed out that the oyster farmers and hippies had a very similar reaction when our cabins first went up decades earlier. What goes around comes around, I guess. Several friends still remained: Handy Candy, who dreamt of staying until she turned eighty; Bulgarian George, who tried to sell but couldn't get the price he wanted; Jeremy, who built a floathouse and hosted legendary barge parties; the friendly lawyer Darrell and his wife, Anita; Jack "Harpoon" Harper; Professor Rick; Prawn Pete; and Packrat Mike, the retired bus driver who was the toughest SOB out there and may have loved the place more than anybody.

Many of my friends who had experienced our cabin on multiple occasions had also fallen in love with Desolation Sound, a few deciding to become permanent owners. Across the bay, the late-night anchor of CBC-TV Vancouver, a co-worker of mine, bought a cabin for her young family to spend their summers in. They became my first friends even remotely in my age range to take up ownership. Rory and Julie got married and had three boys, who have been to the Sound every year of their lives. When a small knockdown came up for sale they made the plunge to buy in. Rory got his ass kicked a couple of times by some southeasterly storms, including one night when he had to watch helplessly from his cabin as a series of gale-force waves picked up *Lil' Buck$* and slammed its aluminum hull down repeatedly on the rocks until it resembled a flattened beer can. Rory quickly learned to respect the wicked force of Mother Nature in the Sound, and restored *Lil' Buck$* to mint condition. One of the members of my hockey team loved the Desolation Sound lifestyle when he visited as well. Scott "Cabo-Wabo" Cabianca was a West Vancouver playboy and international jet-setter who quickly became know as the Dean Martin of Desolation Sound, due to his suave and drunken nature. He could party with the stamina of John Belushi and Bob Marley rolled into one giant doobie and bought the lot right next door to ours. Carrying on Bernard the German's tradition, I gave both Scott and Rory the Desolation Sound housewarming gift: a glistening new machete.

My parents, who used to come up at least once a month through the warmer months, had reduced their trips to sometimes only once a year, and only for a few days. Mom was still game but, strangely, Dad seemed increasingly uninterested. As soon as he got to the cabin he wanted to leave, always bargaining with Mom to head home early. None of us could understand it. This was the place he loved, the place he discovered for all of us. This community was his legacy but he seemingly wanted nothing to do with it, often angered by the ever-emerging politics, gossip and flaunting of the rules that resulted in some of the massive new eyesore cabins. Dad still did most of the major repairs at our cabin, but slowly I started doing more to bring the place up to speed and make it livable for the twenty-first century.

Even though he wasn't around much, Dad seemed resistant to the slightest change or improvement. His reluctance to change was driving a further wedge between us, and neither one of us could figure out a way to talk ourselves through it. My dad was my big and powerful childhood hero, the idol I spent most of my childhood failing to emulate. As a teen I rebelled against him with the ferocity of an S.E. Hinton character, but as an adult I finally mellowed. I had become my own man, and all I wanted from Dad was his pride for my achievements. My heroic father with the strapping chest, wry smile and adventuresome soul had become an old man. I had finally inherited that adventuresome soul and worked my way into a rugged wilderness persona against all odds, but he hadn't waited around for me. I felt an inherent need to maintain his legacy and my passion for it before it collapsed into the ocean. I hoped Dad was proud of me, but I was never completely sure as I kept edging our little place in the wilderness—that two-line ad he spotted in the *Vancouver Sun*—farther into the twenty-first century. Then Gillian came along.

26
Proof of Love

Three years after Captain Vancouver left the gloom of Desolation Sound in his wake, his ships returned to London in the fall of 1795, four and a half exhausting years after they had first set sail. While they were gone, England had gone to war against France, and all eyes and headlines had turned from the scientific explorations of the tall ships in the Pacific to the war in Europe. Captain Vancouver's disintegrating ships limped into port in London to little fanfare; the sailors were paid and went their separate ways. Unlike Captain Cook's voyages of discovery years earlier, Captain Vancouver had returned with the primary news of what *wasn't* there. Captain Vancouver proved there was no viable Northwest Passage, which was an unpopular and decidedly un-sexy discovery. Stephen R. Bown's book *Madness, Betrayal and the Lash* suggests that the dismissive and distracted reaction to Vancouver's epic voyage crushed his already insecure mental state and sank him into a debilitating manic depression that he would never come out of.

Captain George Vancouver died on May 12, 1798 at age forty from the unknown illness that had been plaguing him for years. Mostly from his sickbed, Vancouver wrote his own book of the voyage, entitled (no joke) A *Voyage of Discovery to the North Pacific Ocean and Round the World; in Which the Coast of North-West America Has Been Carefully Examined and Accurately Surveyed*. The title is symbolic of both the ponderous length of the journey and the book, an unedited three-or-four-volume sprawl of thousands of pages, which was published posthumously a few months after his death. According to all accounts, George Vancouver never had any children, or any short- or long-term intimate relationship. He died a depressed, lonesome and broken man. In 1886, eighty-four years after his death, the City of Vancouver was founded, which has famously grown into one of the most cosmopolitan, multicultural and spectacular cities on the planet. The city is Captain Vancouver's true legacy.

Throughout my rediscovery of Desolation Sound, I had always been a bachelor. Part of me thought I always would be, and I was resigned to that fate; there were times when I didn't like it, but I didn't fight it much either. There were plenty of perpetually single people in the Sound, past and present, and I assumed that the environment just attracted a certain type of solitary person, and I was one of them.

Nancy Crowther, the Cougar Lady of Okeover Inlet, spent most of the last thirty years of her life living alone in the Sound. After her parents passed away, Nancy was briefly married to an area man in the mid-twentieth century but that didn't go too well. Nancy was as tough and as wilderness-savvy as any man, probably more so; she likely wasn't willing or able to fit into the traditional role of a housewife, even a wilderness housewife. She quite literally wore the pants and carried the gun. The marriage ended in divorce, which was pretty rare for both the times and the area. Nancy kept the family cabin and quickly reverted back to her maiden name and her introverted lifestyle.

Over Nancy Crowther's several decades of near-solitude, she continued to harvest oysters and clams from her beach, preserve fruit from her orchard, raise and butcher her own chickens and geese, cultivate bees for honey and had her friendly goats for milk and cheese. Those goats and her pack of dogs were her primary social companions. She fought off wolves, bears and the twenty-two cougars she infamously shot and killed; and fought off the encroachment of the hippies, draft dodgers, hobos and oyster farmers who attempted to steal anything they could. Speaking to the *Powell River News,* Nancy once said "the stealing by two-legged animals is far worse than the stealing by those on four legs . . . It's civilization coming. Someone stole more than half of my supply of honey recently. It's endless what they take: my grain, my hay, my groceries. I've moved all my grain inside the house so people can't steal it."

It was for this reason that Nancy Crowther greeted us with her .303 rifle when we trespassed across her property on our first visit. By the time I came back to Desolation Sound as an adult, the Cougar Lady of Okeover Inlet was gone. Whether it was simply old age, dementia or otherwise, over the last decade of life her increasingly eccentric behaviour certainly fit the profile of "going bush." Nancy was rumoured to have taken on bizarre, paranoid conduct such as reporting to what few friends she still trusted that she was being watched. She started sleeping in her truck with her dogs and a loaded rifle, until she was finally hospitalized in Powell River. The Cougar Lady's legendary, unique life came to an end in 1989. The trail that her family bushwhacked back in the 1920s is now called Crowther Road, the sign visible from the turnoff at the foot of Malaspina Road near the Okeover wharf.

Adam Vallance and his young family purchased the Cougar Lady's historic acreage and lovingly restored her log cabin. Cutting through the overgrowth on her property, they discovered towering hazelnut and walnut trees, and Nancy's fruit orchard, which they pruned back to its former vitality. Farther back in the bush, they found her long-abandoned bee boxes and goat corral. The Crowther homestead is now the base of their thriving business, Powell River Sea Kayak, and the launching point for kayak tours of Desolation Sound throughout the sunshine season.

Many of my dear friends had exploded into family-hood as well. The children of Heather and Matt, Nick and Soraya, and new owners Rory and Julie soon filled our yearly seafood summer feast with many more growing and loud mouths to feed. I loved spending time with all the kids, many of whom had been to our cabin every summer since birth. When they all departed back to the city, I was left on my own in a state of silent withdrawal. And while I treasured my adventures in solitude, it made me reflect with a hint of sadness on the solitary existence of so many who have come to Desolation Sound. That feeling of personal regret would surface every time I saw something spectacular in the Sound, wishing it to be a collective experience. I yearned to share the free-spirited boat rides, the lazy days on the deck, the glorious sunsets, shooting stars and romantic fireside nights. I was lonely, but didn't mind drinking alone; I was willing to accept it.

And then one summer, without looking for it, I found it. A girl named Gillian came into my life. She was beautiful, smart, radiant, talented and funny. I was introduced to her in Toronto by our mutual friend Jian Ghomeshi from CBC Radio, and I was immediately smitten with her. We began a long-distance courtship, she from Halifax on the east coast and me from the west. By late July of that summer I had invited her to the cabin in the Sound, an invitation she accepted. It would be a definite test of her mettle. She was very much a downtown city girl, always pretty, made up and well dressed, and if she didn't like it, thought it too wild, too unsafe or just too far, I knew it'd probably be a deal-breaker and I'd go back to my crusty bachelorhood. Her family had a summer place of their own in Wellington, Ontario (which the old-timers called "Wellsies"), located in the upper crust of Prince Edward County, the rolling hills of Ontario wine country on the shores of Lake Ontario. "Wellsies" sounded much closer to the white sands of Savary Island than to the black rocks of Desolation Sound.

A beautiful, smart, radiant, talented and funny girl named Gillian.

Gillian passed with flying colours, swept up by the wild romance of the Sound and my passion for it. Sure, she kayaked in a purple pleather jacket, French beret and high heels, but that was okay with me. Sure, she thought the cabin looked like a rural museum of perfectly preserved early-1980s IKEA memorabilia, but that was fine. It's true that at times she would bring a chilled glass of Chardonnay on hikes through the bush. Yes, she hated my machete, and yes, she most definitely thought many of the neighbours were a little bizarre . . . but I could deal with all of that. Gillian and I fell in love.

One of our first Desolation Sound adventures together was a trial by fire for Gillian. It happened during a stifling, record-breaking heat wave that was forcing the mercury past forty degrees Celsius throughout the Sound, lasting for days and sapping everyone's energy. We barely wore a stitch of clothing and were constantly dripping with sweat. All we could do was collapse on deck chairs in the shade and drink. One of the respites from the heat of the day was taking *Big Buck$* out for a full-speed charge just to feel the ocean breeze on our faces. Gillian and I used the intense hot weather as a good excuse to take *Big Buck$* around the peninsula to Lund for a visit to Nancy's Bakery and a re-stock of ice from the general store. On our way back, the late afternoon swelter made it feel like we were sticking our faces into a hairdryer. We were looking for a place to jump into the ocean and cool off when we saw the column of black smoke.

It was coming from the other side of the peninsula just about exactly where our cabin sat. Many of us around the Sound were still charred with fear from the Lorenzo blaze, and the heat wave was making us even more paranoid than usual; everything seemed readily flammable. It didn't help that the ridge of the peninsula was far too steep and heavily treed for us to see over, which made my brain jump to a worst-case scenario. I quickly forgot about the swim, told Gillian to hang on and threw *Big Buck$* into overdrive. The boat reared up angrily like a spurred pony, then bolted across the water in the direction of the cabin.

I had seen plenty of forest fires in BC, and some small burns right in the Sound, and I knew that forest-fire smoke was a hazy brownish grey. This opaque black smoke was something different. As we made the hairpin turn around the point into our inlet, we were both shocked and frightened to see several black mushroom clouds of smoke rise up over the trees against the azure summer sky. It had to be fuel tanks exploding. I pushed down hard on the throttle and *Big Buck$* gave us all she had. Soon the first few of our neighbouring cabins were in view; thankfully none of them were on fire but the black smoke column continued to rise straight up in the exact direction of home. A sick, panicked lump grew in the pit of my stomach as Gillian tried to calm me down.

Our cabin finally came into view, sitting as it always has on its stilts on the rocks, looking like the national park lodge my Dad had intended in his design. I slowed up *Big Buck$* and heaved a huge sigh of relief, my arms collapsing over the windshield of the boat. But where was the smoke coming from? As we motored closer, we saw several yachts and sailboats streaming out of Kahkaykay Bay. Closer to the entrance of the ancient natural harbour we saw it: a yacht was fully engulfed in flames in the dead centre of the bay. It was a fifty-four-foot vintage wooden cabin cruiser based out of Vancouver Island that had cruised the Sound for years. The orange flames from the boat crackled straight up in the air. The mushroom-cloud explosions we had seen were the boat's diesel and propane tanks exploding. As the other yachts and sailboats pulled up anchor and high tailed it to get away from the explosions, local skiffs driven by oyster farmers, neighbours and curiosity seekers were pouring in. I of course wanted to get as close to the action as possible.

As I steered *Big Buck$* toward the flames, Gillian grabbed my arm. "No! We are not going in there. Did you know that most of the people who died in the Halifax Explosion were curiosity seekers who gathered to watch the fire?" I very reluctantly steered clear. The Coast Guard arrived within thirty minutes of the blaze and let the yacht burn spectacularly into the summer night until the ocean eventually doused it and there was nothing left but floating debris. The cause of the fire was somewhat ironic. The heritage boat that had sailed the coast for so many decades on its vintage equipment without fail was a victim of modern technology. A powered-up laptop left unattended on a pillow had overheated and burst into flame. The owners had been onshore at the time and were unharmed; the only casualty was their pet cat. The stifling air was filled with lingering acidic smoke that made sleeping even more difficult, and our nerves were on edge for the rest of that insufferable night.

The next morning the entire bay and our surrounding inlet reeked of diesel fuel. We could see the sheen on the water and the fuel-soaked charred wood washed up on the shoreline. Because the yacht which was carrying hundreds of litres of diesel fuel, which had exploded in a provincial marine park, many of the extremely concerned local oyster farmers and neighbours thought for certain that some government body, or the owner of the boat, would show up to contain the fuel spillage and clean up the debris. To the shock of all concerned, that didn't happen until days later, allowing several tides to flush the diesel fuel and debris back and forth through the ecosystem of the Sound. When we realized to our dismay that no immediate help was coming to clean up our pristine coastal waterways filled with countless animal and plant species above and below the surface, two hardy oyster farmers named Don and Karen rallied several farmers and neighbours to attempt a cleanup ourselves.

When they swung by our place, Gillian, Handy Candy, Rick the English Professor and I were trying to stave off the heat and the diesel stench with some cold champagne, all of us in various states of undress. When Don and Karen asked for our help we agreed, and in typical Desolation Sound fashion, we simply freshened the flutes and climbed aboard the oyster skiffs, including Gillian in her heels, oversized designer sunglasses and particularly lovely summer dress. And so, with one hand dragging an oil-spill cleanup boom through the water and the other daintily holding a glass of champagne, Gillian gamely did her part in our attempted cleanup of the boat explosion.

Gillian is a Canadian singer-songwriter who performs under the name Jill Barber, and it didn't take long for our little coastal community to figure out who she was. At my persistent begging, she once performed a concert on a hot night under a full moon at our local fine-dining establishment, the Laughing Oyster Restaurant, to the pin-drop-silent delight of the restaurant full of locals and yachting tourists from around the world. Another time, she gave me one of the best birthday gifts of my life when she performed an intimate acoustic concert for all our friends and neighbours on the deck of our cabin. People came from all over the Sound to hear Jill sing, gathering together on a gorgeous night as the sun set over the western treeline, and the moon rose over the eastern hills. Jill's music brought all the families, neighbours, oyster farmers, oddballs and recluses together in harmony as a community and I loved it.

During our trips to town I would often try to track down the old hermit Russell Letawsky so I could proudly introduce him to Jill. We eventually found him at the end of a steep dirt road overcrowded with alder trees, just north of the Sliammon First Nation reserve. He was living alone in a little house that looked threatened to be engulfed by the rainforest immediately behind it. When we pulled into the driveway he was sitting just inside the open door of his home listening to CBC Radio. We parked the car and Gillian and I stepped out. He stood on the doorstep but didn't recognize me. His hair was still long, in a ponytail, and he still had a beard, but it was now mostly white, save for his moustache that was stained dirty yellow by his pipe smoke. He wore glasses and moved a little slower, but he was still the same old Russell. "Russell? It's Grant Lawrence."

After I discovered where Russell was living "in town," we would sometimes meet for a drink and a chat at the Lund Pub. If you ever see him there, please send over a half-litre of red wine or a pint of Guinness to his table, where he's likely playing euchre.

He squinted at us, and stepped down into the yard. Recognition crossed his face. "Oh! Grant, hello!"

"Russell, I want you to meet my girlfriend, Gillian." We sat together for an hour or so, reminiscing about our days together in the Sound. He was upset that his shack had been torn down, but visibly pleased when he heard we had named his former residence Russell Cove. He lit his pipe and I let the smoke drift up my nostrils, its pleasant burnt-cherry scent taking me back twenty-five years. Russell was still as passionate and philosophical as ever, quoting Nietzsche, and reminding us of his credo: *Amor fati* . . . love your fate. Russell gestured to Jill with his pipe. "Did you know that this beautiful lady is your *Amor fati*?" I told him that I had never thought of her that way, but I would from now on. And when Jill and I eventually got up to leave, we promised that we would see him again.

Jill and I spent as much time as I could convince her to be there at the cabin in the warmer months. We would wake up together, in each other's arms, looking out the window for sun on the arbutus tree just outside the master bedroom, a sure sign of a beautiful day ahead. If it was chilly, Jill would refuse to get out of bed until I had a crackling fire in the cast-iron fireplace warming up the drafty cabin. Then she'd make us any breakfast I'd ask for: bacon and eggs, blueberry pancakes or avocado omelettes. Gone were the days when out of hungover, dry-heaving bachelorhood desperation I would be forced to warm up leftover spaghetti on the BBQ for breakfast just for sheer sustenance. I bought Jill a little red kayak to match my blue one, and together we'd paddle the inlets of the Sound. I'd eagerly show her all my favourite swimming and snorkelling spots, and try to capture her imagination with the ghost stories of the Sound . . . the Cougar Lady, Arthur Jones, Captain Vancouver, Gus Bloom and the others. Some she believed, some she didn't.

On one bright and sunny Canada Day, we packed up a picnic lunch and prepared the kayaks for a day out on the water. Without her noticing, I slipped a few other items into *Little Blue*. We paddled to one of our favourite spots and unfurled our picnic blanket on a nice, hot slab of shoreline granite on the north side of Edith Island, a spectacular, supernatural location with nary a human being in sight. Before Jill could sit down, I dropped down on one knee in my shorts and dirty V-neck T-shirt and took out the little box I had stowed in the kayak. When I looked up at Gillian she was already crying, looking down at me. I opened up the box to show her the diamond engagement ring, and I asked her to marry me.

Happiness shared: at long last, I had finally found someone to share the wild boat rides, the pink sunsets, the soggy picnics and the fireside nights with. Gillian and I fell in love.

Through tears she said yes, and then we both started crying. We hugged, we kissed and I popped the bottle of champagne I had also slipped into the kayak without her seeing. We got drunk, skinny-dipped and made love on the rocks. Eventually we paddled back to the cabin, and on the way home I looked down into the calm blue ocean water and saw my grizzled, happy reflection . . . and I saw the frightened, fragile bespectacled nerd I once was, and thought of all the others who had gazed into this ocean and had seen their own reflections change over the curve of time: the First Nations in their dugout canoes, Captain Vancouver in his tall ship, the European settlers in their rowboats, the Cougar Lady, the hippies and the oyster farmers, my father, my mother, my little sister, the hermit Russell Letawsky, Handy Candy, Bernard the German, George, Lorenzo, all our friends and neighbours, and Gillian. Ever since the Ice Age carved dramatic mountain peaks and ocean depths into the west coast of Canada, Desolation Sound has always been the same, and will remain the same long after we're gone. It simply and grandly offers us a reflection of who we were, and who we are, bound together by our adventures in solitude.

The student finally becomes the teacher. Nick held a Desolation Sound fishing derby for my stag weekend . . . and I won! But I had insider knowledge . . . Russell's fishing secrets are still paying off, twenty-five years later. Nerd to bushman transition now complete.

"These adventures in solitude, never done"
– Carl "AC" Newman, The New Pornographers

Recommended Reading

When it comes to books on Desolation Sound, for many, the starting and end point is M. Wylie Blanchet's 1968 classic, *The Curve of Time.* It's proven time and time again to have a magical effect on its readers, literally altering the course of lives. *The Curve of Time* even spawned a direct tribute, *Following the Curve of Time: The Legendary M. Wylie Blanchet* by Cathy Converse. Powell River writer Heather Harbord has written some very detailed books about the Sound, including *Desolation Sound—A History*, and the best kayaking guidebook available for the area, *Sea Kayaking Desolation Sound and the Sunshine Coast.* Other fine books that were invaluable to me when cross-referencing the history of the area were *Upcoast Summers* by Beth Hill; *Boats, Bucksaws, and Blisters: Pioneer Tales of the Powell River Area* by Bill Thompson; *Spilsbury's Coast* by Jim Spilsbury and Howard White; *Magnetic Isle:*

Gladys Bloomfield's Savary by Gladys Bloomfield; and what I consider to be an extremely important, breakthrough book, *Clam Gardens: Aboriginal Mariculture on Canada's West Coast* by Judith Williams.

Though there are many books written about the often misunderstood life and times of Captain George Vancouver, the one I consider the most fascinating and which I recommend strongly is *Madness, Betrayal and the Lash: The Epic Voyage of Captain George Vancouver* by Stephen R. Bown. Others are Sam McKinney's *Sailing With Vancouver*, and George Vancouver's own tome, *A Voyage of Discovery to the North Pacific Ocean and Round the World, 1791–1795*. Also, Tom Gallant's rich and loving descriptions of east coast boats and sailing in his book *A Hard Chance: Sailing into the Heart of Love* was an inspiration; Andrew Scott's *The Encyclopedia of Raincoast Place Names: A Complete Reference to Coastal British Columbia* was handy if heavy; and Taras Grescoe's *Bottomfeeder* told me everything I ever wanted to know about fish. *The Darien Gap: Travels in the Rainforest of Panama*, by Lund's own Martin Mitchinson, helped explain the road from Lund to Quellon.

Fueling my ever-growing interest in solitude, the fine line between sanity and madness, and "going bush," were a few very good books on the subject, first and foremost *Descent into Madness* by Vernon Frolick, as well as *The Eden Express: A Memoir of Insanity* by Mark Vonnegut and *Into the Wild* by Jon Krakauer. Helping me picture the hippie communes and outlaw biker gangs were books like *Apple Bay (or Life on the Planet)* by Paul Williams, *Policing the Fringe: The Curious Life of a Small-Town Mountie* by Charlie Scheideman and Hunter S. Thompson's *Hell's Angels*.

And finally . . . take time out for Herge's *Adventures of Tintin*.

Recommended Listening

I love rock 'n' roll music, and there are many "shout-outs" to some of my favourite musicians, bands, singers, songs and albums throughout this book. Some are obvious, some not so much, and I want to give credit where credit is due. It all starts with the title of the book, which is also the title of a beautiful song by Vancouver band the New Pornographers. You can find "Adventures in Solitude" — the song — on the New Pornographers' fourth album, *Challengers*. Much appreciation to lead singer and songwriter Carl "AC" Newman for his permission to use this song title that I love so much. Many of the chapter titles in *Adventures in Solitude* are musical references. "A Little Place In The Wilderness" is a song by Canadian band Memphis (a project of Torquil Campbell, lead singer of Stars). Fjord Rowboat is a band from Toronto. "C'mon Sea Legs" is a song by Victoria band Immaculate Machine, which can be found on their album *Fables*. "Shine A Light" is an oft-repeated title in rock 'n' roll (Rolling Stones, Constantines), but here I was thinking of the anthemic song by Montreal band Wolf Parade. The song is found on their near-iconic first album, *Apologies To The Queen Mary*.

"The Beautiful Failure" is a poetic phrase uttered by my long-time friend and mentor, Vancouver author Michael Turner, while we sat and discussed hippie culture in his backyard. "Smoke On The Water" is a classic song by English stoner band Deep Purple and the first song every banger learns to play on guitar. Easiest/best riff ever. "Harvest Moon" is a perfect tune by Neil Young. It's also the title of a 1992 Neil Young album. "Blood's Too Rich" is a rousing sing-along by Canada's best guitarist, Luke Doucet. It can be found on the album of the same name. "Wishing Well" is a song by my wife, Jill Barber. It's one of the many timeless, "radiant" songs found on her record *Chances*.

Captains Courageous is both a Rudyard Kipling book and an exciting 1937 movie starring Spencer Tracy (I try to follow similar themes in this book. Thanks to Dad for showing me this and so many great old movies that shaped my love of pop culture). "Take Me To The Riot" is a song by Montreal band Stars, found on their album *In Our Bedroom After the War*. "Somewhere Else" is my favourite song about place, written and sung by Ottawa artist Jim Bryson on his album *The North Side Benches*. "Cloudy With A Chance of Drunk" is a Desolation Sound weather report that I first heard from my friend, co-worker and D-Sound neighbour Natalie Clancy. "Hangover Days" is a brilliant duet (my favourite element of pop music) between the songwriter — Toronto's long, tall cool one, Jason Collett — and the lovely Emily Haines, lead singer of Metric. This song can be found on Jason's best album, *Idols of Exile*. Thanks to Jason for his early support of this book. *Welcome To The Night Sky* is the title of the best album by Halifax band Wintersleep. "My Sword Hand's Anger" is by a band called Apostle of Hustle, the best band name in Canada. "Purple Haze" = Jimi Hendrix. "Stormy High" is an outrageous reefer-rocker from Vancouver band Black Mountain that can be found on their epic record *In The Future*. "Left and Leaving" is the best song by my favourite Canadian band, The Weakerthans, from Winnipeg. It can be found on their must-have album of the same name. And finally, "Proof of Love" is a song, and an album, by Canada's favourite banjo player, Old Man Luedecke from Chester, Nova Scotia. I love all of these artists and songs and records and I hope you'll take the time to listen to many or all of them. All of the Canadian songs listed above can be heard at www.cbcradio3.com.

And don't forget the Gruesomes, Young Fresh Fellows, NoMeansNo, Hard Rock Miners, D.O.A., Violent Femmes, Evaporators, Joel Plaskett and, of course, The Smugglers.

Thank You

Garth, Jean and Heather Lawrence, Jill Barber, Russell Letawsky, Nick and Soraya Thomas, Rory Brown and Julie Mendgen, Samantha Haywood, Lindsey Love, Carl "AC" Newman and the New Pornographers, everyone at Harbour Publishing, Silas White, Holland Gidney, Naomi MacDougall, Christy Nyiri, Five Seventeen, DavidChristyInternet, Ken Beattie, Dave Bidini, Michael Barclay, Bill Richardson, Michael Turner, Chris Murphy, Steve Pratt and everyone at CBC Radio 3, Jo-Ann Roberts, Jian Ghomeshi, Shelagh Rogers, Stuart McLean, Kevin Sylvester, Steve Burgess, *Sounds Like Canada*, *All Points West*, *On The Coast*, CBC Radio, Chip Sutherland, Candyce Anderson, Bernard Krieger, Richard Brent, Mike Mullen, Darrell and Anita Dick, Jack and Pat Harper, Rick Johnson and Tracie Smith, George and Christina Dessev, Adam and Laurie Vallance, Nancy and Ben Bouchard,

Bill, Lola and Justus DeKort, David Bowes and the Laughing Oyster Restaurant, Nancy's Bakery, the Boat Stop Café, Heather Harbord, Dr. Elsie Paul, Al and Amy Sharp, Jeremy Duggan, Bad Karen Skadsheim, Rick Turrell, Evelyn Pollen, Megan Barnes, Scott Cabianca, the Thomas Family, the Brown Family, the Vancouver Flying Vees Hockey Club, The Smugglers, Nardwuar the Human Serviette, Don and Karen Carto, Jason Collett, VancouverIsAwesome.com, Brian and Joyce Barber, Bill Baker, Angus Stuart, Connie Blundy, Lund Automotive, Phillips Beer and to Chris Kelly, who persistently urged me to write it all down.